Partners for Development

New Roles for Government and Private Sector in the Middle East and North Africa

Samiha Fawzy
Ahmed Galal
Editors

THE WORLD BANK
WASHINGTON, D.C.

© 1999 The International Bank for Reconstruction
and Development/THE WORLD BANK
1818 H Street, N.W.
Washington, D.C. 20433

Cover design by Chris Komisar, Auras Design.

ISBN 0-8213-4482-X

Library of Congress Cataloging-in-Publication Data
Partners for development : new roles for government and private sector in the Middle East
and North Africa / Samiha Fawzy, Ahmed Galal, editors.
    p.cm
    ISBN 0-8213-4482-X
    1. Middle East--Economic conditions--1979-2. Africa, North--Economic conditions. 3.
Middle East--Economic policy. 4. Africa, North--Economic policy. 5. Privatization--Middle
East. 6. Privatization--Africa, North. I. Fawzy, Samiha, 1951- II. Galal, Ahmed, 1948-

HC415.15.P37 1999
338.956 21--dc21   99-045102

Contents

FIGURES

Preface

"In a world of 5.7 billion people, we at the Bank deal with 3 billion people who live under two dollars a day and 1.3 billion people who live under one dollar a day. A billion and half of those people don't have clean water, and in this region of the world, you know full well the impact of not having clean water, an impact on the lives of families, an impact on the opportunities for women and girls, a destructive impact on the lives of our people. We are concerned with the issues of health and we are concerned with the issues of education. We have concluded in our institution that we cannot do this alone, and we have come to a ... partnership around the world.

We've also learned that it's necessary in order to have growth, which is a prerequisite to human development, that we must be partners with business, with the private sector. (Not just the private sector internationally, although that has grown enormously.) To give you an idea, seven years ago, foreign investment in developing countries was 30 billion dollars a year and the loans from institutions such as the World Bank totaled 60 billion dollars a year, which means that the official institutions were twice the size of the private sector. Today, the official institutions are around 45 billion and the private sector overseas investment is 260 billion. So from being half the size, it's now five to six times the size, and for every dollar invested from overseas, four or five dollars are invested locally. So the private sector is not a gloss, it's not an institutional group that we can forget, it's a group that is central to the activities of development."

— Remarks at the Opening Ceremony of the Second Mediterranean Development Forum by James D. Wolfensohn, President, The World Bank Group, Marrakech, September 3, 1998.

List of Contributors

Özer Ertuna
Professor of Economics, Bogaziçi University, Ankara, Turkey

Samiha Fawzy
Professor of Economics, Cairo University, Egypt
Principal Economist, The Egyptian Center for Economic Studies (ECES), Egypt

Ahmed Galal
Economic Adviser, The World Bank, Washington, D.C.
Member of the Board, The Egyptian Center for Economic Studies (ECES), Egypt

Bernard Hoekman
Principal Trade Economist, The World Bank, Washington, D.C.

Taher H. Kanaan
Minister of State for Foreign Affairs, Jordan

Mokhtar Khattab
Undersecretary, Ministry of Public Enterprise Sector, Egypt

Lahouel Mohamed El Hédi
Professor of Economics, University of Tunis III, Tunisia

John Nellis
Senior Manager, The World Bank, Washington, D.C.

Edmund O'Sullivan
Editor in Chief, *Middle East Economic Digest*, London

Sahar Tohamy
Senior Economist, The Egyptian Center for Economic Studies (ECES), Egypt

Foreword

On behalf of the Mediterranean Development Forum (MDF) partnership of 10 Middle East and North Africa Region (MENA) think tanks and the World Bank Institute, I am happy to present the first book of an MDF publication series. The series is based on conferences that the MDF partnership holds every 18 months. This particular volume entitled *Partners for Development: New Roles for Government and Private Sector in the Middle East and North Africa* includes papers on the theme of public–private partnerships discussed at the second Mediterranean Development Forum (MDF2). The MDF2 took place in Marrackech, Morocco, on September 3 – 6, 1998.

This publication hopes to capture the magnitude of the MDF2 conference by publishing papers on some of the most noteworthy presentations. Over 100 speakers debated innovative and cutting-edge development issues with an audience of over 500 of the region's most influential thinkers and practitioners ranging from high-level government officials to think tank representatives to private sector leaders to academics, and to civil society.

We would like to express our thanks to those who contributed to this book. We would like to acknowledge Samiha Fawzy of the Egyptian Center for Economic Studies (ECES) and Ahmed Galal of the World Bank, as well as the authors who provided us with a unique perspective on public–private partnerships in the region. Like the other partners, the ECES organized the workshops and coauthored publications in the MDF series. We hope that the papers presented here will contribute to the ongoing debate on the development opportunities and challenges facing the countries in the Middle East and North Africa.

Vinod Thomas, Director
World Bank Institute

About MDF

The Mediterranean Development Forum (MDF) partnership, launched in 1997, is composed of 10 Middle East and North Africa Region (MENA) think tanks and the World Bank Institute. The partnership is dedicated to providing policy support among development actors, research, and capacity-building of think tanks, and creating networks in the MENA region. The partnership's work culminates in a Forum held every 18 months.

"The ultimate purpose of the initiative," said Kemal Derviş, World Bank Vice President for the Middle East and North Africa, "is to boost economic growth in the region, improve integration in the world economy, and reduce poverty and inequality." To that end, MDF represents a vital opportunity for some of the region's most influential thinkers and practitioners to impact regional policy.

A crucial component of the MDF partnership is the Forum because it provides a rare opportunity for MENA experts, high-level government officials, and civil society representatives to meet and engage in a dialogue to set the region's development agenda. The Mediterranean Development Forum already has a unique impact on the region. Its first conference, MDF1—held in May 1997—focused on the interplay of civil society, business, and government in order to boost the region's competitiveness. The discussions at MDF2 in September 1998 broke new ground on the most crucial issues facing the developing world: how to enhance public participation in the development process.

As a direct result of the MDF partnership, the following projects have emerged in the last two years: programs on decentralization and governance in the West Bank and Gaza; programs on quality education emphasizing gender; the Network on Women Evaluators; the Network of Lawyers Reforming NGO Laws; the "Meet the Civil Society Initiative"; the MENA Data Initiative; and the MDF publication series.

The next Forum, MDF3, will take place in Cairo, Egypt, on March 5 – 8, 2000. Based on the theme, "Voices for Change, Partners for Prosperity," MDF3 will emphasize an inclusive approach toward development and the importance of partnerships in the wake of the new millennium. For more information on the conference, please contact the partner in your region listed on the back cover of this publication.

CHAPTER 1

Overview

Samiha Fawzy
Ahmed Galal

There is a growing consensus that the time has come for governments and private sector leaders of the Middle East and North Africa to forge a new partnership for development (see, for example, World Bank 1995). The question is: what kind of partnership should the two parties seek in order to ensure sustainable economic development? This volume attempts to address this question. To make the investigation tractable, the papers deal with four key facets of the government–private sector interface: the business environment, privatization, infrastructure, and two activities that induce transaction costs—tax administration and government procurement.

Three themes guide much of the analysis. First, sustainable development requires the participation of key economic actors in society, especially the government and the private sector. On the one hand, without government commitment and capacity to provide pro-growth economic policies and institutional arrangements, the private sector will not invest up to its potential. On the other hand, without private investment, government policies do not create new jobs and more goods and services. A partnership between both actors could be beneficial to society.

Second, the world is changing, and so should the region. After decades of state domination of economic activity, many governments around the world are increasingly relying on the private sector to foster economic growth. Governments are becoming less engaged in the direct provision of goods and services, while becoming more active in developing market mechanisms, creating supporting institutions, and providing safeguards to ensure equitable distribution. This trend is seen in the Middle Eastern and North African countries as well, but the policy and institutional environment remain less than fully supportive of the development of an efficient private sector. Progress on privatization has also been slow. Private sector participation in infrastructure is modest. And the government–business interaction continues to involve excessive transaction costs, especially in tax administration. Further realignment of the roles of governments and the private sector is needed.

Third, not all government–private partnerships are beneficial to society. It is indeed possible, as the East Asian experience shows, that bureaucrats, corporations, and banks collude, eventually bringing economic growth to a halt. To avoid such mishaps, several conditions have to be met. These conditions are not elaborated here, as they form the body of the papers in this volume. The point worth noting, however, follows from the old saying: "The devil is in the details." How well these details are specified ultimately determines the usefulness of the new public–private partnership to society.

The rest of this chapter offers a number of broad conclusions from the papers themselves. Its organization mirrors that of the volume, which moves from the business environment, to privatization, to infrastructure, and finally to transaction costs.

The Business Environment

An increasing number of countries in the region are committed to a private sector–led growth strategy. Morocco, Tunisia, Turkey, Jordan, Lebanon, and Egypt are prime examples. Beyond reforms on the macroeconomic front, these countries are making the business environment more friendly, reducing direct government involvement in the economy through privatization, encouraging private sector participation in infrastructure, and reforming their institutions to make them more hospitable to private investment. Progress has been uneven, however, and the state of the business environment in these economies is generally less attractive than in East Asia, Latin America, and Eastern Europe. Investors in the region claim that several obstacles continue to hinder the efficient operation of firms, exports, and investment. This view is supported by the survey results reported in this volume.

More specifically, Samiha Fawzy, Lahouel Mohamed El Hédi, and Taher H. Kanaan (chapters 2 through 4) provide an assessment of the business environment in Egypt, Tunisia, and Jordan, respectively. Their analyses reveal a consistent pattern. On the positive side, producers and consumers in all three countries face more rational incentive structures in the 1990s than they did in the 1980s, thanks to macroeconomic reforms and the initiation of structural reforms in the financial sector, trade regime, and state-owned enterprises. As reforms are aging without policy reversal, uncertainty is also diminishing. On the negative side, the authors note that the size and composition of the private sector remains modest and thin compared to the private sector in other developing countries. In Egypt, Tunisia, and Jordan, the share of the private sector still falls within a narrow range of 64–66 percent of GDP, compared with 80 percent in Brazil, 74 percent in Uruguay, and 72 percent in Indonesia. Finally, the authors identify, on the basis of firm-level surveys, the most binding constraints on private sector operation and expansion.

These are the inefficient tax administration, the costly judicial system, the scarcity of skilled labor, elaborate collateral requirements to access finance, and weak support systems.

Privatization

Privatization is the most visible feature of the new partnership between governments and the private sector. It is fundamentally a process of redrawing the boundaries that define the ownership and management of productive assets in the economy. If well implemented, it has the potential of improving static and dynamic efficiency, with an acceptable distribution of the benefits among the seller, buyers, workers, and consumers (Galal and others 1994).

In the Middle East and North Africa region, progress on privatization has been slow. The proceeds from major privatization transactions averaged about 3 percent of the total worldwide over the period 1991–98 (Privatization International, various editions). The region is doing better, with Egypt in the lead, but the world is moving faster. One possible explanation for this state of affairs is that the case for privatization has not been made convincingly. Another is that the political, institutional, and implementation-related constraints are too difficult to overcome. A third is a combination of both factors. Part II of this volume attempts to sort out this puzzle.

In chapter 5, John Nellis reviews the extensive literature that analyzes the impact of privatization on the performance of firms. He concludes that ownership matters. In the majority of cases, the evidence shows that privatization improves the performance of firms, across manufacturing and infrastructure enterprises, with positive gains at the macroeconomic level. But he also concludes that these gains are not automatic; policy and institutions matter as well. What governments do or do not do to promote competition, adopt regulation when necessary, and ensure a transparent sale process, are just as important.

In chapters 6 and 7, Mokhtar Khattab (covering Egypt) and Özer Ertuna (covering Turkey) assess progress on privatization to date, identify the constraints encountered in the process, explain how policymakers dealt or failed to deal with them, and conclude with policy recommendations. Khattab highlights the significant progress made by Egypt since 1996, which led to the sale of 29 percent of all state-owned enterprises (SOEs), or 35 percent of the book value of total assets. He attributes this success to the ability of the Egyptian government to mobilize the support of key economic actors (the executive branch, the public, the press, and parliamentarians) and to overcome the problems of excess labor, valuation, and the limited absorptive capacity of the capital market.

In Turkey, Ertuna notes that progress on privatization has been very slow. The size of the SOE sector remained stable at 11 percent of GDP over the period 1985–91, despite the formulation of a detailed master plan in 1984. The process gained momentum in the last couple of years, leading to cumulative sale revenues of US$4 billion. He attributes the limited success in the past to the failure of policymakers to address the political and legal constraints, labor opposition, and the lack of implementation capacity.

Infrastructure

If progress on privatization has been relatively modest in the Middle East and North Africa region, private sector participation in infrastructure (for example, power, telecommunications, gas, or water) is even more modest (figure 1.1). With the exception of Sub-Saharan Africa, the region has the lowest share of private sector participation in infrastructure. Most of the power, gas, transport, water, and other utilities are run inefficiently under state ownership and control. In the few cases in which the private sector participates in infrastructure, governments have focused on individual transactions (of the build-operate-transfer [BOT] variety) rather than on a sector-wide approach to reform. Egypt and Morocco are two examples. These observations raise two sets of questions. First, why do governments in the region rely almost exclusively on themselves to provide infrastructure services? Are they concerned that replacing public by private providers will not benefit most groups in society? Is such an outcome inevitable? Second, why do governments follow the transaction-by-transaction approach rather than sectoral reforms to engage the private sector in infrastructure? Is it because the transactions approach is more beneficial? These questions are addressed in Part III.

FIGURE 1.1 INVESTMENT IN PRIVATE INFRASTRUCTURE PROJECTS IN
DEVELOPING COUNTRIES
by region, 1990–97
1997 US$ billion

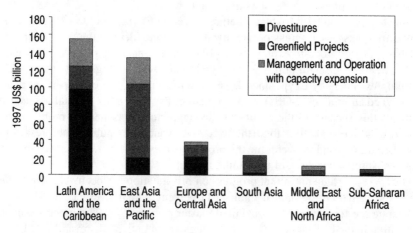

Source: PPI Project Database.

Taking up the first set of questions, Galal (chapter 8) explores the consequences of replacing public by private providers in utilities, using Telecom Egypt as a case study. The analysis shows that competition, incentive regulation, and privatization of utilities could benefit consumers, workers, the seller (government), and buyers. These benefits are possible because reforms are associated with improvements in productivity, more rational pricing of services, and greater investment. However, they are not automatic. The benefits and their distribution depend on the nature and sequence of reforms, which can be assessed using the "ex ante stakeholder analysis" applied to Telecom Egypt.

Turning to the second set of questions, Edmund O'Sullivan (chapter 9) summarizes the arguments surrounding the debate over the sequence of engaging the private sector in infrastructure. The main arguments for the transaction-by-transaction approach can be stated as follows. First, policy reforms take time, while transactions can be undertaken expeditiously. As a result, expansion of badly needed services is possible. Second, the transactions are likely to trigger policy and institutional reforms down the road, as new investors demand a better regulatory framework. Finally, the transactions often embody new technology, know-how, and finance, all of which improve productivity. The case for policy and institutional reforms before engaging the private sector is equally compelling. First, while transactions are likely to bring about some benefits now, these benefits could be at the expense of larger gains tomorrow. After all, the lasting benefits from engaging the private sector do not merely follow from injecting new capital; they follow from a combination of competition, incentive regulation, and private ownership. Second, rather than speeding up sector reform, transactions may delay reforms because they relax the resource constraint and create a false sense of achievement. Further, they could complicate reform later if, for example, the government decides to increase competition but finds it too costly because it has to renegotiate existing contracts with independent power producers. Finally, the benefits of new technology, know-how, and finance also follow from sector reforms, as observed, for example, in Chile, Argentina, and Mexico. Which of the two approaches is more valid and relevant for the Middle East and North Africa countries? The judgment is left to the reader.

Transaction Costs

Finally, part IV of the volume focuses on two government activities that affect the private sector in a significant way: tax administration and government procurement. The reason for focusing on tax administration is that it is often cited by the private sector as the most binding constraint on firm operation and expansion. At the same time, tax evasion and avoidance are often cited by government officials as the most encountered problem with the private sector. The reason for focusing on government procurement is that the government is a big spender both in the region and elsewhere. The process is often complicated, nontransparent, and discriminatory—leading to uncertainty, corruption, and waste of resources. In addition, by not signing the World Trade Organization (WTO) Government Procurement Agreement (GPA), most developing countries have opted not to subject their procurement to international discipline and multilateral surveillance.

In dealing with tax administration, Sahar Tohamy (chapter 10) attempts to answer two questions: First, what is the magnitude of tax evasion and transaction costs in the Egyptian case? Second, how can both problems be ameliorated? Her answer to the first question is based on a comparative cross-country analysis. Her conclusion is that tax evasion exists in Egypt, but its level is consistent with the country's economic and institutional conditions. Similarly, the transaction costs associated with tax administration for business in Egypt are relatively high, supporting similar findings elsewhere. In response to the second question, Tohamy examines the relationship between taxpayers and the tax authority as a contractual arrangement. To remedy the weaknesses of this arrangement, she draws a number of policy recommendations, including investing in taxpayer education, targeting voluntary compliance, and streamlining tax collectors' incentives.

Finally, Bernard Hoekman (chapter 11) attempts to explain the rationale for the choice by developing countries to forego the signing of the WTO GPA. He cites the following possibilities: unfamiliarity with the existence of such mechanisms, a perception that the payoff is small, a desire to discriminate in favor of domestic firms for infant industry and related reasons, and the successful opposition by groups favoring the status quo. He argues that the GPA provides a useful mechanism for governments to ensure that public procurement procedures are efficient. It also provides an opportunity for reducing uncertainty and anchoring the expectations of the parties involved in the procurement process by increasing transparency, surveillance, and accountability.

Conclusions

This volume argues for a new partnership between the public and private sector in the Middle East and North Africa region. Although significant progress has been made in this direction, the new alliance for development requires further alignments in the roles of the government and the private sector.

- To make the business environment more supportive of the efficient operation, exports, and investment, the reform agenda facing governments in the region is fundamentally institutional in nature. Beyond macroeconomic stability and opening up to world markets, reforms are needed to strengthen the supervision of banks, improve the efficiency of the judicial system, and reduce red tape.

- To restore balance to the roles played by the government and the private sector in the direct ownership and management of resources, privatization is a must. The case for privatization is apparent, and governments have no comparative advantage producing and selling chocolate, cement, clothing, and cellular phones. The issue is how to speed up the process without compromising on efficiency and equity.

- With respect to private sector participation in infrastructure, the question is not whether such a realignment is desirable; the financing gap alone justifies moving in this direction. Rather, the question is how. In particular, should governments continue to follow the approach of transaction-by-transaction, or should they instead focus on sectoral reforms first to attract private capital?

- Finally, tax administration and government procurement seem to be two important institutional issues that deserve special emphasis. While difficult to deal with, they cannot be ignored.

On all these challenges, this volume offers some insights. But insights are just a beginning. The next step is action.

Notes

We would like to thank the contributors to this volume for their dedicated efforts and responsiveness to suggestions. Our thanks also go to the participants at the Cairo and Marrakech workshops for sharing their insights and criticisms. In particular, we would like to mention Mahmoud Abdel Fadil, Hanaa Kheir El Din, Abdel El Monem Abdel Rahman, Kemal Derviş, Adel El Labban, Heba Handoussa, Ahmed Hassan, Taher Helmy, Steve Kelman, Guy Pfeffermann, Roger Leeds, John Page, Alfonso Revollo, A. Saaidi, Jamal Saghir, Nemat Shafik, Alex Shalaby, William Wiggleworth, and Jaime Vazquez-Caro. Hisham Fahmy and his team at the Egyptian Center for Economic Studies (ECES), especially Dina Shawki, provided critical support, without which this volume could not have been possible. Last, but not least, we thank Aziz Gökdemir for editing, Carol Levie for typesetting and layout, and Heather Worley for production.

References

Galal, Ahmed, Leroy Jones, Pankaj Tandon, and Ingo Vogelsang. 1994. *Welfare Consequences of Selling Public Enterprises: An Empirical Analysis*. Oxford: Oxford University Press.

Privatization Yearbook. Various editions. London: Privatization International.

World Bank. 1995. *Claiming the Future: Choosing Prosperity for the Middle East and North Africa.* Washington, D.C.: World Bank, Middle East and North Africa Regional Office.

PART I
The Business Environment

CHAPTER 2

The Business Environment in Egypt

Samiha Fawzy

After decades of state-dominated economic activity, governments around the world are increasingly relying on the private sector to foster economic growth. They are becoming less engaged in the direct provision of goods and services and more active in developing markets, creating supporting institutions, and providing safeguards to ensure equitable distribution.

While this broad observation is hard to dispute, the question arises as to what is necessary to engender greater and more efficient private sector participation in economic growth. Searching for an answer to this question, economists have come to believe that private sector decisions depend on the incentive structure that reflects the relative scarcity of resources, as well as the incentive structure provided by the prevailing institutional framework (Serven and Solimano 1993; Clague 1997; Ul Haque 1995). This broad understanding of the incentive structure is often referred to as "the business environment."

Based on the premise that it takes a combination of economic and institutional reforms to persuade the private sector to be more active, this paper assesses the business environment in Egypt.[1] The analysis addresses three questions: Is the Egyptian private sector taking the lead in economic growth at present? Does the macroeconomic environment offer the necessary conditions for private sector development? And finally, does the institutional climate encourage private firms' growth and competitiveness? These questions are relevant to Egypt today, given that the government has recently taken significant steps to improve the business environment. The state of private sector development, however, is still far below the level needed to boost Egypt's growth, to foster its integration in the world market, and to ensure a decent living standard for Egyptian citizens.

This chapter is organized as follows. The first section offers a brief analysis of the private sector development in Egypt to date, which is followed by a section that assesses the macroeconomic environment with a view to identifying the most critical areas that require further reforms. The section titled "Institutional Environment" relies on the findings of a survey conducted on a random sample of firms to identify the most binding institutional constraints to private sector operations in Egypt. This section also provides a detailed analysis of these constraints for companies of varying economic activities, size, and ownership structures. The chapter ends with a concluding section.

Private Sector Development in Egypt

In the early 1990s, the government of Egypt introduced more liberal policies to boost the private sector. Have these policies produced an agile and vibrant private sector that can bear the responsibility of economic growth? This section briefly reviews the evolution of the private sector's relative importance, composition, and characteristics.

Relative Importance

Recent figures suggest that the role of the private sector in the Egyptian economy is expanding. But much remains to be done considering both the scope of the sector in other emerging markets, and the Egyptian government's goal of achieving a sustainable annual GDP growth rate of 7 to 8 percent.

Table 2.1 indicates that the private sector's contribution to GDP increased from 61 percent during 1991–92 to 66 percent during 1996–97, and from 53 percent to 60 percent excluding agriculture. But the private sector has neither regained the pre–1952 Revolution level of its contribution to GDP of 85 percent, nor does it compare well to the private sector's share of GDP in such countries as Brazil (80 percent), Uruguay (74 percent), and Indonesia (72 percent) (Moore 1995; World Bank 1994). Although its share in investment rose from 46.5 percent to 51.5 percent during the same period, it is still low compared with an average of 73.8 percent in developing countries (table 2.2).

At the same time, the size of the government in economic activity is relatively large while the flow of foreign direct investment (FDI) is relatively low. It is true that the share of government expenditure in GDP has been reduced from 36 percent in 1993 to 28 percent in 1996. However, table 2.2 indicates that this level of government expenditure is still above an average of 22 percent in other countries. On FDI, there has been a noticeable decline of almost 50 percent between the years 1991–92 and 1996–97. The current FDI-to-GDP ratio of less than 1 percent is much lower than what Egypt needs to grow at 7–8 percent annually and the corresponding 1996 average of 3 percent in other developing countries (table 2.2).

TABLE 2.1 PRIVATE SECTOR CONTRIBUTION TO THE EGYPTIAN ECONOMY
in percent age unless specified otherwise

Private shares in sectors	1987–88	1991–92	1992–93	1993–94	1994–95	1995–96	1996–97
Private share in GDP	62.4	61.2	61.8	61.7	62.6	63.3	66.4
Excluding agriculture	54.0	53.8	54.4	54.4	55.6	56.6	60.4
Private share in investment	36.7	46.5	33.3	33.5	40.9	49.2	51.5
Private share in bank loans[a]	71.7	64.2	62.7	61.2	66.8	69.7	72.3
FDI (US$ millions)	1,124.7[b]	1,152.0	1,139.6	1,320.8	782.7	626.9	769.7

a. Total bank loans extended to the business sector at the end of the fiscal year.
b. 1990–91.
Sources: Central Bank of Egypt (CBE), Economic Bulletin, various issues; and Ministry of Economy (1997a).

TABLE 2.2 PRIVATE SECTOR INDICATORS: CROSS-COUNTRY COMPARISON, 1996
percentage

Country	Share of private investment in gross domestic fixed investment	Share of FDI in GDP	Share of government expenditure in GDP
Egypt	59.1	0.9	28.4
Chile	80.0	5.5	16.8
Mexico	79.1	2.3	22.6
Thailand	77.6	1.3	18.0
Korea	76.0	0.5	24.8
Malaysia	69.8	4.5	35.1
Indonesia	60.5	3.5	16.6

Source: World Economic Forum (1997) (share of government expenditure in GDP); World Bank (1998).

Composition

Table 2.3 shows that the private sector generates more than 50 percent of value added in all activities, with the exception of petroleum, money and banking, electricity, and insurance.

It also indicates that the private sector's share in GDP in all economic activities has increased in the period between 1991–92 and 1996–97, again with the exception of petroleum and electricity. The sector in which the private sector gained a decisive upper hand is industry.

The change in the contribution of the private sector to GDP reflects even more significant changes in investment patterns between 1996–97 and 1991–92 (table 2.4). Most noticeably, private firms are increasingly turning away from the commodity sector to transportation, communications, and tourism for investing. This trend is expected to continue, especially because the government announced last year that all future power generation projects will be constructed by the private sector on a build-

TABLE 2.3 SHARE OF PRIVATE SECTOR IN GDP BY ECONOMIC ACTIVITY
percentage

Sector	1991–92	1996–97
Commodity sectors	62.8	68.8
Agriculture	98.8	98.7
Industry and mining	58.1	74.0
Petroleum and its products	17.3	13.3
Electricity	0.0	0.0
Construction	70.8	73.8
Productive services	62.1	68.6
Transportation and Suez Canal	47.9	55.8
Trade	89.7	94.4
Money and banking	29.3	30.4
Insurance	39.5	41.2
Hotels and restaurants	84.7	85.3
Social services	54.9	55.3
Total GDP	61.2	66.4
Total GDP excluding agriculture	53.8	60.4

Note: GDP is at factor cost.
Source: CBE, *Economic Bulletin*, various issues.

TABLE 2.4 DISTRIBUTION OF PRIVATE INVESTMENT BETWEEN ECONOMIC
SECTORS
percentage

Sector	Share in total private investment	
	1991–92	1996–97
Commodity sectors	58.9	55.9
Agriculture	7.7	10.1
Industry and mining	23.6	27.5
Petroleum and its products	25.5	14.9
Electricity	0.0	0.6
Construction	2.1	2.8
Productive services	14.5	22.1
Transportation and Suez Canal	4.3	7.4
Trade, banking and insurance	3.3	3.5
Hotels and restaurants	6.9	11.2
Social services	26.6	22.0
Total	100.0	100.0

Source: CBE, *Economic Bulletin*, various issues.

own-operate-transfer (BOOT) basis. In addition, there have been three bids for BOOT in airport projects and two planned BOOT projects to develop roads. Moreover, cellular phone concessions have been sold to private firms and port services opened to private investors (The United States Embassy 1998). To date, 12 new industrial cities with 2,000 productive factories have been developed, the majority of which are privately owned (Ministry of Economy 1998).

Characteristics

Three salient features characterize the private sector in Egypt and are likely to influence its impact on the economy: the dominance of small and micro firms ("small" firms employ 10–50 workers, whereas "micro" firms employ fewer than 10), the prevalence of the legal partnership form, and the presence of a large informal sector.

The structure of the private sector in Egypt has a dual nature in terms of size; on one end, there is a large number of small and micro firms, but on the other end, there is a limited number of large firms. Small and micro enterprises represent nearly 98 percent of private economic units, they create nearly three-quarters of all private jobs and produce an estimated 80 percent of the country's private value added (Guigale and Mobarak 1996). If the agriculture sector were excluded, the figures will decline; however, the magnitude of small and micro firms will still be significant. Despite their dominance, small and micro firms are not participating efficiently in Egypt's growth. First, small firms suffer more than large firms from institutional constraints, as will be discussed in the section on the institutional environment. Second, they serve mainly low-income consumers and provide low-quality, low-price products. Third, most of these firms use obsolete technologies. Conversely, while large-size firms are relatively well-developed, they are too few to foster large private-sector-led growth.

As for the legal status of private firms, in 1992, most private establishments in non-agricultural activities were incorporated either in the form of individual proprietorships (47 percent) or partnerships (48 percent), while private joint-stock firms represented only 4.4 percent of all private firms (World Bank 1994). The implication is that more than 90 percent of private firms take the form of a partnership and are run on a family rather than on a corporate basis. In addition, most private firms in Egypt are not traded on the stock market, and although some have been listed recently, this is done for tax reasons and not to enlarge the shareholders' base.

Another important characteristic of Egyptian private investment is the large informal sector. Despite the lack of accurate figures on the size of the informal sector in Egypt, the majority of small and micro enterprises are informal. For example, in 1991, there were estimated to be 2.28 million informal enterprises (Alexandria Businessmen's Association 1996). Egyptian Financial Group (EFG)-Hermes estimates that the informal sector represents nearly 40 percent of the total Egyptian economy (EFG-Hermes 1997). The large share of the informal private sector may be attributed to the legacy of socialist policies, cumbersome regulatory regimes, and high transaction costs. The implication is that informal assets can neither be used in efficient and legally secure transactions nor be used as collateral (De Soto 1997).

Based on this analysis, it is evident that despite some positive signs of development, the Egyptian private sector is not yet able to act as a catalyst to growth. The moderate growth rate of private investment, the decline of FDI inflows, the dominance of weak and underdeveloped small and micro enterprises, the large informal sector, the family-based management strategies, and the inward orientation of most private firms, all reflect a shallow state of development in Egypt's private sector.

Two major problems in the business environment seem to be responsible for the limited contribution and efficiency of the private sector: a distorted macroeconomic incentive structure and cumbersome institutional constraints. The former problem results in weak incentives for investing and the latter in high transaction costs and a lack of competitiveness. The following sections identify the macroeconomic and institutional constraints that are still impeding private sector operations in Egypt.

Macroeconomic Reforms: Uneven Progress

The experiences of other countries, particularly in East Asia and Latin America, suggest that a high degree of macroeconomic stability, credibility, and sustainability is key to a strong private sector response (Serven and Solimano 1993). This section investigates the status of macroeconomic reforms, covering both the stabilization and structural reform efforts to date. It also attempts to identify the most critical areas requiring further reform.

Successful Stabilization

Reforms under the Economic Reform and Structural Adjustment Program (ERSAP) starting during 1990–91 focused mainly on stabilizing the economy. These reforms produced positive results. The public deficit-to-GDP ratio shrank to 1 percent, double-digit inflation was broken, and the current account balance deficit as a percentage of GDP decreased significantly (figure 2.1). The exchange rate was devalued and unified, and the Egyptian pound kept stable between £E3.33 and £E3.39 to the U.S. dollar over the last few years. Under conditions of fiscal adjustment, open-capital account, and higher interest rate on Egyptian pound deposits than on dollar-denominated deposits, foreign reserves increased from $6.1 billion to $20 billion, covering more than 16 months of imports (Ministry of Economy 1998). As a result of reforms and attractive returns on the stock market, portfolio inflows have increased from an average of only $4 million in the early 1990s to $654 million during 1996–97 (Ministry of Economy 1997b). External debt indicators also improved during the same period (figure 2.2).

FIGURE 2.1 STABILIZATION INDICATORS

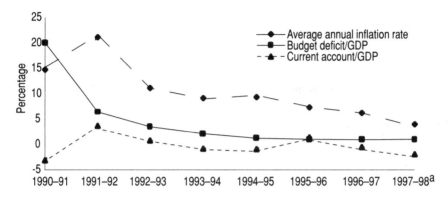

Note: a. Estimated.
Source: Ministry of Economy (1998).

FIGURE 2.2 DEBT INDICATORS

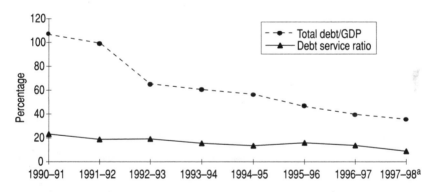

Note: a. Estimated.
Source: Ministry of Economy (1998).

Uncompleted Structural Adjustments

The government has also initiated significant structural reforms. These reforms covered the financial sector, privatization, deregulation, and trade liberalization. However, they have not gone far enough.

FINANCIAL LIBERALIZATION

Reforming the financial sector has led to several positive improvements, including greater efficiency in financial intermediation, reversal of the dollarization
phenomenon, and revival of the stock market as apparent in the market capitali-
zation and trading volume indicators (figure 2.3). Despite these tangible developments, Egypt's financial system still suffers from deficiencies: 70 percent of
bank assets are controlled by state-owned banks; most private banks concentrate on short-term commercial lending mainly to large and medium-sized private firms; the insurance industry is underdeveloped and highly concentrated;
and the stock market does not participate effectively in private sector finance
(World Bank 1997).

FIGURE 2.3 FINANCIAL INDICATORS

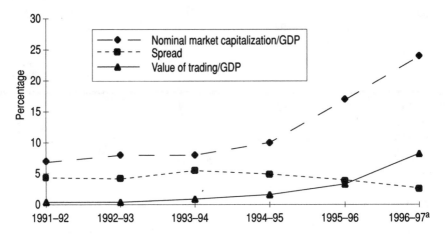

Note: a. Estimated.
Source: Subramanian (1997).

PRIVATIZATION

The privatization process has been accelerated in the last two years. By July
1998, the government had privatized 91 of 314 companies (only 9 were sold to
anchor investors), with total sales proceeds of £E9.1 billion, representing almost 14 percent of the total book value of state-owned enterprises (SOEs), which
are estimated to be worth £E63.8 billion.[2] More important, the privatization process has been expanded to include joint venture banks, public banks, and public
insurance companies.[3] The government has also adopted build-operate-transfer
(BOT) schemes to attract private investment in infrastructure, particularly elec-

tricity generation, transportation, and telecommunications. Nevertheless, the size of SOEs relative to GDP in Egypt is about 30 percent, compared with an average of 11 percent for other developing economies (Anderson and Martinez 1998). In addition, the limited sales to anchor investors leaves the governance structure of privatized firms largely unchanged, and hence undermines the potential welfare effects of privatization.

TRADE LIBERALIZATION

The Egyptian government has implemented serious unilateral, regional, and multilateral measures to open its trade regime. These measures have included a reduction in the maximum tariff from 160 percent prior to 1990 to 50 percent in 1997, and hence narrowed dispersion significantly. The nominal unweighted average tariff fell from 33 percent in 1988 to 24.6 percent in 1998, while the weighted average tariff was estimated at 28 percent in 1998 (Ministry of Commerce and Supply 1998). In addition, the Egyptian pound has been made convertible, although it is not traded abroad. Foreign exchange restrictions were abolished, and foreign currency transfers are now completely free.

Egypt also is adhering to the World Trade Organization's requirements and is close to signing an association agreement with the European Union. The Egyptian government has joined efforts to revive the Arab common market and is discussing with the United States the possibility of a free trade agreement.

Notwithstanding these reforms, the average tariff of 28 percent exceeds the world average (8.2 percent) and even the average tariff of other developing countries (21.4 percent). This protection contributes to low productivity and threatens efficient resource allocation. The cascading nature of the tariff structure creates an anti-export bias estimated at 19.4 percent in 1997 (Ministry of Commerce and Supply 1998). Finally, administrative and foreign trade practices have not moved in the same direction as tariff reform, thus increasing trade-related transaction costs.

DEREGULATION

To induce more private sector contribution to economic activity, the Egyptian government has launched a comprehensive deregulation program. This includes simplifying company registration, customs procedures, and approval processes, and issuing laws to facilitate business operations (Ministry of Economy 1998).

In response to Egypt's successful financial stabilization and the prospect of improved structural adjustment, real GDP growth increased from 1.9 percent during 1991–92 to 4.7 percent during 1994–95 and then to almost 5 percent during 1996–97 and 1997–98 (Ministry of Economy 1998). Despite these positive developments, Egypt's competitive position, compared with countries in East Asia and Latin America, is not satisfactory in terms of economic growth, trade performance, openness, saving, and investment (table 2.5).

TABLE 2.5 SELECTED INDICATORS FOR EGYPT AND SOME FAST-GROWING
ECONOMIES

Country	Average annual growth rate of GDP 1990–96	Trade/ GDP 1996	Average tariff rate 1996	Gross national savings/GDP 1996	Gross domestic investment/GDP 1996
Egypt	3.7	0.43	22	16.7	16.89
Chile	7.2	0.46	11	23.81	25.07
Hong Kong	5.5	2.66	0	33.07	30.46
Mexico	1.8	0.58	11	18.95	16.74
Korea	7.3	0.64	7.9	34.07	38.29
Singapore	8.7	2.99	0.4	49.99	35.83
Thailand	8.3	0.75	9.3	35.48	43.19
Indonesia	7.7	0.47	6	30.75	28.48
Malaysia	8.7	1.62	15	35.48	41.37

Sources: World Bank, *World Development Indicators*, 1998; The World Economic Forum, *The Global Competitiveness Report*, 1997.

Reforms Ahead

Looking ahead, Egypt's challenge is to maintain financial stability while pursuing further structural reforms. To this end, increasing the pace of privatization, trade liberalization, financial sector development, and deregulation are crucial. A more rapid and wider privatization process including infrastructure and public monopolies is important for increasing competition, allaying fears of policy reversal and encouraging private sector investment and capital inflow. Future privatization efforts should include changing the management as well as the ownership of firms in order to maximize the benefit of the shift from public to private ownership. In this regard, sales to anchor investors should be encouraged.

On other reforms, greater openness through continued reduction of trade barriers, deeper regional integration schemes, and a more flexible exchange rate system will correct the bias in the relative prices, encourage firms to produce for global markets, help upgrade technology, and stimulate greater competition. Further financial sector reforms will help mobilize savings, fuel accumulation of physical and human resources, and thereby provide necessary inputs for private sector operations. Deregulation, through simplifying bureaucratic procedures, eliminating red tape, increasing market contestability, reducing transaction costs, and securing property rights, is likely to induce more private investment.

In addition to these reforms, evidence suggests that without efficient institutions and effective enforcement mechanisms, macroeconomic reforms will fail to deliver private sector-led growth. An enabling and competitive institutional environment is widely acknowledged as an indispensable complementary condition for encouraging private investment, promoting high market specialization and competitiveness, and reducing uncertainty and transaction costs (North 1990; Olson 1997). The following section identifies those institutions that are impeding the private sector the most in Egypt.

Institutional Environment

Despite the significant steps taken to improve the business environment in Egypt, private firms claim that many institutions still hamper their operations. This section analyzes these constraints in general and individually. It also compares the Egyptian institutional environment to other countries.

The analysis relies primarily on a survey conducted by the Egyptian Center for Economic Studies (ECES) in early 1998 on 154 private firms. The sample was selected randomly from different economic activities including trade, manufacturing, oil, tourism, and construction. Firms of varying sizes[4] and ownership[5] structures were included to determine whether institutional constraints fall disproportionately on smaller firms and foreign companies. Variations in economic activities are meant to explore whether certain constraints are sector-specific (see figures 2.4, 2.5, and 2.6).

FIGURE 2.4 SAMPLE DISTRIBUTION BY ECONOMIC ACTIVITY

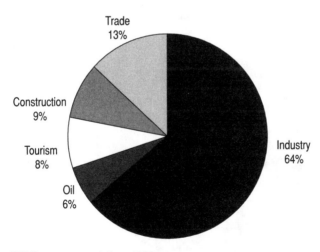

Source: ECES survey population, 1998.

FIGURE 2.5 SAMPLE DISTRIBUTION BY SIZE OF ENTERPRISE

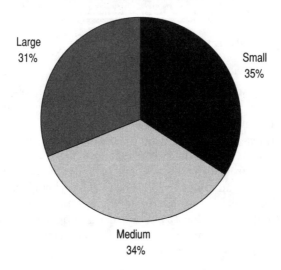

Source: ECES survey population, 1998.

FIGURE 2.6 SAMPLE DISTRIBUTION BY OWNERSHIP

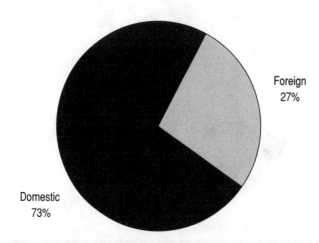

Source: ECES survey population, 1998.

Survey Results

The survey findings show that tax administration, commercial dispute settlement, and support services, respectively, are the primary constraints limiting the operation and growth of the private sector in Egypt (figure 2.7). The least binding constraints include unofficial payments, input procurement, and local demand. Constraints rated as moderate include difficulties related to workers, exporting, cost, and access to finance, and economic policy uncertainty.

A comparison between the constraints faced by Egyptian entrepreneurs in 1994 and in 1998 reveals that some problems have remained while others have been ameliorated (World Bank 1994). The problems of complicated tax administration, inefficient dispute settlement, unqualified labor, and weak support services have persisted over time. In fact, their relative importance has increased and they are ranked as the most severe constraints to private investment today. However, the severity of some problems, including cost and access to finance, bureaucratic procedures, and policy uncertainty, seems to have been reduced since 1994. The lower ranking of these constraints confirms the positive achievements of Egypt's reform program, particularly in terms of financial liberalization and deregulation.

FIGURE 2.7 OVERALL RANKING OF INSTITUTIONAL CONSTRAINTS

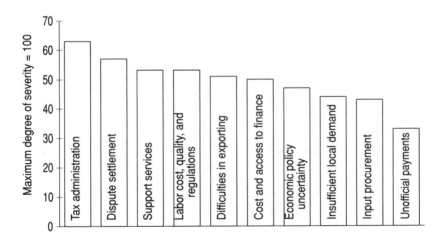

Source: ECES survey results, 1998.

SEVERITY OF CONSTRAINTS ACROSS ECONOMIC ACTIVITIES

The severity of constraints is highest in the trade sector—followed by construction, manufacturing, and tourism—and is lowest in the oil sector (figure 2.8). Individual constraints also affect sectors differently (table 2.6). For example, while tax administration is most binding to the trade sector, it is less constraining for the oil sector. Commercial dispute settlement is the primary constraint impeding investment in the construction sector, but this constraint ranks relatively low for the tourism sector. Unofficial payments are the primary complaint of firms in the construction sector, perhaps because these firms are involved in government procurement. Labor problems are felt more acutely by firms in the oil sector because foreign firms operating in the oil industry are more likely to adhere to rigorous domestic labor laws.

FIGURE 2.8 INSTITUTIONAL CONSTRAINTS BY ECONOMIC ACTIVITY

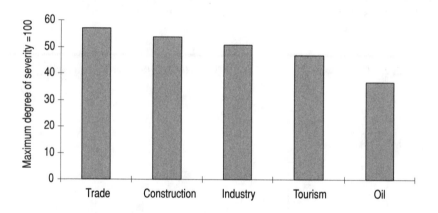

Source: ECES survey results, 1998.

SEVERITY OF CONSTRAINTS BY SIZE OF FIRM

On average, small firms suffer more than large ones from institutional constraints[6] (figure 2.9). This is especially apparent in tax administration and dispute settlement, because small firms cannot afford accountants and lawyers; in addition, their lack of collateral restricts their access to affordable credit. The only constraint that has proved to be less problematic for small firms is labor issues. This is mainly because most small firms are family businesses, and the enforcement of labor regulations is weak in small firms, especially those employing fewer than 10 workers.

TABLE 2.6. RANKING OF INSTITUTIONAL CONSTRAINTS BY OWNERSHIP, SIZE, AND ECONOMIC ACTIVITY
(Maximum degree of severity = 100)

	Economic policy uncertainty	Labor cost, quality, and regulations	Cost of access to finance	Input procurement	Tax admin- istration	Insufficient local demand	Difficulties in exporting	Support services	Unofficial payments	Dispute settlement
Ownership										
Local	51	52	53	44	65	43	56	na	na	59
Foreign	37	54	40	39	56	46	36	na	na	51
Size										
Small	50	48	56	44	73	46	54	50	35	63
Medium	38	54	59	43	62	43	58	62	38	58
Large	49	57	44	43	56	43	47	52	29	52
Activity										
Industry	46	51	49	43	64	46	51	53	33	56
Oil	38	58	25	39	42	25	13	44	10	54
Trade	58	64	54	48	74	46	50	65	28	63
Tourism	48	55	64	29	50	45	44	41	28	39
Construction	52	43	46	52	69	36	63	51	39	70

Source: ECES survey results, 1998.

25

FIGURE 2.9 INSTITUTIONAL CONSTRAINTS BY SIZE OF ENTERPRISE

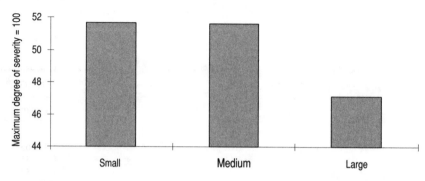

Source: ECES survey results, 1998.

SEVERITY OF CONSTRAINTS ACCORDING TO OWNERSHIP

Institutional constraints also differ according to the ownership structure of the firm. Figure 2.10 shows that domestic firms suffer more from regulatory and institutional constraints than foreign firms. This could be attributed to the fact that most foreign firms included in the sample were operating in the oil sector, which is subject to international contracts.

FIGURE 2.10 INSTITUTIONAL CONSTRAINTS BY OWNERSHIP

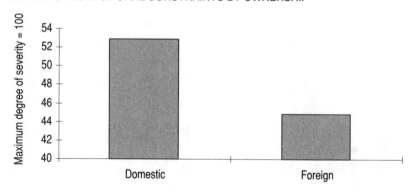

Source: ECES survey results, 1998.

Diagnosis of Institutional Constraints

While the overall ranking of constraints is useful, it conceals details that could be important for policymaking. Table 2.7 reveals some interesting details, which are elaborated on below.

TABLE 2.7 DETAILED RANKING OF OBSTACLES TO PRIVATE OPERATIONS IN EGYPT

Constraint	Ranking[a]	Constraint	Ranking[a]
Tax administration		*Finance*	
a. Lack of trust between tax collectors and		a. Cost of finance	63
tax payers	69	b. Collateral requirements	55
b. Inefficiency of the dispute system	67	c. Time to obtain approvals	53
c. Arbitrary estimation of taxable profits	65	d. Required documentation	44
Supporting services		e. Availability of finance	27
a. Domestic transportation	63	*Local demand*	
b. Information services	59	a. Lack of information on domestic	
c. Availability and quality of training services	58	market	60
d. Availability of technical assistance services	57	b. Complexity of government	
e. Marketing and distribution	56	procurement regulations	59
f. Airports and maritime port services	55	c. Inefficiency of marketing	
g. Laboratories for testing standards	53	and distribution	50
h. Qualified warehousing facility	52	d. Demand insufficiency	44
i. Maintenance and repair services	51	*Input procurement*	
j. Health certification and procedures	42	*Imported inputs*	
k. Telecommunications	36	a. Tariffs and surcharges	68
Labor		b. Customs procedures	65
a. Lack of skilled labor	61	c. Port services	58
b. Difficulties in firing labor	37	d. Information about suppliers	49
c. High cost of labor	35	*Domestic inputs*	
d. Union activities	12	a. Quality and specification	49
Difficulties in exporting		b. Price	47
a. Marketing and distribution companies	57	c. Delivery on time	45
b. Tariffs on imported inputs	56	d. Availability	39
c. Drawback and temporary admission system	51	*Unofficial payments*	
d. Export procedures	44	a. Each import transaction	43
e. Absence of export credit	42	b. Tax collectors	38
f. Insurance services	38	c. Each export transaction	37
Economic policy uncertainty		d. Labor insurance inspector	24
a. Lack of transparency in lawmaking	69	e. Loans from banks	20
b. Lack of respect for property rights	56		
c. Policy instability	53		

Note: a. Maximum degree of severity = 100
Source: ECES survey results, 1998.

TAX ADMINISTRATION

Tax administration has been cited as a chronic constraint to private sector development in Egypt for years (World Bank 1992, 1994; Galal 1996). Investors do not complain about the extent of taxes as much as the complicated tax administration itself. Trust is lacking between tax collectors and taxpayers, disputes are settled inefficiently, and estimation of taxable profits is arbitrary. Investors report that they do not know how much taxes they actually have to pay. The criteria for tax assessment is ambiguous, and tax collectors have significant discretionary powers, which lead tax officers and taxpayers to extreme initial bargaining positions. Investors also complain that the process of tax assessment and collection is time-consuming and costly. In many instances, it leads to underreporting of taxable income or tax evasion and often takes years to resolve in court. Finally, taxpayers complain that tax collectors tend to overestimate taxes to meet the collection targets (World Bank 1992; Hassan 1996).

DISPUTE SETTLEMENT

Table 2.8 indicates that the average time needed to resolve disputes in court is four and a half years compared to one year outside of court. The survey also shows that the main reasons for disputes are bankruptcy, broken agreements, problems with the tax authority, and quality of supplies, ranked according to their importance. Nearly two-thirds of disputes take place between private firms, while disputes with government bodies represent 22 percent of the total. The remaining disputes are with banks, labor, and SOEs. Apart from being time-consuming, investors also complain that litigation is expensive and that the judicial system is not well-acquainted with commercial disputes related to market economies. Much of the existing legislation was developed during the period of centralized control, inwardness, and direct government participation in the economy, which makes it incompatible with a dynamic, private sector-dominated, open market economy. New trade agreements and the growing importance of intellectual property rights also require that the current laws be revised. In addition, investors complain about the lack of contract enforcement mechanisms and the poor enforcement of laws. In their view, the judicial system must be reformed and improved to cope with their needs in a global market-oriented economy.

SUPPORTING SERVICES

Interviews with private firms suggest that the high cost and poor quality of support services are important impediments to productivity growth. According to the survey results, the most important problems are as follows:

- *High cost and low quality of domestic transportation.* Investors' activities are hampered by the poor maintenance of transport vehicles, lack of equipment, and inefficient handling and loading services. Businesspeople point out the need for improving the transportation services by lowering tariffs

TABLE 2.8 DISPUTES SETTLEMENT

	Small	Medium	Large	Average
Time needed to resolve a dispute				
In court (years)	4	5	5	4.5
Out of court (years)				
Less than 1 year (% of responses)	92	87	87	90
More than 1 year (% of responses)	8	13	13	10
Distribution of disputes across different actors (% of total disputes)				
Private	21	61	59	61
Public	0	7	4	5
Labor	0	0	7	5
Banks	0	1	3	2
Government	4	22	26	22

Source: ECES survey results, 1998.

on transport vehicles, increasing refrigerated transport modes, and introducing new freight lines.

- *Absence of adequate information about suppliers and markets.* Despite the remarkable development in information services, access to information remains a problem in Egypt. Information is not accurate and is costly to obtain, especially for small and micro enterprises, which constitute the bulk of firms in Egypt.

- *Shortage of marketing and distribution skills and networks.* Private firms complain that marketing, distribution services, and after-sales services are scarce and inefficient.

- *Lack of technical assistance.* Evidence suggests that Egyptian firms require technical assistance in production planning, quality management, and technology upgrading.

- *Poor training services.* Private firms rate the inadequacy of training centers as a major obstacle.

- *Inadequate port services.* Investors claim that the high cost, low quality, and complicated procedures of port services are among the major factors hampering their productivity growth. A recent study indicates that Egypt's seaport charges for imports are triple those of competing countries, which raises the cost of insurance and freight (CIF) for imports to Egypt by over 10 percent (World Bank 1997).

LABOR

Although the Egyptian labor force is internationally competitive in terms of cost, the lack of high-quality human resources is one of the most acute challenges facing firms. Private investors rank the lack of skilled and semi-skilled labor and qualified local managerial staff as the most binding labor constraint. Education and vocational training do not produce the skills demanded in the local labor market.

Next to the quality issue, the survey results show that restrictive labor laws are also problematic. Egypt's job security law is among the most stringent in the world. Firms are not allowed to lay off workers without governmental approval, which renders dismissals costly or even impossible when operations must be downsized or new technologies must be introduced to maintain competitiveness. Although many firms have succeeded in circumventing labor regulations, this constraint still affects firms' competitiveness negatively.[7] These regulations give investors a strong incentive to shift production to capital-intensive techniques, which puts Egyptian firms in a disadvantageous position in an increasingly competitive world economy. They may also discourage firms from investing in training since disciplinary actions against misconduct and low productivity are not enforceable.

DIFFICULTIES IN EXPORTING

The investors surveyed regarded difficulties in exporting as a moderate problem because most of them produce for the domestic rather than international markets.

For exporting firms, the primary concern is high tariff rates on imported inputs. The average nominal tariff rate is still high in Egypt, and the cascading tariff structure creates an anti-export bias. The lack of distribution and marketing companies ranks second. As for drawback and temporary admission systems, investors complain that these systems involve many steps that are costly in both time and money. Finally, firms complain about complicated export procedures and the absence of export credit and insurance services, in that order.

FINANCE

Firms complain that the cost of credit is their leading financial constraint. The second constraint is collateral requirements, followed by the excessive time needed to obtain approvals, and finally the lack of available and accessible finance. Availability of finance is the least reported problem related to finance, perhaps because the high cost of capital and the complicated, and often impossible, collateral requirements deter firms from seeking formal credit, especially in the case of small and micro firms. The result is a reliance on informal sources of finance, which are more costly and hence negatively affect firms' profitability.

The survey highlights the constraining features of the financial system from a private-sector perspective. First, most private commercial banks concentrate on short-term commercial lending (70 percent of total consolidated loan volume) mainly to medium-sized and large companies. The result is that large firms lack long-term finance, and small and micro enterprises are excluded from the formal credit system. Given that almost 90 percent of the firms operating in Egypt are small or micro enterprises, this raises the cost of production. Second, the small but rapidly growing stock market does not yet play a significant role in private sector finance. Although many large companies are listed on the stock exchange, few are actually traded stocks. In fact, seeking listing on the stock market is motivated by tax preferences rather than the possibility of raising capital by floating shares. In addition, derivative markets (futures and options) are virtually nonexistent. Third, the insurance industry is underdeveloped and highly concentrated. The ratio of total assets to GDP of all insurance companies in Egypt (life and non-life) was about 4 percent in 1995, while life insurance assets alone were 38 percent of GDP in a sample of developed economies. Moreover, the reserves and surplus of the social insurance and public pension fund systems, nearly 29 percent of total financial assets, are beyond the reach of the private sector. Insurance companies hold the bulk of their funds, 77 percent, in fixed-term bank deposits and government bonds (American Chamber of Commerce in Egypt 1996; World Bank 1997).

ECONOMIC POLICY UNCERTAINTY

One of the most interesting results of the 1998 survey is that uncertainty of economic policy ranks relatively low as a constraint, while it ranked as the most binding constraint in the early 1990s (World Bank 1992; Galal 1996). Seven years of the ERSAP seem to have provided sufficient time to establish an acceptable degree of credibility and safeguarding against policy reversal. Moreover, recent years have witnessed closer coordination between the private sector and the government in the process of decisionmaking. Nevertheless, businesspeople still complain about ad hoc policies and sudden changes, lack of respect for property rights, and asymmetry of information.

INSUFFICIENT LOCAL DEMAND

Local demand does not present a serious obstacle to private sector development according to interviews with entrepreneurs. Egypt's large population, estimated at 61.7 million in 1997, and a substantial informal sector suggest a potentially large home-demand base. Moreover, the local demand rate of growth, which is more important than its absolute size, indicates an upward trend in demand in the past two years, which is likely to continue with the expected acceleration of private sector participation in economic activities. Interviews with entrepreneurs, however, indicated that the most binding problems were related to the complexity of government procurement regulations and the inefficiency of marketing and distribution channels, in that order. Data also show that local demand is highly concentrated in basic goods, which explains the low level of home-demand sophistication (Fawzy and Galal 1997). Unsophisticated demand explains, partly, why Egyptian firms are not strict about quality; the lack of laws to protect consumers contributes as well. Consumer protection law (Law 57 of 1939 as amended Trademarks Law) is underdeveloped in Egypt. This limits contestability as unprotected consumers tend to avoid new brands, thus making the cost of reputation-building for new entrants particularly high and hampering any attempt to innovate.

INPUT PROCUREMENT

The survey results concerning inputs or supplies highlight serious challenges to firms' competitiveness. Investors complain more about imported inputs than about domestic ones, especially with respect to tariffs and surcharges, complicated customs procedures and port services. As for domestic inputs, investors stated that the most binding constraint is the poor and inconsistent quality of products, followed by late delivery.

UNOFFICIAL PAYMENTS

Bribes were cited as the least severe problem facing businesspeople in Egypt today. The survey findings indicate that bribery is more widespread in import and export transactions, tax collection, labor insurance inspection, and loans from banks, in that order. This seems to conform with the overall ranking of institutional constraints. Results also indicate that the construction sector suffers the most from unofficial payments, while the oil sector suffers the least. This is understandable when one takes into consideration that a high percentage of construction transactions is with the government and that the value of these transactions is usually high, which positively correlates with grand corruption. Conversely, the oil sector is subject to international contracts, and foreigners are usually more apprehensive about bribery than locals.

To sum up, the survey results support the conclusion that despite ongoing reforms, institutional reforms are crucial to private sector development. Tax administration, the judicial system, support services, education, and vocational training are priorities for reform.

Cross-Country Comparison

Comparing the institutional environment in Egypt with that of other countries helps to gauge whether investors' complaints represent actual constraints or not. A cross-country analysis also gives investors and policymakers a reference point in negotiating for more reform and deregulation, attracting foreign direct investment, and setting growth targets. More important, in an increasingly liberalized and competitive global market, international technology, management skills, and capital will flow to economies that offer the most competitive and rich environment. Lagging behind international performance levels will be costly for Egypt.

In evaluating Egypt's institutional constraints, *The International Country Risk Guide* (ICRG) (1997) is a useful index that measures to what extent the institutional environment is business-friendly. It focuses on five institutional variables: contract repudiation, expropriation risk, corruption, rule of law, and bureaucratic quality.

Figures 2.11 and 2.12 indicate that although Egypt's rating has improved somewhat during the period from 1991 to 1996, reflecting an improvement in its institutional framework, institutional constraints are still significant in Egypt compared
with many developing countries. This may partially explain the low level of private
sector growth in Egypt, as well as the limited FDI inflows to the country over the
past five years.

FIGURE 2.11 INSTITUTIONAL CONSTRAINTS IN EGYPT OVER TIME

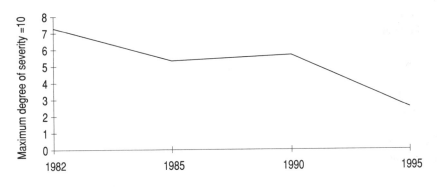

Source: International Country Risk Guide (1997).

FIGURE 2.12 INSTITUTIONAL CONSTRAINTS IN EGYPT AND SELECTED COUNTRIES

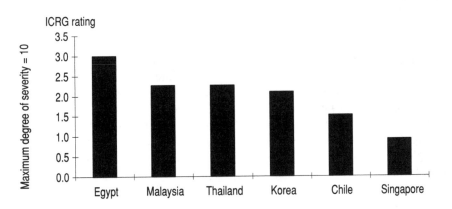

Source: International Country Risk Guide (1997).

In short, this cross-country comparison shows that the business environment in Egypt is less attractive than many of its competitors, and that investors' complaints are likely to be real constraints. Therefore it is necessary to identify which institutions impede private sector development the most in Egypt.

Conclusion

This paper investigated whether the private sector is leading economic growth in Egypt, whether the macroeconomic environment offers the necessary conditions for private sector development, and whether the institutional climate is amenable to firms' growth and competitiveness. The underlying argument of the analysis is that it takes both economic and institutional reforms for the private sector to flourish and play that role. Several conclusions can be drawn from this analysis.

First, despite recent aggressive economic reforms, the private sector's initiatives are insufficient to drive Egypt's growth and are far behind the private sector contribution to economic activity in other developing countries. Although this unsatisfactory response could be a manifestation of the "wait and see" behavior of investors, other factors in both the macroeconomic and institutional environments seem to be responsible for this inadequacy.

Second, while the stabilization reforms in Egypt have been successful by international standards, the structural component of the reform program is lagging behind. The slow pace of privatization, high tariff levels, young stock market, and underdeveloped insurance and pension systems hamper private sector efficiency.

Third, the survey results show that the institutional climate deprives private firms of the means to compete in a highly competitive global market. The most critical reform areas to promote private sector development are tax administration, the judicial system, support services, education, and vocational training.

Fourth, private sector development is only one element of Egypt's growth. Complementary public investment in social services, infrastructure, and environment are essential. The health of the private sector also hinges on a competent, capable government.

Finally, a solid public–private partnership is indispensable for growth. It helps overcome private sector concerns about policy reversals and eliminates any constraints to private sector development.

Notes

1. The author would like to express her thanks to Amal Refaat for research assistance and Dina Shawki for help throughout the course of preparing this study.

2. Unpublished data from the Ministry of Public Enterprises.

3. The Commercial International Bank (CIB) was the first joint venture bank to be privatized in 1993, followed by the Egyptian American Bank (EAB) in 1996.

4. The number of employees was used as an indicator of size. Firms employing between 10 and 50 workers were considered small. Firms employing between 51 and 100 workers were considered medium size. Firms with more than 100 workers were considered large.

5. Foreign ownership refers to firms with any foreign participation.

6. Small firms are defined as employing fewer than 50 workers, medium-sized firms employ from 50 to 100 workers, and large firms are those that employ more than 100 workers.

7. Firms can circumvent layoff restrictions in many ways such as requiring their employees to sign undated letters of resignation upon employment, developing contractual arrangements whereby employees are recognized only as part time, and so on.

References

Alexandria Businessmen's Association. 1996. "Small and Micro Enterprises in Egypt." In Marcello Guigale and H. Mobarak, eds., *Private Sector Development in Egypt*. Cairo: The American University Press.

American Chamber of Commerce in Egypt. 1996. "The Role of the Private Sector." In Marcello Guigale and H. Mobarak, eds., *Private Sector Development in Egypt*. Cairo: The American University Press.

Anderson, Robert, and Albert Martinez. 1998. "Supporting Private Sector Development in the Middle East and North Africa." In Nemat Shafik, ed., *Prospects of Middle Eastern and North African Economies: From Boom to Bust and Back?* London: Macmillan Press.

CBE (Central Bank of Egypt). *Economic Bulletin*, various issues. Cairo.

Clague, Christopher. 1997. "The New Institutional Economics and Economic Development." In Christopher Clague, ed., *Institutions and Economic Development: Growth and Governance in Less Developed Countries*. Baltimore: The John Hopkins University Press.

De Soto, Hernando. 1997. "Dead Capital and the Poor in Egypt." Distinguished Lecture Series 11. ECES (Egyptian Center For Economic Studies), Cairo.

EFG (Egyptian Financial Group)-Hermes. 1997). *Egypt: A New Economic Horizon*. Cairo: EFG-Hermes.

Fawzy, Samiha, and Ahmed Galal. 1998. "Egypt: Competitiveness of Firms and the National Diamond." ECES (Egyptian Center for Economic Studies), report submitted to the Ministry of Economy, Egypt.

Galal, Ahmed. 1996. "Which Institutions Constrain Economic Growth in Egypt the Most?" Working Paper No. 001. ECES (Egyptian Center For Economic Studies), Cairo.

Guigale, Marcello, and Hamed Mobarak. 1996. "The Rationale for Private Sector Development in Egypt." In Marcello Guigale and H. Mobarak, eds., *Private Sector Development in Egypt*. Cairo: The American University Press.

Ul Haque, Irfan. 1995. "The Macroeconomic Environment and Competitiveness." In Irfan Ul Haque, Martin Bell, Carl Dahlman, Sanjaya Lall, and Keith Pavitt, eds., *Trade, Technology, and International Competitiveness*. Washington, D.C.: Economic Development Institute, World Bank.

Hassan, Hazem. 1996. "A PSD-Friendly Tax System." In Marcello Guigale and H. Mobarak, eds., *Private Sector Development in Egypt*. Cairo: The American University Press.

ICRG (*International Country Risk Guide*). 1997. Produced by Political Risk Services, Inc.

Ministry of Commerce and Supply. 1998. *Enhancing Egypt's Exports*. Cairo: Development Economic Policy Reform Analysis Project.

Ministry of Economy. 1997a. *Recent Economic Statistics*. Cairo: Ministry of Economy.

Ministry of Economy. 1997b. *The International Competitiveness of Egypt in Perspective*. Inaugural Yearbook 1997. Cairo: Development Economic Policy Reform Analysis Project.

Ministry of Economy. 1998. *Recent Economic Statistics*. Cairo: Ministry of Economy.

Moore, Philip. 1995. *Egypt: Investment and Growth*. London: Euromoney.

North, Douglass. 1990. *Institutions, Institutional Changes and Economic Performance*. Cambridge: Cambridge University Press.

Olson, Mancur, Christopher Clague, Philip Keefer, and Stephen Knack. 1997. "Institutions and Economic Performance: Property Rights and Contracts Enforcement." In Christopher Clague, ed., *Institutions and Economic Development: Growth and Governance in Less Developed Countries.* Baltimore: The John Hopkins University Press.

Serven, Luis, and Andres Solimano. 1993. "Private Investment and Macroeconomic Adjustment: A Survey." In Luis Serven and Andres Solimano, eds., *Striving for Growth after Adjustment: The Role of Capital Formation.* Washington, D.C.: The World Bank.

Subramanian, Arvind. 1997. "The Egyptian Stabilization Experience: An Analytical Retrospective." ECES Working Paper No.18. ECES (Egyptian Center For Economic Studies), Cairo.

The United States Embassy. 1998. *Foreign Economic Trends and Their Implications for the United States.* Report for the Arab Republic of Egypt. Cairo.

World Bank. 1992. *Arab Republic of Egypt: The Private Sector Regulatory Environment (Volume II: Main Report).* Washington, D.C.: World Bank.

World Bank. 1994. *Private Sector Development in Egypt: The Status and the Challenges.* Washington, D.C.: World Bank.

World Bank. 1995. *Bureaucrats in Business.* Oxford: Oxford University Press.

World Bank. 1997. *Arab Republic of Egypt, Country Economic Memorandum, Egypt: Issues in Sustaining Economic Growth (Volume II: Main Report).* Washington, D.C.: World Bank.

World Bank. 1998. *World Development Indicators.* Washington, D.C.: World Bank.

World Economic Forum. 1997. *The Global Competitiveness Report.* Geneva: World Economic Forum.

CHAPTER 3

The Business Environment in Tunisia

Lahouel Mohamed El Hédi

By concluding a Free Trade Agreement with the European Union, Tunisia will face a major challenge over the next 10 years. Removing all trade barriers on the bulk of imports from European suppliers will expose firms to intense competition. Tunisian firms will thus have to undergo major restructuring, which is unlikely to be carried out successfully and at a low transition cost unless the local business environment shows further improvements.

Tunisian state policy towards the private sector has improved over time. In the 1960s, economic management was dominated by centralized planning, an overwhelming role for the public sector, and the building of cooperatives in agriculture. In spite of the declared objective of fostering the development of the private sector, along with the public and the cooperative sectors, there was a clear bias in favor of the latter sectors and against the former. Policy and behavior towards the private sector have of course improved since then, but there is still room for more trust and cooperation between the public and the private sectors.

The socialist strategy was abandoned at the end of the 1960s when the authorities realized that the overall strategy was discouraging private initiative in almost all economic activities, and that the cooperative program—which was the cornerstone of that strategy—was in fact perceived by landowners and businessmen as a disguised form of collectivization. Beginning in the 1970s, a new economic policy was put in place, consisting of the promotion of the private sector while continuing to support an expanding public sector. Trade policy continued to strongly protect Tunisian manufacturing, but important incentives were also granted to the offshore sector, thus attracting significant domestic and foreign investment to exporting activities, mainly to textiles, and resulting in a significant expansion of manufacturing exports. Public enterprises continued, however, to dominate many import-substituting activities, and manufacturing investment was highly regulated by a state agency— the Investment Promotion Agency (API).

This policy remained in effect until the mid-1980s. Beginning in 1987, the government embarked on a structural adjustment program leading to the liberalization of the Tunisian economy and its integration into the world economy. This program has many components: gradual trade liberalization, domestic price deregulation, fiscal reforms involving the substitution of a value added system in place of a highly complex sales tax system, as well as significant cuts in income tax rates, gradual state divestiture from many economic activities, and so on. The prior approval of manufacturing investment by the state agency API was removed in 1987. In the case of FDI, there are no restrictions on investment in offshore activities but prior approval is still needed for all investment in activities serving the domestic market. Domestic price deregulation was enacted in 1991 and a shift from a positive list to a negative list regime was introduced in trade policy in 1994.

In 1995 Tunisia concluded a free trade agreement with the EU, stipulating the gradual removal of all barriers to trade in industrial goods by the year 2010. This agreement constitutes the biggest challenge that the Tunisian economy and private firms have faced in modern times.

Reforms have gone in the right direction. However, as argued in this paper, the development of an efficient private sector still faces some constraints that need to be addressed. The paper is organized in four sections. The first section reviews the importance in the economy and the evolution of the private sector in Tunisia. The major economic reforms carried out since 1987 and having a bearing on the private sector are reviewed in the next main section. Then, the section on business constraints analyzes important remaining constraints. The final section summarizes the main conclusions and policy recommendations.

Size and Evolution of the Private Sector in Tunisia

How important is the private sector in the Tunisian economy? How did it evolve over time? This section deals with both of these questions.

Importance in Value Added

The share of the private sector in GDP has steadily increased since the beginning of the 1980s (table 3.1). This sector is heterogeneous, comprising both organized private firms and individual micro firms, with the latter defined as those with fewer than 10 employees for industry and services other than commerce, and fewer than 5 employees for commerce. The total share of all private firms increased from an average of 57.7 percent during the period 1983–86 to about 64.6 percent in the more recent period 1992–95.

Micro enterprises have held the largest share of output throughout the whole period but the bulk of the increase in the share of the private sector is attributable to the expansion of organized firms, which raised their GDP share from about 19 percent in the period 1983–86 to over 22 percent in the period 1992–95 and to 23.5 percent in 1996. In contrast, state-owned enterprises (SOEs) have seen their share decrease from 28.5 percent to 22.5 percent between the two periods. However, the share of SOEs is still large in Tunisia compared to several other countries. For all developing countries it stood, already in the late 1980s, at an average of 11 percent (World Bank 1995).

The declining share of the public sector is due both to the new dynamism shown by private firms and to the gradual implementation of the privatization program. The pace of privatization was initially slow, with only 6 firms privatized during the period 1987–94; since then, it has accelerated somewhat, the state divesting itself of 15 other firms during 1995–97. Divestiture on a much larger scale is planned for the years 1998–99, involving about 50 firms operating in various activities such as cement, tourism, trade, food, and textiles. The implementation of this program will result in a more significant increase in the GDP share of the private sector.

The private sector has been the dominant sector in all activities, with the exception of non-manufacturing industry (mining, energy, and public utilities), in which the state continues to hold the largest share, even though the private share has also increased significantly in this sector, from less than a third in the late 1980s to almost 46 percent in the years 1992–95. The private sector generates 98 percent of agricultural and fishing output and almost three-quarters of the value added of manufacturing and nonadministrative services (table 3.2).

TABLE 3.1 PRIVATE AND PUBLIC VALUE ADDED AS A SHARE OF GDP (1983–96)
(share of GDP at factor cost, percentage)

Period	Share of all private sector[a]	Share of private firms[b]	Share of SOEs[c]
1983–86	57.7	19.2	28.5
1987–91	59.1	19.0	27.4
1992–95	62.5	22.4	23.5
1995	63.1	22.7	22.5
1996	64.6	23.5	21.3

a. The private sector includes private firms, micro enterprises and households.
b. Private firms are defined in the National Accounts as those firms with more than 10 employees in industrial activities or in services other than commerce, and more than 5 employees in commerce.
c. SOEs are defined in the National Accounts as those enterprises in which the State holds an equity share of at least 34.
Source: National Statistical Institute. National Accounts (various issues).

TABLE 3.2 SHARES OF THE PRIVATE SECTOR IN VALUE ADDED BY SECTOR
(1983–95)
percentage

| Sector | Share of the private sector in value added | | |
	1983–86	1987–91	1992–95
Agriculture and fishing	n.a.	97.4	98.1
Manufacturing	n.a.	69.0	72.7
Other industry	n.a.	32.5	45.7
Services (financial not included)	n.a.	70.4	73.1
Total nonfinancial sector	66.0	67.6	72.8
Firms	(22)	(22)	(26)
Micro enterprises[a]	(44)	(45.6)	(46.8)

a. Defined as those enterprises with less than 10 employees for industry and services other than commerce, and with less than 5 employees for commerce.
Source: Estimates based on data provided by National Statistical Institute. National Accounts (various issues).

Importance in investment

Tunisia's total investment has undergone wide fluctuations since the early 1980s. The overall investment–GDP ratio was relatively high during the first half of the 1980s, averaging over 29 percent over the years 1983–86. It declined, sharply, during the following stabilization period (1987–91) to an average of 22.6 percent, recovered to an average of 26.6 percent during the period 1992–95, then showed again some weakness in more recent years, particularly in 1996 when it declined to less than 23 percent (table 3.3). Compared with other developing countries, Tunisia's investment ratio has stood at a higher level than the average for all regions, with the exception of East Asia where it averaged over 34 percent over the period 1990–95 (table 3.3).

Private investment followed more or less the same pattern as total investment, declining, as a ratio to GDP, during the stabilization period (1987–91), recovering strongly in the period 1992–95 and weakening again in the more recent years (table 3.3). The share of the private sector in total investment, barely exceeding 46 percent in the pre-adjustment period, rose above 50 percent since the late 1980s and has fluctuated since, around an average of 52 percent. This share stands well below what is observed in many regions of the world, including the Middle East and North Africa region, and is particularly much lower than in East Asia and in Latin America where it averages 75 percent. The public sector thus continues to play a much bigger role in physical capital formation than in most other developing countries. Even though there has been a decline in the total investment–GDP ratio in recent years, Tunisia's overall investment is still high compared with all developing countries outside East Asia—which

makes the relatively small share of the private sector the most salient feature of investment there.

The private sector has lagged behind in infrastructure investment, which
continues to be dominated by the public sector, but it has become the leading investor in the other activities. Its most significant expansion since the
start of structural adjustment took place in manufacturing, in which its share
increased from about 45 percent in the period 1983–86 to an average of
more than 78 percent in the period 1992–95 (table 3.4). This trend will be
reinforced by the privatization of the bulk of the cement industry planned
for the next three to four years. The private sector has also increased its
share in non-manufacturing investment, from about 40 percent prior to structural reforms to more than half in the years 1992–95, thanks to the expansion of foreign direct investment in petroleum exploration and in gas. This
share is also expected to rise in the future because of the greater projected
involvement of foreign firms in activities that have been hitherto kept exclusively in the hands of public firms, such as power generation and sewage
treatment. By contrast, the investment share in services has remained low
since the early 1980s, hovering around 40 percent. The reason is that this
sector is dominated by activities such as transport and telecommunications—
areas in which privatization and private sector participation have made the
least progress.

TABLE 3.3 PRIVATE INVESTMENT IN TUNISIA (1983–97)
percentage

Period	Total investment/ GDP	Private investment/ GDP	Private investment/ Total investment
1983–86	29.3	13.5	46.3
1987–91	22.6	11.7	51.9
1992–95	26.6	13.6	51.0
1995	24.2	13.0	53.8
1996	22.9	11.7	51.2
1997	24.4	12.9	53.0
Other countries (1990–95):			
All developing countries	23.3	16.5	70.8
Europe, Middle East, and			
North Africa	21.3	12.3	57.7
East Asia	34.3	25.6	74.6
Latin America and			
the Caribbean	19.1	14.6	76.4

Sources: For Tunisia: Ministry of Economic Development (1998); National Statistical Institute, National Accounts
(various issues). For other countries: World Bank (1996b).

TABLE 3.4 SECTORAL SHARES OF THE PRIVATE SECTOR IN FIXED INVESTMENT, 1983–95
percentage of total investment in each sector

Sector	1983–86	1987–91	1992–95
Agriculture and fishing	81.7	84.3	92.8
Manufacturing	45.3	71.7	78.2
Non-manufacturing industry	40.4	46.2	50.4
Services (financial services excluded)	40.1	40.7	40.4
Total	45.5	56.8	56.4

Source: Estimates based on data provided by National Statistical Institute. National Accounts (various issues).

Reforms Favorable to the Development of an Efficient Private Sector (1987–96)

The business environment has certainly improved since structural reforms were introduced in 1987. Investment has been liberalized in most activities. The financial sector has also undergone significant reforms with the liberalization of interest rates and the strengthening of prudential regulation. All these reforms have fostered a more competitive and efficient environment, favorable to the private sector. This section is a brief review of major reforms favorable to business.

A major achievement of Tunisia's economic policy since the start of structural reforms in the middle of 1996 has been macroeconomic stability. The appreciation of the dinar throughout the first half of the 1980s was offset by a 20 percent devaluation in 1996—and the Central Bank has since managed to stabilize the real exchange rate. There is no doubt that the devaluation played an instrumental role in the significant and quick response of exports during the period 1987–90. The stabilization of the real exchange rate thereafter has also played an important role in fostering a stable macroeconomic environment. The budget deficit has been significantly reduced from an average of over 5 percent of GDP in the pre-adjustment period to an average of 3 percent in the 1990s. Inflation has also been reduced, from an average of 9 percent in the period 1981–86 to 5 percent in the 1990s and to 3.7 percent only in the years 1996 and 1997. This deceleration is certainly due to the slowdown of inflation in Tunisia's main trading partners, but also to prudent monetary and budgetary policies.

Financial liberalization is likely, along with prudential regulation, to foster efficiency in the private sector. The gradual liberalization of interest rates and removal of the preferential rate system, beginning in 1987 and accelerating in 1992, ended the era of extremely low and even negative real interest rates. Prudential regulation based on capital adequacy, strict classification of loans according to the degree of risk, and adequate provisioning has also contributed to reducing the proportions of bad loans and nonperforming projects. We should remember that the objective is not to promote the private sector at any cost, but to foster the development of an efficient private sector.

Trade reforms have also been important. Import licensing and quantitative restrictions have been gradually removed on the bulk of imports, beginning in 1992 and accelerating in 1994. Today, the negative import list covers less than 8 percent of total imports. Effective tariff dispersion has been greatly reduced since 1987, with maximum rates cut from over 200 percent to 43 percent, even though tariff bindings concluded with OMC allow for a much wider dispersion, particularly for agricultural commodities. Imports of capital goods with no close domestic substitutes have been exonerated from import duties since 1996, which should be favorable to investment. Trade-related transaction costs have also been reduced through the current convertibility of the dinar, introduced in 1994, which removed the requirement for Central Bank foreign exchange transfer authorization, thus eliminating undue import delays.

Import transactions have been greatly liberalized over the last five years. The most significant liberalization step was taken, however, when Tunisia concluded a Free Trade Agreement (FTA) with the EU in 1995, stipulating the removal of all trade barriers on non-agriculture commodities over a 12-year period. The effective implementation date is 1998, since the ratification of this agreement by the last European parliament took place in March 1998, but Tunisia began implementation in 1996. According to the schedule set, all trade in non-agricultural sectors with the EU will be completely liberalized by the year 2008, or 2010 at the latest. Since about 75 percent of Tunisia's imports already originate in the EU, trade liberalization with the latter will amount to liberalization of most Tunisian imports. The conclusion of the FTA with the EU thus constitutes an important commitment to trade liberalization and to the promotion of a competitive environment for Tunisian firms.

A more favorable business environment has also been fostered through the removal of domestic price control on most goods and services. A competition and price reform, introduced in 1991 and further strengthened since 1994, has done away with a complex and inefficient price control system that discouraged domestic competition and distorted business decisions. Price controls currently involve no more than 10 percent of goods and services at the wholesale level and less than 13 percent at the retail level.

Investment undertaking has been greatly facilitated by abolishing the administrative authorization since 1987 and through the establishment of a one-stop shop at which all the administrative and legal services involved in the opening of a business are gathered: the Treasury Department, the court, the Investment Promotion Agency, and so on. This reform has shortened the delays involved in setting up a company from several months to about a week. A unified investment incentive code was also put in place in 1994, replacing sectoral codes with fiscal and financial incentives varying across economic activities. The new code set incentives based on the cross-cutting objectives of exports, regional development, and acquisition of new technology. The unified code "Code Unique" has its own shortcomings, complexity, and some sectoral differentiation, but has certainly reduced distortions across economic activities. The incentive system includes schemes that are extremely favorable to investment, a 10-year tax holiday, total exemption from import duties, the value added tax for totally exporting projects, and generous income tax exemption measures on reinvested income.

Taxation also has undergone major reforms involving both indirect and direct taxes. In 1989 a value added tax scheme replaced a cascade sales tax system, which favored, unintentionally, some activities over others. In 1990 direct taxation was greatly simplified, owing to marginal rates being brought down for individuals from levels exceeding 60 percent to a maximum rate of 35 percent. The statutory rate for business was reduced from 44 to 35 percent.

Finally, some flexibility has been brought to the labor market since 1994, through two important reforms involving firing and the limited duration contract. The firing law of February 1994 came to fill a vacuum in the area of firing procedures and compensation. Prior to this law compensation was left completely to the judge's decision, which created a lot of uncertainty for both employees and employers. This law set a scale that limited compensation to between one and two months per year worked and to a maximum of three years of salary. The limited duration work contract has been generalized since 1996, regardless of the nature of the work involved. According to a law enacted in 1996, an employer can conclude with an employee a work contract for a limited duration, provided that the total period of work does not exceed four years, including renewals. At the end of the four-year period, the employer has to either fire the employee or grant him the permanent worker status. These reforms of labor legislation allow for both a great deal of employment flexibility and minimum job security and compensation in case of firing.

Business Constraints

Despite the significant improvements in the business environment, firms in general, and private firms in particular, claim that serious obstacles to the development of economic activity remain. Their concerns have been documented in surveys and have been brought very often to the attention of policy makers in various meetings and forums.

Survey Results

Two surveys have been conducted with firms to find out how they assess the quality of their environment and what they think are the major obstacles they face. The first survey, conducted by the Institute of Quantitative Economics (IEQ 1996a), covered 179 Tunisian firms operating in various manufacturing activities as well as in tourism. About half of these firms employed more than 200 persons and are considered of relatively large size by Tunisian standards. The other half employs between 20 and 200 persons. About a third of interviewed firms have offshore status. The results of this survey are summarized in table 3.5.

TABLE 3.5 MAIN OBSTACLES OF THE BUSINESS ENVIRONMENT IN TUNISIA:
SURVEY RESULTS

Nature of the obstacle	Percentage of firms considering it very serious or fairly serious
High level of costs of production	76
Rigidity of administrative procedures	68
Low level of skills	61
Tough price competition	61
Difficulties of penetrating foreign markets	59
Strong competition in the local market	54
Weak local demand	50

Source: Institute of Quantitative Economics (1996b).

Most respondents (76 percent) consider high factor costs a very serious or fairly serious constraint. The second biggest constraint is red tape and the regulatory framework, according to 68 percent of the respondents. The low level of skills comes in third, followed by difficulties encountered to penetrate foreign markets and increasing competition on the domestic market. Inadequate infrastructure and the high cost of international transportation were also mentioned as serious impediments to business.

The survey also contains questions concerning actions that the firm has taken or plans to take in order to face foreign competition following liberalization. The answers reveal interesting findings: about three-quarters of the respondents declared that they have started or intend to bring adjustments to their enterprises in the area of technology, skills, and management and internal organization. The results thus show that they are readying themselves for a more competitive business environment, even though many of them fear trade liberalization and declare publicly that they are not optimistic about its outcome.

The second survey, undertaken by the Ministry of International Cooperation in 1995[1] concerns foreign investors' perceptions of the Tunisian environment. A questionnaire was addressed to 124 European investors, potentially interested in investing or currently operating in Tunisia. Investors were asked to rank what they consider as the most important actions to be taken in order to make Tunisia more attractive to FDI. The majority (40 percent of the respondents) ranked reducing red tape and liberalizing the regulatory framework among the five leading actions that need to be taken; 20 percent said that they consider trade liberalization and deregulation as the two most effective actions; and 8 percent thought that reducing red tape was the most important action to be taken. Production-related constraints were also mentioned as impediments to foreign investment but each one of them, taken separately, ranked well below the trade, red tape, and regulatory constraints.

The results of these surveys highlight the perceptions that private investors, national or foreign, have of the domestic business environment. They bring out clearly the importance of competition policies, particularly with respect to trade, of skills and of the reduction of red tape. Other aspects are emphasized by businessmen and representatives of business associations: delays incurred in investment undertakings, availability of industrial estates, legal gaps, the quality of infrastructure, and the quality of technical and economic information support. The most important issues involved are briefly reviewed below, with a focus on how the private sector itself can be more efficiently associated in improving the business environment.

Analysis of Constraints to the Development of an Efficient Private Sector Trade Liberalization

As stated above, important reforms have been introduced since 1987 in order to liberalize foreign trade. However, trade policy and regulation still have some serious drawbacks that need to be addressed.

First, additional duties have been introduced since 1995 in order to offset the effects of the removal of licensing. These duties, labeled compensatory temporary duties, set initially at rates of 30 percent on several liberalized goods, were to be gradually removed over a period of three years following their introduction. According to the timetable, they are to be completely removed by the end of 1998. However, they resulted, in the meantime, in nominal rates of protection of more than 70 percent for many finished goods.

Moreover, even though licensing has been removed on more than 90 percent of imports, import transactions continue to be submitted to various types of control and regulation. Some of these are also used in most countries—developing and developed as well—and they are reasonable, but others unduly restrict imports. Sanitary, environmental, and technical controls exist in most countries and they impose tougher standards in developed than in developing countries. However, for goods on which import licensing has been removed, new regulatory devices (*cahiers de charge*) have been established, amounting to import restrictions that the removal of licensing was intended to eliminate. Furthermore, technical control discourages imports to the extent that it takes too long, thus raising transaction costs.

These restrictive measures may be conceived by decisionmakers as temporary measures needed to ride out the transitional period. However, they may be sending wrong signals to the private sector that liberalization can be delayed and that most domestic activities may still be protected by one type of restriction or another. The continuation of excessive protection for highly inefficient activities can only delay the much needed reallocation of resources.

The Development of Education and Skills

In spite of the progress made, the Tunisian labor force is still falling behind in terms of education and skills. The 1994 population survey (table 3.6) shows that almost one-fourth of the total working labor force had no schooling at all and two-thirds had either no schooling or at most a completed primary level. Only 7 percent of the labor force reached the higher education level. With the exception of the chemicals industry, in which 60 percent of the labor force has either secondary or higher education, manufacturing activities follow more or less the same skill composition as in the other sectors. Consequently, the ratio of staff to blue-collar workers is also low, averaging 2 to 3 percent in manufacturing.

The level of skills is also very low in the textiles and clothing sector, which is the main manufacturing exporting sector. More than 70 percent of the labor force has completed at most primary education and only 1 percent has reached the university level. The development of the offshore textile sector has therefore been based, so far, on low wage and relatively unskilled labor. This advantage is being eroded by competition from lower labor-cost countries—and Tunisia cannot continue to count on this advantage for long. Furthermore, integration into the world economy requires a labor force endowed with much higher education and skills, capable of rapid mastery of new technologies and of adjustment to changing patterns of production and specialization. Tunisia has thus, a lot of catching-up to do with respect to Europe in order to fully benefit from trade liberalization and to sustain competition in manufacturing and related services.

TABLE 3.6 LEVELS OF SCHOOLING IN TUNISIAN MANUFACTURING, 1994
percentage of working labor force

Sector	No schooling	Primary	Secondary	Higher	Total
Food	16	52	28	3	100
Construction materials	19	47	30	4	100
Mechanical and electrical industry	7	46	41	5	100
Chemicals	7	33	50	10	100
Textiles, leather, and shoes	17	56	26	1	100
Other manufacturing	7	56	26	1	100
Whole economy	24	40	29	7	100

Source: National Statistical Institute (1994).

Given the significant education and skill gap, the government is increasing its training capacity both for formal and vocational training. The formal education system has been reformed in order to guarantee a minimum of nine years of education to all children. The current ratio of school enrollment at the university level is on the order of 12 percent, which is still low compared with many countries with similar per capita income. This ratio is projected to increase to 25 percent by the year 2010, which will constitute a major improvement compared with the current situation but which will still put Tunisia at a big disadvantage with respect to its major European trading partners. Vocational training capacity is also expected to increase in significant proportions, from 10,000 trainees presently to 60,000 trainees by the year 2002.

Important and ambitious as they are, these efforts need to be complemented by those of the private sector, both in formal education and in vocational training. The private educational system is still marginal in Tunisia. There are good private primary schools but their number is still very limited. At the secondary level, private schools train the dropouts of the public system. At the higher education level private institutes face the problem of diploma recognition by the government, which has so far limited their student population also to the dropouts of the public system. It is fair to say that private participation in human capital formation has been only tolerated at best by the government—and a more encouraging policy is needed. A transparent certification and control system needs to be instated and all safeguard measures have to be taken, but adequate incentives should also be granted in order to foster the development of a private educational sector. For example, an education voucher system may be gradually introduced, enabling the beneficiary to choose between private and public schools. Fiscal incentive schemes should also be designed in order to encourage donations to both public and private schools.

Private initiative should also be encouraged in vocational training. Without some public financial and organizational support, chances of its development will remain small. The idea of a voucher system with the choice left to the beneficiary between private and public institutions is as applicable to this kind of training as to formal education. It is worth emphasizing that it is in the area of human capital formation and skill enhancement that the public–private partnership should be most sought. This partnership applies both within the formal training activity itself and to the interface between the educational system (vocational training and university) and firms.

There is thus ample room for fruitful cooperation between the private and the public sectors in the area of training. However, the Tunisian economy in general and the manufacturing sector in particular have shown a stubbornly low ratio of staff and skilled to unskilled labor. The projected increase in the supply of skills will not bear fruit fully if the private sector's demand does not follow suit. The absorption of high skills and staff has been handicapped so far by the extremely limited size of most Tunisian firms. The share of enterprises with less than six employees has remained constant at about 82 percent since 1987. In 1996 there were about 1,400 firms out of a total of about 87,000 with more than 100 employees (table 3.7). Apart from a few dozen that can be considered as large enterprises employing more than 500 persons and belonging mostly to the public sector and the financial sector, the majority of Tunisian firms are thus very small units for which highly qualified personnel is too costly.

TABLE 3.7 DISTRIBUTION OF TUNISIAN ENTERPRISES BY SIZE
measured by employment

	Number of firms	Percentage of total	Number of firms	Percentage of total	Number of firms	Percentage of total
	1987		1990		1996	
Less than 6	31,995	81.8	43,874	81.0	71,984	82.4
6–10	2,771	7.1	3,987	7.3	5,983	6.9
11–20	1,793	4.6	2,600	4.8	3,892	4.5
21–50	1,264	3.2	1,931	3.6	2,830	3.2
51–100	535	1.4	788	1.4	1,217	1.4
More than 100	727	1.9	1,023	1.9	1,420	1.6
Total of more than 6	(7,090)	(18.2)	(10,329)	(19.0)	(15,342)	(17.6)
All sizes	39,085	100	54,203	100	87,326	100

Source: Caisse Nationale de Sécurité Sociale (various issues).

The limited size of firms is due to two main factors, family ownership and the highly protectionist policy that lasted over more than three decades. Tunisian entrepreneurs have so far been very reticent to opening ownership outside family ties. Given limited financial resources, this attitude has restricted their choice of investment projects to small projects. The existence of high barriers to entry of imports has made many of such projects artificially profitable. Moreover, the lack of foreign competition has avoided the pressure on local firms to upgrade the skills of their workers and to improve their ratio of skilled and white-collar employees to blue-collar workers.

The ongoing trade liberalization is likely to introduce much greater competition in the Tunisian economy and put pressure on firms to increase their demand for skills. Trade liberalization may also push them to open their capital to investors outside the family. There are already some signs of this happening, particularly in terms of partnership with foreign firms, but the legislation on mergers and acquisitions, which needs to be amended, remains an obstacle.

IMPROVING THE CONDITIONS OF STARTING UP A BUSINESS
Firms are faced with great difficulties in securing finance from banks. The latter still take too long to evaluate investment projects and require guarantees and collateral that many new entrepreneurs are not able to meet. Prudential regulation has induced banks to take a more conservative attitude in lending, perhaps because of their still-limited capacity to assess the profitability submitted to them.

Firms tend also to face difficulties in getting access to industrial or commercial land. Until recently a public institution (ALI: Industrial Land Agency) held the monopoly as industrial land developer. Its performance showed some serious limits, in terms of both quantity and quality. Indeed, it has been incapable of following the pace of demand. According to estimates, about 1,000 applications remained unsatisfied by the end of 1996. Furthermore, entrepreneurs have complained of the poor quality of roads and the sewerage system in estates developed by this agency.

The lifting of restrictions on the private sector to develop land for industrial use has thus been welcomed by private investors as a means to speed up the process and to improve the quality of land development. It is too early to tell to what extent these expectations will be fulfilled, in terms of increased availability, and cost and quality of services, since the experience of private sector participation is just starting. However, there is no doubt that private sector participation will make a big difference, just as it has been observed in the case of housing development—which used to be, until the mid-1970s, mainly in the hands of the public sector.

If we add to the delays involved in securing finance and land, those needed to seek the construction permit and to meet other administrative requirements, the effective period to start a project may exceed two years. For existing well-established firms the delays are much shorter. It is new firms that are faced with the longest delays in starting their projects.

IMPROVING INFRASTRUCTURE WITH GREATER PARTICIPATION OF THE PRIVATE SECTOR

Government efforts in strengthening the infrastructure of the country have been very important over the last few years. As stated earlier, it is infrastructure investment that has been relatively steady while directly productive investment has lagged behind. These efforts have focused on roads, telecommunications, ports, and so on. However, many of these activities remain in the hands of the public sector, often holding a monopoly position. There is thus large room for private sector participation, particularly of foreign firms endowed with highly important technical know-how and easy access to international finance. Tunisia has just started taking advantage of new arrangements for a greater involvement of FDI in infrastructure development, such as the BOT-type of contracts. It is expected that an important power plant will be built (at a cost of US$300 million) and run in the near future by a foreign firm under a BOT contract. A similar contract is envisaged for a sewage treatment plant. These are steps in the right direction but they need to be followed, or better yet preceded by a larger opening of infrastructure development and management to the private sector in general, and to foreign investment in particular, given the limited financial resources and technical expertise that still characterize the domestic private sector. This liberalization will generate high benefits for the economy, particularly in the area of telecommunications.

LEGAL GAPS

Given the ongoing liberalization program and the important restructuring of the Tunisian economy that will follow, the needed resource reallocation as well as the expansion of investment are bound to be influenced by the degree of flexibility of the system—or the lack thereof—and by the constraining nature of barriers to exit and to adjust. Some legal gaps persist in three areas: bankruptcy, mergers and acquisitions, and labor legislation.

Bankruptcy legislation and procedures are ill-adapted to the increasingly competitive environment in which the private sector operates. First, the existing legislation stipulates harsh sanctions, going as far as the withdrawal of civil rights. Secondly, the procedures do not provide a sufficient degree of flexibility to allow debtors to compose with creditors in order to forestall bankruptcy. Finally, procedures tend to be too long, dragging bankruptcy cases for years. These obstacles explain why many owners tend to liquidate their enterprises outside courts, thus foregoing the chance to keep them in activity.

Merger and acquisition legislation needs also to be reformed. Anti-trust law discourages actions that, in the context of liberalization, should be facilitated in order to induce a more efficient management of resources by the better-performing owners and managers. Such actions are likely to ease business conversions and reduce the cost of restructuring.

Firms also consider labor legislation as somewhat constraining. They consider that firing is an action too costly for them and that the labor disputes settlement council (Conseil de Prud'hommes) sides most of the time with the worker. Firing for reason of absenteeism was not allowed until 1994. Firing prompted by economic difficulties faced by the firm can be very costly for the latter, resulting in a severance payment of up to one year of salary in some sectors. Because of the adverse effects that such restrictions may have on investment and employment, the labor code has been recently amended by allowing firms to lengthen the duration of temporary contracts as opposed to the indefinite duration contracts. This amendment is meant to enable firms to avoid firing costs in the case of indefinite contracts and at the same time to give workers a chance to accumulate skills and experience in the hope that they will be able to keep their jobs beyond the period of their temporary contracts.

SUPPORT SERVICES TO THE PRIVATE SECTOR

Throughout the world the private sector has access to support services rendered by state or state-affiliated institutions and more recently by professional associations and the private sector. These services, often of a public-good nature, can have a significant impact on competitiveness. They concern essentially technology and research and development—as well as dissemination of economic information.

There are presently six public technical centers entrusted with the mission to promote and disseminate new technology, and to provide technical assistance to firms in their respective areas of expertise. Entrepreneurs think that their services can become much more useful than they are now provided the centers become more efficient and they attract better expertise. The government is making more resources available to these centers and has associated the private sector with their management by granting them the majority of seats on governing boards.

However, these centers continue to act as public institutions, and they are not responsive enough to the needs of private firms. Even though decisionmakers are well aware of the limited expertise they have, the problem of attracting more experienced and skilled experts is still unresolved, the centers' salaries being still not competitive in comparison to those offered by the private sector for the expertise needed. This is considered as a major obstacle to making the centers' services better appreciated and valued by private firms. Ultimately, if the quality of these services improves, their cost can be covered to a large extent by the fees charged to beneficiaries. This will ease their burden on state budget, but more important, it will make the centers' activities demand-driven, responding to needs highly valued by firms. The centers have not reached that stage yet and reforms are still needed to upgrade their services and make them highly sought by firms.

The same conclusions apply to public institutions in charge of gathering and disseminating economic information, especially with regard to business opportunities in Tunisia and abroad. These institutions include the Investment Promotion Agency (API), the Export Promotion Center (CEPEX), and so on. Some important restructuring has been brought to these institutions but more needs to be done in order to integrate them into the market of economic information and to make them more tuned to the needs of the private sector.

Conclusions and Policy Recommendations

Policy towards the private sector in Tunisia has improved significantly, since the beginning of structural adjustment in 1987. Several reforms have led to the development of this sector, essentially at the expense of SOEs. However, the latter's share in GDP remains too high by comparison with most developing countries with similar levels of development. The private sector's share in total investment has also increased since the first half of the 1980s, but it is still much lower than the shares observed in most parts of the world, particularly in East Asia and Latin America. The role of the private sector is still limited in scope; the private sector is hardly involved in many important activities such as mining, telecommunications, power generation and distribution, water and sanitation, and much of transportation and education.

Important reforms, implemented since 1987, have contributed to the creation of a more favorable environment to business: macroeconomic stability, trade liberalization, financial liberalization, the replacement of a complex and distortions-ridden sales tax system by a value added tax, the reduction of tax rates on income both for business and households, the harmonization of tax and financial investment incentives over different economic activities, the start of privatization, and the introduction of some flexibility in hiring and firing.

Commitment to a more open economy has been clearly made by concluding an FTA with the EU, the country's major trading partner. Many enterprises are readying themselves, during the transition period and with the support of the government, to become more competitive and to face this challenge. Others have to undergo major restructuring, or be wiped out by competition or absorbed by better performing firms. However, there is a consensus among business managers as well as decisionmakers that the adjustment process cannot succeed unless the business environment is further improved in order to meet the conditions of competitiveness.

Trade liberalization is bound to give rise to resource reallocation costs that can be reduced both in terms of size and duration only by following a steady policy. Some activities are likely to suffer from liberalization, but others will gain—and any temptation to revert to trade restrictions to protect threatened activities should be avoided. Following a steady course will strengthen credibility and push firms to take the efficient redeployment actions.

Privatization should proceed at a faster pace. The government's intention is to do so and plans are under way to privatize major SOEs, but the process is taking too long. Many SOEs continue to suffer from poor performance and any delays in privatization will only make their situation worse. Telecommunications, in particular, remains in the hands of the public sector with hardly any competition playing to put pressure on prices and raise the supply and the quality of services.

The private sector's participation in education and vocational training should also be sought and encouraged through various incentives, along with the provision of an adequate regulatory framework in order to promote quality training. One option to be envisaged is that of a voucher system whereby the beneficiary would have the choice between a public and a private school.

Tunisia is not fully benefiting from private sector participation in the building or management of infrastructure such as in power generation, or water and sanitation, either. Such participation is still in an experimental stage while it has proven highly successful in many parts of the world.

The shortage of industrial estates with adequate infrastructure and good location is of concern to existing as well as potential entrepreneurs. The opening of industrial land development to the private sector has been a rational decision, but it is important to speed up the process of implementation in order to meet demand in a relatively short period of time.

Given the urgent need for the technical and managerial upgrading of the majority of Tunisian firms, organizations supplying support services, especially the technical centers, can play an important role towards that end. However, major reforms have to be introduced in their incentive and pay schemes to enable them to attract highly skilled engineers and experts.

The most difficult obstacle to be addressed and the one considered the most serious by many firms is red tape and the rigidity of administrative procedures. Further liberalization of the economy will certainly lessen the impact of this problem, but it can be dealt with in a more structural way only through improvements in the quality of training of public employees and the design of a better incentive system in the civil service.

Note

1. The results of this survey are taken from Page and Underwood 1997.

References

API (Agence de Promotion de l'Industrie). 1998. "Note de Synthèse sur les réalisations des projets déclarés durant la période 1994–96." Agence de Promotion de l'Industrie, Tunisia.

Caisse Nationale de Securité Sociale (CNSS). Various issues. Tunisia.

IEQ (Institute d'Economie Quantitative). 1996a. "Compétitivité, restructuration, diversification et ouverture sur l'extérieur des industries manufacturières et des services." Rapport n° II. Institut d'Economie Quantitative, Tunisia.

IEQ (Institute d'Economie Quantitative). 1996b. "L'Entrepreneur face à l'ouverture." Note de l'IEQ IEQ/AFB/960708. Institut d'Economie Quantitative, Tunisia.

Ministry of Economic Development. 1998. Economic Budget. Tunisia.

National Statistical Institute (NSI). 1994. Population Survey (Main Characteristics of the Working Labor Force). Tunisia.

National Statistical Institute. National Accounts. Various issues. Tunisia.

Page, J., and J. Underwood. 1997. "Growth, the Maghreb and Free Trade with the European Union." In Ahmed Galal and Bernard Hoekman, eds., *Regional Partners in Global Markets: Limits and Possibilities of the Euro-Med Agreements*. CEPR (Center for Economic Policy Research), London/ ECES (Egyptian Center for Economic Studies), Cairo.

World Bank. 1994. "Republic of Tunisia, Private Sector Assessment." World Bank, Washington, D.C. June.

————. 1998. "Tunisie: Intégration mondiale et développement durable, Choix Stratégiques pour le 21ᵉ siècle, Etudes Économiques de la Banque Mondiale sur le Moyen Orient et l'Afrique du Nord." World Bank, Washington, D.C.

————. 1995. *Bureaucrats in Business: The Economics and Politics of Government Ownership.* Oxford University Press.

————. 1996b. Trends in Private Investment in Developing Countries. International Finance Corporation (IFC) discussion paper, no. 31. Washington, D.C.

CHAPTER 4

The Business Environment in Jordan

Taher H. Kanaan

The economy of Jordan experienced extremely high rates of investment and growth during most of the 1970s and the early 1980s, financed mainly by remittances of Jordanians working in the oil-exporting countries, and by official assistance from these same countries. The sources helped to finance not only a high rate of investment but also a high level of public and private consumption, which together exceeded GDP, leaving domestic savings in the negative.

That decade and a half of good times ended in the mid-1980s with the fall in oil prices and consequent decline in official assistance and workers' remittances. Average annual growth during 1983–89 was under 1 percent. During 1988–89 a major crisis erupted as Jordan became unable to meet external obligations, which led to an IMF-supported stabilization program and a major debt rescheduling at the Paris Club.

The hope for economic recovery and future growth was pinned on the new faith in the private sector, market forces, and foreign investment. The stabilization program was accompanied with policies to reform economic governance all round and to make the economy more attractive to private sector investment, domestic as well as foreign.

With the breakout of the Gulf crisis in 1990, Jordan faced major disruption of its international trade and the economic challenge of adjusting to the return of 300 thousand Jordanians from the Gulf countries. In 1992, real GDP rebounded with a 16 percent growth, fueled mainly by the repatriated savings of the returnees, but also by external debt relief and new official development assistance. The boom and real growth continued during 1993–95, with a yearly average of over 6 percent. However, the growth momentum came to a virtual halt in 1996 and 1997, with real growth not exceeding 1 percent and 3 percent, respectively. This setback was mainly due to the vanishing of the euphoria associated with the peace process, the continued economic sanctions on Iraq, the collapse of oil prices, and the economic recession in the Far East, constraining the three major markets for traditional Jordanian exports. However, part of the blame must be assigned to the delay in dealing effectively with certain major impediments to Jordanian competitive advantage. These impediments are in three categories—(a) the high transaction costs imposed on entrepreneurs by adverse bureaucratic practices, (b) the qualitative shortcomings of the education and training systems, and (c) the oligopolistic and other rent-seeking interests still dominating many important markets.

As will be shown in the following sections, considerable progress has been made in legislative, regulatory, and institutional reforms that are necessary to make the economic environment more friendly to business. However, important as they are, these reforms have been lacking the teeth of being carried out through clear and decisive executive action by members of the civil service at all levels.

The Scope of the Market in the Economy

The Jordanian economy is traditionally private sector-oriented. Direct state ownership has been relatively small, significant only in the mining sector (phosphates and potash), public utilities (water, energy, and telecommunications), and transport services (public bus transport, air transport, and port services).

The proportion of GDP at factor cost originating in public sector establishments excluding "producers of government services," that is, the conventional public administration sector, was 15.5 in 1990, marginally declining to 13.5 percent in 1995. In the latter year, the private sector share was predominant in agriculture (100 percent) construction (almost 100 percent), manufacturing (92 percent), as well as in financial, business, community, and other private services (almost 100 percent). (See table 4.1.)

The role of the public sector in aggregate investment has also been declining, shrinking from about 40 percent of gross fixed capital formation and 10 percent of GDP in 1990 to 20 percent of gross fixed capital formation and 6.6 percent of GDP in 1996. (See table 4.2.)

The impact of the public sector on the economy is believed to be much larger than indicated by GDP figures, to wit:

a) The public sector is the largest employer in the country, engaging in 1995 more than 300 thousand employees, equivalent to more than 40 percent of the total employed population. In 1996 wages and salaries paid by the public sector constituted about 45 percent of the total compensation of employees, declining from about 52 percent in 1990.

TABLE 4.1 GROSS DOMESTIC PRODUCT IN PUBLIC AND PRIVATE SECTORS (AT CURRENT PRICES)

millions of Jordanian dinar

Economic activity	1990 Total	1990 Private	1990 Public	1991 Total	1991 Private	1991 Public	1992 Total	1992 Private	1992 Public	1993 Total	1993 Private	1993 Public	1994 Total	1994 Private	1994 Public	1995 Total	1995 Private	1995 Public
Agriculture	187.8	187.8	0.0	213.5	213.5	0.0	246.9	246.9	0.0	193.3	193.3	0.0	193.2	193.2	0.0	171.8	171.8	0.0
Mining and quarrying	148.8	7.3	141.5	124.9	17.0	107.9	130.5	13.5	117.0	106.9	13.9	93.0	102.4	8.5	93.9	157.7	7.8	149.9
Manufacturing	345.3	314.5	30.8	343.7	312.1	31.6	406.3	383.8	22.5	427.3	413.4	13.9	561.4	527.0	34.4	579.7	531.5	48.2
Electricity and water	53.9	17.9	36.0	62.0	13.6	48.4	66.6	15.8	50.8	78.7	15.3	63.4	84.0	21.1	62.9	98.1	24.3	73.8
Construction	105.6	105.6	0.0	125.7	125.7	0.0	215.3	215.3	0.0	283.7	283.5	0.2	299.4	299.2	0.2	297.5	297.2	0.3
Trade, restaurants, and hotels	216.8	285.6	-68.8	254.7	280.6	-25.9	278.7	325.7	-47.0	317.2	365.7	-48.5	377.0	422.5	-45.5	414.6	515.1	-100.5
Transport and communications	362.0	140.8	221.2	382.7	149.8	232.9	450.0	187.5	262.5	487.1	179.7	307.4	520.1	224.6	295.5	572.3	241.3	331.0
Finance, insurance, real estate, and business services	407.0	410.7	-3.7	472.2	477.6	-5.4	520.4	529.6	-9.2	622.7	629.9	-7.2	658.9	668.6	-9.7	721.7	752.8	-31.1
Social and personal services	51.1	47.6	3.5	66.2	61.3	4.9	86.9	82.6	4.3	88.8	83.9	4.9	109.6	105.9	3.7	128.5	124.3	4.2
Total	1,878.3	1,517.8	360.5	2,045.6	1,651.2	394.4	2,401.6	2,000.7	400.9	2,605.7	2,178.5	427.2	2,906.0	2,470.6	435.4	3,141.9	2,666.2	475.7
Producers of government services	449.1	0.0	449.1	474.4	0.0	474.4	554.7	0.0	554.7	619.1	0.0	619.1	666.9	0.0	666.9	756.4	0.0	756.4
Producers of private nonprofit services for																		

(Continued on next page.)

TABLE 4.1 (CONTINUED)

Economic activity	1990 Total	1990 Private	1990 Public	1991 Total	1991 Private	1991 Public	1992 Total	1992 Private	1992 Public	1993 Total	1993 Private	1993 Public	1994 Total	1994 Private	1994 Public	1995 Total	1995 Private	1995 Public
households	30.8	30.8	0.0	34.0	34.0	0.0	39.2	39.2	0.0	38.9	38.9	0.0	47.0	47.0	0.0	50.4	50.4	0.0
Domestic household services	6.2	6.2	0.0	5.3	5.3	0.0	7.2	7.2	0.0	7.6	7.6	0.0	6.0	6.0	0.0	5.9	5.9	0.0
Total	2,364.4	1,554.8	809.6	2,559.3	1,690.5	868.8	3,002.7	2,047.1	955.6	3,271.3	2,225.0	1,046.3	3,625.9	2,523.6	1,102.3	3,954.6	2,722.5	1,232.1
Less: Input bank service charge	−39.9	−39.9	0.0	−53.7	−53.7	0.0	−41.8	−41.8	0.0	−66.4	−66.4	0.0	−73.9	−99.0	25.1	−75.0	−123.2	48.2
GDP at factor cost	2,324.5	1,514.9	809.6	2,505.6	1,636.8	868.8	2,960.9	2,005.3	955.6	3,204.9	2,158.6	1,046.3	3,552.0	2,424.6	1,127.4	3,879.6	2,599.3	1,280.3
Net indirect taxes	343.8	116.8	227.0	349.5	127.5	222.0	532.1	156.2	375.9	596.8	183.0	413.8	666.0	264.2	401.8	739.7	339.9	399.8
GDP at market prices	2,668.3	1,631.7	1,036.6	2,855.1	1,764.3	1,090.8	3,493.0	2,161.5	1,331.5	3,801.7	2,341.6	1,460.1	4,218.0	2,688.8	1,529.2	4,619.3	2,939.2	1,680.1

PERCENTAGES

Economic activity	1990 Total	1990 Private	1990 Public	1991 Total	1991 Private	1991 Public	1992 Total	1992 Private	1992 Public	1993 Total	1993 Private	1993 Public	1994 Total	1994 Private	1994 Public	1995 Total	1995 Private	1995 Public
Agriculture	100.0	100.0	0.0	100.0	100.0	0.0	100.0	100.0	0.0	100.0	100.0	0.0	100.0	100.0	0.0	100.0	100.0	0.0
Mining and quarrying	100.0	4.9	95.1	100.0	13.6	86.4	100.0	10.3	89.7	100.0	13.0	87.0	100.0	8.3	91.7	100.0	5.0	95.0
Manufacturing	100.0	91.1	8.9	100.0	90.8	9.2	100.0	94.5	5.5	100.0	96.8	3.2	100.0	93.9	6.1	100.0	91.7	8.3
Electricity and water	100.0	33.2	66.8	100.0	21.9	78.1	100.0	23.7	76.3	100.0	19.4	80.6	100.0	25.1	74.9	100.0	24.8	75.2
Construction	100.0	100.0	0.0	100.0	100.0	0.0	100.0	100.0	0.0	100.0	99.9	0.1	100.0	99.9	0.1	100.0	99.9	0.1
Trade, restaurants and hotels	100.0	131.7	−31.7	100.0	110.2	−10.2	100.0	116.9	−16.9	100.0	115.3	−15.3	100.0	112.1	−12.1	100.0	124.2	−24.2

Transport and communications	100.0	38.9	61.1	100.0	39.1	60.9	100.0	41.7	58.3	100.0	36.9	63.1	100.0	43.2	56.8	42.2	57.8
Finance, insurance, real estate, and business services	100.0	100.9	-0.9	100.0	101.1	-1.1	100.0	101.8	-1.8	100.0	101.2	-1.2	100.0	101.5	-1.5	104.3	-4.3
Social and personal services	100.0	93.2	6.8	100.0	92.6	7.4	100.0	95.1	4.9	100.0	94.4	5.6	100.0	96.6	3.4	96.8	3.2
Total	100.0	80.8	19.2	100.0	80.7	19.3	100.0	83.3	16.7	100.0	83.6	16.4	100.0	85.0	15.0	84.9	15.1
Producers of government services	100.0	0.0	100.0	100.0	0.0	100.0	100.0	0.0	100.0	100.0	0.0	100.0	100.0	0.0	100.0	0.0	100.0
Producers of private nonprofit services for households	100.0	100.0	0.0	100.0	100.0	0.0	100.0	100.0	0.0	100.0	100.0	0.0	100.0	100.0	0.0	100.0	0.0
Domestic household services	100.0	100.0	0.0	100.0	100.0	0.0	100.0	100.0	0.0	100.0	100.0	0.0	100.0	100.0	0.0	100.0	0.0
Total	100.0	65.8	34.2	100.0	66.1	33.9	100.0	68.2	31.8	100.0	68.0	32.0	100.0	69.6	30.4	68.8	31.2
Less: Input bank service charge	100.0	0.0	100.0	100.0	0.0	100.0	100.0	0.0	100.0	100.0	0.0	100.0	100.0	134.0	-34.0	164.2	-64.2
GDP at factor cost	100.0	65.2	34.8	100.0	65.3	34.7	100.0	67.7	32.3	100.0	67.4	32.6	100.0	68.3	31.7	67.0	33.0
Net indirect taxes	100.0	34.0	66.0	100.0	36.5	63.5	100.0	29.4	70.6	100.0	30.7	69.3	100.0	39.7	60.3	45.9	54.1
GDP at market prices	100.0	61.2	38.8	100.0	61.8	38.2	100.0	61.9	38.1	100.0	61.6	38.4	100.0	63.7	36.3	63.6	36.4

Source : Hashemite Kingdom of Jordan, Department of Statistics, Amman (1998).

TABLE 4.2 GROSS FIXED CAPITAL FORMATION BY KIND OF ECONOMIC ACTIVITY, 1990–95
millions of Jordanian dinar

Economic activity	1990			1991			1992			1993			1994			1995		
	Total	Private	Public	Total	Private	Public	Total	Private	Public	Total	Private	Public	Total	Private	Public	Total	Private	Public
Agriculture, hunting, forestry	0.0	11.7	11.7	0.0	17.4	17.4	0.0	20.2	20.2	0.0	19.5	19.5	0.0	17.6	17.6	0.0	27.6	27.6
Mining and quarrying	9.8	0.3	10.1	49.7	0.7	50.4	11.4	0.0	11.4	12.0	0.8	12.8	92.3	0.1	92.4	11.6	0.0	11.6
Manufacturing	0.9	12.1	13.0	3.4	22.8	26.2	0.6	44.3	44.9	4.1	26.6	30.7	35.7	76.9	112.6	14.0	63.9	77.9
Electricity and water	20.4	3.8	24.2	25.1	3.6	28.7	38.8	0.0	38.8	57.1	0.5	57.6	59.8	10.1	69.9	83.8	9.8	93.6
Construction	0.0	3.3	3.3	0.0	3.0	3.0	0.0	15.2	15.2	0.0	20.4	20.4	0.0	32.4	32.4	0.0	15.2	15.2
Wholesale and retail trade, restaurants and hotels	0.6	4.0	4.6	0.9	9.2	10.1	0.3	16.4	16.7	0.1	11.6	11.7	7.1	14.9	22.0	4.1	13.9	18.0
Transport, storage and communication	114.4	73.4	187.8	12.9	49.6	62.5	10.9	63.4	74.3	-54.5	37.2	-17.3	24.1	16.3	40.4	20.0	35.8	55.8
Finance, insurance, real estate, and business services	0.0	309.6	309.6	1.5	332.2	333.7	0.2	625.5	625.7	0.6	910.2	910.8	0.5	709.3	709.8	1.8	750.0	751.8

Community, social and personal services	1.5	1.3	2.8	0.8	6.1	6.9	1.8	14.5	16.3	3.0	15.2	18.2	2.8	27.0	29.8	6.8	48.9	55.7
Producers of government services	124.0	0.0	124.0	135.9	0.0	135.9	180.9	0.0	180.9	234.7	0.0	234.7	257.2	0.0	257.2	280.7	0.0	280.7
Producers of private nonprofit services for households	0.0	2.9	2.9	0.0	3.2	3.2	0.0	4.8	4.8	0.0	1.3	1.3	0.0	6.9	6.9	0.0	7.1	7.1
Total	271.6	422.4	694.0	230.2	447.8	678.0	244.9	804.3	1049.2	257.1	1046.4	1303.5	479.5	911.5	1391.0	422.8	972.2	1395.0

Source: Hashemite Kingdom of Jordan, Department of Statistics, Amman (1998).

b) In organized economic activity, defined as establishments employing five or more persons, public sector establishments are shown to have accounted for 61.1 percent of the total employment in those establishments in 1992, marginally declining to 57.8 percent in 1995. (See table 4.3.)

c) Exports originating in enterprises with dominant government ownership accounted for 29 percent and 25 percent of total commodity exports in 1993 and 1995 respectively. The enterprises concerned are the Jordan Phosphates Company, the Arab Potash Company, and the Jordan Cement Company. The decline of the share of these enterprises in total exports between the two years is significant, particularly in view of the fact that exports increased by 54 percent over that period. Exports of private sector enterprises were the better performers, since their share in the increase amounted to 83 percent.

Macroeconomic Reforms

The reform agenda since 1989 consisted of the following: debt and credit worthiness, trade policy, the financial sector, and competitiveness and privatization. Progress on these fronts is described below.

Debt and Creditworthiness

The debt crisis in 1989 triggered negotiations with the Paris and London Clubs for debt rescheduling. This, together with reduced new borrowing, debt buybacks at substantial discounts, and debt reductions totaling US$1.2 billion by the end of 1997, led to the reduction of the net present value of debt-to-GDP ratio to below the 80 percent mark, and to the reduction of the debt service-to-exports ratio to well below the 25 percent mark above which liquidity concerns rise.

TABLE 4.3 EMPLOYMENT IN ORGANIZED ACTIVITIES
in thousands of establishments employing five or more persons

Institution	1992 Public	1992 Private	1992 Total	1995 Public	1995 Private	1995 Total
Government institutions	166.4	0.0	166.4	207.7	0.0	207.7
Public shareholding companies	14.3	20.0	34.3	6.2	34.3	40.5
Other companies	0.8	64.4	65.2	0.2	84.5	84.7
Sole proprietor businesses	0.0	21.1	21.1	0.0	25.3	25.3
Non-governmental organizations	0.0	10.2	10.2	0.0	12.3	12.3
Total	181.5	115.7	297.2	214.1	156.4	370.5
Percentages	61.1	38.9	100.0	57.8	42.2	100.0

Source: Hashemite Kingdom of Jordan, Department of Statistics, Employment Survey for Establishments Engaging Five Persons or More, Amman (1992, 1995).

Accordingly, Jordan became qualified as a moderately indebted country (World Bank 1997).

Trade Policy and Exports Development
Trade liberalization covered both imports and exports.

IMPORTS
Jordan has recently undertaken significant trade liberalization measures. One such extremely important measure was the Law on Unification of Taxes and Fees No.7 of 1997. According to this law, a maximum customs rate of 40 percent was instituted. As a result, the maximum tariff rate was lowered from 50 to 40 percent (excluding alcohol and tobacco), and the number of tariff bands was reduced from 10 to 6. The tariff on cars was lowered to 40 percent, offset by an additional general sales tax (GST).

Tariffs on capital goods were eliminated with respect to 492 items, and reduced to 10 percent with respect to 216 other items. Import tariffs on 46 raw materials and intermediate products were reduced from 20–23 percent to 5–10 percent. Processed food and several other consumer products were made duty-exempt. The mean trade-weighted tariff was reduced from an estimated 16.8 percent in 1987 to an estimated 13.7 percent in 1996, and Jordan's overall tariff variance was significantly lowered. (The figures are likely to be underestimated, since goods totally exempted from tariff are not included in calculating the average.) Further reductions in tariff rates are scheduled to take effect in 1998.

To offset the loss in public revenue resulting from reduction of tariffs on luxury goods that used to carry very high duties (above 40 percent), these goods were made subject to equally high sales taxes.

To improve the public administration of customs and facilitate customs clearance, a new Customs Law has just been enacted by Parliament. The same objective was pursued through computerization and adoption of the Automated System for Customs Data and Management (ASYCUDA), implementation of a green channel for imports, and allowing importers to apply pre-shipment valuation by an internationally reputed institution.

With regard to non-tariff barriers, it is estimated that about 16.8 percent of goods imported are subject to non-tariff barriers such as quotas and licenses. The imports subject to such barriers are mostly cereals, vegetable oils and oil seeds, pharmaceuticals, manufactured fertilizers, transport equipment, and nonmetallic mineral products.

Other non-tariff trade restrictions are those associated with bilateral trade protocols. Jordan has trade protocol agreements with Bahrain, Egypt, Iraq, Kuwait, Lebanon, Libya, Morocco, Oman, Saudi Arabia, Syria, Tunisia, the United Arab Emirates, and Yemen. More recently such agreements were concluded with Palestine, and Israel. In the context of the Partnership Agreement with the EU, the trade protocols with Morocco and Tunisia are expected to become more liberal. Jordan will be phasing out of such agreements upon accession to the World Trade Organization (WTO) in compliance with the requirements of Most Favored Nation (MFN) treatment.

Jordan is a member of Arab regional trade arrangements since their inception.

Discussions to activate the Arab Free Trade Area (AFTA) are likely to pick up momentum in the latter part of 1998 with the objective of completing the setting up of AFTA by 2007. This will replace the present restrictive trade protocols with Jordan's neighboring Arab countries with all-round liberal relations.

Jordan earns the highest score of 4 for the average tariff rate category. (SRII 1998a, p. IV-4).

In November 1997, the government signed an Economic Association Agreement with the European Union (EU), aiming to establish free trade relations between Jordan and the EU by 2010. Jordan has also applied for WTO membership, and is already participating in working group discussions for this purpose.

EXPORTS

Exports are not subject to taxes, with the exception of minor fees on the exports of scrap metal, 2 percent on the value of re-exported imports, and a small fee for the mandatory subscription to the Trade Centers Corporation, a body for the promotion of exports. Most exports of Jordanian origin do not require export licenses, the exceptions being agricultural products, cereals, milk, pasta, and precious metals.

Earnings from the exportation of most goods are exempt from income tax, the exceptions being exports of phosphates, potash, and fertilizers. Service exports, which are almost as significant in value as exports of goods, do not enjoy such exemption.

Two important initiatives to reduce anti-export bias and facilitate trade are under way, namely (a) the establishment of an export credit guarantee mechanism to insure exporters against commercial and political risks within the Credit Guarantee Corporation, which was initially set up for encouraging credit to micro borrowers; and (b) the strengthening of the Jordan Institute of Standards and Metrology that attends to the maintenance of high-quality standards for goods made in Jordan and facilitates for Jordanian exporters the receipt of ISO 9000 certification.

Financial and Banking Policies

The financial system of Jordan is dominated by commercial banks whose assets reached about JD (Jordanian dinar) 9.7 billion by the end of 1997. The role of the financial market (for equities as well as bonds) is still very small. Total value traded in the Amman financial market in 1997 was about JD 304 million, equivalent to 5.4 percent of GDP. The financial role of insurance companies also has been small. Of some significance is the role of the Social Security Corporation whose assets reached almost JD 1 billion at the end of 1997. As a consequence, the overall efficiency of the resource mobilization is determined mainly by the performance of the banking system.

The maturity of banks' loans is an important indicator of how banks contribute to the efficiency of the investment and growth process. Figures of recent years indicate that overdrafts represented between 35 and 40 percent of banking credit. Credit extended for more than 12 months accounted for about 41 percent of total credit in 1989, 35 percent in 1992, and down to 27 percent in 1996, with a definite bias toward shorter-term maturities. Accordingly, long-term investment has been adversely affected by the inadequacy of longer-term financing, especially in an environment in which capital markets remain underdeveloped.

Reform of the financial system focused on the following areas:

(a) Reinforcement of banking supervision at the Central Bank by reforming the Banking Law to provide the Central Bank with more authority to deal with problem banks independently from the Companies Law, and to enforce compliance with modern banking practices—especially provisions compatible with Basle Agreements.

(b) Liberalization of current account transactions. In this context, the distinction between resident and nonresident accounts for several types of operations was removed, and SWAP operations in foreign exchange became permissible. For all practical purposes the JD is fully convertible into any other major currency, being pegged at US$/JD 1.41.

(c) Enhancement of competitiveness and assurance of a level playing field in banking services. In this context a process of phasing out of the privileges of specialized credit institutions (SCIs) was started with abolishing the privileges of the Housing Bank and reducing the rediscount subsidies to the other two SCIs, namely the Agricultural Credit Corporation and the Industrial Development Bank.

BANKING

Enhancement of the efficiency of the banking sector was pursued by adopting such measures as:

(a) Requiring banks to meet the new 12 percent capital adequacy requirements by the end of June 1997 and to raise their minimum capital from JD 10 million to JD 20 million by the end of 1997.

(b) Improving the reporting requirements of banks to bring them closer to internationally accepted standards.

(c) Consolidating international reserves, and adopting an interest rate policy supportive of investment and growth. Reserve requirements, which were lower for investment banks, have been brought in line with those applied to commercial banks.

(d) Lowering reserve requirements on foreign currency deposits to bring them into line with those applied to the JD deposits, thus eliminating discrimination against the JD.

(e) Creating a General Bank Deposit Insurance Corporation to replace the informal practice of giving depositors *de facto* almost full protection.

(f) Automating payment, transfer, and transactions settlement systems.

THE CAPITAL MARKET

The repatriated savings of 300 thousand returnees from the Gulf in the aftermath of the Gulf crisis and war lead to an unprecedented rise in the stock values of the Amman Financial Market in 1992–93. Since then stock prices have been falling, and liquidity in the market has been scarce. These developments, together with the Central Bank policy of consolidating international reserves by offering CDs at high rates of interest, prompted the banks to buy CDs instead of channeling funds to productive investments.

A modern Securities Law, which was enacted in 1997, separates the regulatory functions from the operations side of the Amman Financial Market. Accordingly, the Jordan Securities Commission (JSC) was created with broad regulatory powers to see to it that the capital market does function in an efficient and transparent manner, that its operations conform to internationally accepted standards and to practices that increase investors' confidence and protect their lawful interests, and that information flows between market institutions, participants and investors are transparent and efficient. In addition to the JSC, the Securities Law provides for the establishment of a private sector stock exchange (bourse) corporation for brokerage and dealing with financial papers.

Overall, management reform measures were taken to improve the automation of the financial market by the computerization of trading, clearing, settlement, and the centralized depository systems.

Also envisaged is the establishment of a private sector depository to act as a clearing house and bookkeeper, a training institute to upgrade skills in dealing with securities, an association to represent the private sector participants in the securities industry in its interaction with the JSC.

The Jordan Mortgage Refinance Company (JRMC) was created in 1997 to encourage the bond market and expand the availability of medium- and long-term finance. The company provides a secondary mortgage facility and a source of liquidity for mortgage lending, and so helps to build investor confidence in Jordan's emerging bond market by offering bonds of transparently low risk.

INSURANCE

The current insurance law and regulations suffer from a number of shortcomings that make it inadequate to ensure solvency and sound financial status of insurance companies. Accordingly, a new Insurance Law is being drafted that, among other reforms, will adopt European Union solvency margins and provide for the creation of an independent Insurance Supervision Agency.

SECURED FINANCING AND LEASING, AND REGISTRATION OF MOVABLE PROPERTY

A vacuum exists in the legal and regulatory environment to enable the development of leasing, factoring, and venture capital companies, and the registration of lease and security interests in movable property. Currently, a Secured Financing and Leasing Law is in preparation. Similarly, a Register of Interests in Movable Property should be established to comprise a computer-based system with registration and inquiry functions. This should facilitate the extension of credit on the security of the enterprise's own productive assets.

Competitiveness of Markets and Privatization

By 1995 the government had decontrolled nearly all prices including interest rates. A new Competition and Anti-Trust Law is being processed through Parliament. The enactment of this law should not only protect consumer welfare but also enhance competition and promote efficiency in domestic markets.

The government's economic strategy calls for reducing public sector involvement in the production and distribution of goods and services, in exchange for consolidating and streamlining the government's role as supervisor and regulator against market distortions and other abuses and excesses (Kanaan 1998). The strategy involves mainly the conversion of public utilities in the energy, telecommunications, and public transport sectors into commercially oriented public shareholding companies owned temporarily by the government. Other planned moves include the divestiture of large blocs of government equity in various PLCs that were originally established as public–private joint ventures—and last, but not least, steps towards a more level playing field in the financial sector through abolishing the privileges that had been enjoyed by the Housing Bank as a quasi-official specialized financial institution.

An institutional framework for privatization has been established in the form of the interministerial High Committee for Privatization, and the Privatization Implementation Unit (EPU) set up in the Prime Ministry in 1996. The objective is to oversee the implementation of the privatization program in a rapid and transparent manner.

The Business Environment

The business environment, to be conducive to entrepreneurial initiative and attractive to investment, requires a legislative framework designed to be supportive of that objective. By itself, however, appropriate legislation is necessary but by no means sufficient. Of decisive importance is the actual practice in enforcing legislation, applying regulations, and executing administrative directives. The following section describes progress in the legislative framework relevant to the business environment, while the subsequent section takes up the actual practices affecting the "transactions costs."

The Legislative Framework

After the economic crisis in 1989, a number of important laws and regulatory initiatives have been taken that markedly improved the legislative framework for business, making it "among the most business friendly in the world," as judged by a prominent international center (SRII 1998b, p. IV-1). These include the following:

(a) The General Sales Tax Law No. 6 of 1994, which reduced the dependence of fiscal revenue on customs duties, and formed the first step towards a modern value added tax system;

(b) The Income Tax Law No. 14 of 1995;

(c) The Encouragement of Investment Law No.16 of 1995;

(d) The Labor Law No. 8 of 1996;

(e) The Law of Unification of Tariff Taxes and Fees No. 7 of 1997, which lowered import tariffs and consolidated tariffs and fees for increased transparency; and

(f) The Customs Law of 1998, which streamlined and simplified customs procedures, increased transparency and reduced bureaucratic discretion.

Further, draft laws with significant liberalization impact are pending completion of the legislative cycle. These include the amended Companies Law, a new Securities Law, a new Competition (antitrust) Law, a new Leasing and Secured Financing law, and a new Intellectual Property Rights Law.

Certain items of the above-mentioned legislation were described earlier as part of the review of the economic reform. The following paragraphs attempt to highlight key aspects of the legislative framework not covered by earlier discussion.

THE COMPANIES LAW

The Companies Law (No.1 of 1989) is a fairly modern piece of legislation. It contains, among other things, detailed provisions regarding the formation and incorporation of partnerships and companies, public offerings and sales, bond issues, mergers and acquisitions of companies, transformation of companies from one form into another, and dissolution and liquidation of companies. It also contains detailed provisions dealing with the rights, obligations, and responsibilities of the external auditors of companies as well as the powers of the controller of companies and his or her authority to supervise the conduct and affairs of companies in order to ensure full and strict compliance with the law.

A new Companies Law was drafted in 1995 with provisions to amend the Companies Law currently pending in the legislative process. The amendments purport to resolve a number of ambiguities, to simplify procedural aspects and to generally improve the regulatory environment for corporate governance and finance.

TAXATION LAWS

The taxation system in Jordan has a high level of transparency. It consists of a well-defined set of laws describing the tax system. All new tax legislation approved by the Parliament, and new regulations and procedures that have been agreed upon by the Council of Ministers are published in the official gazette, which is widely available. Furthermore, the tax laws that apply to income, imports, and the general sales tax on domestic products, are regularly published in English as well as Arabic. Included in the articles of each tax law is a set of guidelines related to tax enforcement. These documents are relatively concise and straightforward to understand for the average citizen. In addition, several private organizations such as the Jordanian Businessmen Association, the Exporters Association, as well as leading auditing firms, produce pamphlets that provide the essential elements of tax laws. Within the coming short period, the Ministry of Finance will have the GST and Customs Laws available on the Internet. Although the laws are transparent, there are several areas that should benefit from reform.

The Income Tax Law No. 14 of 1995 lowered the general tax rates for corporations and individuals. Previous corporate income tax rates varied between 38 and 55 percent. The new corporate tax rates on income, net of allowable expenses, are as follows:

- 15 percent for companies in mining, manufacturing, hotels, hospitals, transportation, and construction projects with paid-up capital above JD 1 million.

- 35 percent for banks, financial companies, insurance companies, exchange companies, and brokerage companies.

- 25 percent for all other businesses, including trading and service companies.

ENCOURAGEMENT OF INVESTMENT LAW

The Encouragement of Investment Law No. 16 of 1995, together with recent regulations based on it, provides for a generous incentive regime for both Jordanian and foreign investors, to wit:

- A minimum of 25 percent of income and social service tax is waived for a 10-year period on approved new investments. If they are located in designated development zones B and C, the rate of tax exemption rises to 50 percent and 75 percent, respectively.

- The law provides for further tax exemptions to companies re-investing profits, and allows deductions for company expenditures on staff training, marketing, and research and development. However allowances for capital depreciation are less generous than in some other countries (SRII 1998a, p. IV-16).

- Import duty exemptions on capital equipment and intermediate inputs are conceded to firms that invest in a wide range of industrial, agricultural, and service activities. The exemptions apply as follows: (a) fixed assets for a period of three years for new projects, and for modernization and expansion of existing projects, provided that such modernization results in 25 percent of expansion of productive capacity; (b) spare parts up to 15 percent of the total value of the fixed assets utilizing the spare parts, provided that such parts have been imported within the first 10 years of starting the project; and (c) furniture and similar supplies for hotels and hospitals every seven years.

The law provides for equal treatment of foreigners and Jordanians in all respects except one, namely that foreign equity is not to exceed 50 percent in companies operating in three specific sectors—mining, wholesale and retail trade and commercial services, and construction contracting.

Companies interested in conducting export-oriented activities or trading operations have the choice to set up their business inside any of the public or private free zones in the country where they enjoy exemption from duties on their imports, and from all income and social service taxes for a period of 12 years.

LABOR POLICIES

The Labor Law No. 8 of 1996 introduced flexibility in hiring and firing of workers by private enterprise. Employees may be let go for any justifiable reason without liability by the enterprise beyond the terms of contract.

Jordan has no minimum wage or wage control. However, the government keeps minimum wages for several professions set on the recommendations of an advisory panel.

Restrictions exist in connection with expatriate labor. There are several occupational categories in which the hiring of foreigners is restricted. In categories in which it is permitted, per-head taxes are imposed on expatriate labor. In the current climate of widespread unemployment and economic slowdown, there are significant pressures on the government to increase such restrictions.

PRICING POLICIES

As part of the program for structural adjustment and economic reform, the government has been implementing a gradual policy of reducing price controls and bringing the previously managed prices more in line with market conditions. An apparent breakthrough was the removal of food subsidies. However, the cash compensation that was decided to alleviate the social effect of abolition of the subsidies is still in force. It does not only burden the budget and aggravate its deficit, but it suffers from the same inequity as did the subsidies it replaced because its benefits are widely distributed to the needy and the less needy alike.

Transaction Costs

BUSINESS START-UP PROCEDURES

Business start-up procedures include the completion of all the bureaucratic steps and obtaining all the necessary approvals and permits necessary for a business to start operations. If these are complicated and costly in time and resources the transaction cost of doing business shoots up to form a major deterrent to investment. A recent assessment of these procedures in Jordan report the following issues.

Ten years ago cumbersome registration procedures used to consume anything from four to eight weeks, and necessitated sizable preparatory paperwork to obtain a license to start a business from the Ministry of Industry and Trade. Since the abolition of such requirements in 1988 registration of a company with the Controller of Companies became a simple matter that could be completed in a single day. Other start-up procedures, however, relating to getting other relevant permits from a variety of public entities are perceived to remain time-consuming and cumbersome.

Several studies have analyzed some of the general problems associated with the business start-up regime, including the existence of too many layers of officials in too many agencies needing to approve and review documents with little coordination among them. These difficulties are often exacerbated by the lack of clear rules regarding all necessary permits, as well as by the lack of specific guidelines on the documents and processes required for obtaining them. Even when the processes are understood, the required documentation for approval can be onerous to obtain.

According to private sector business leaders, an overstaffed but undertrained bureaucracy with a rigid view of laws and regulations exacerbates the complexity of the investment start-up process. In the view of many investors, the staff at government agencies act too much like enforcers of narrow laws and not enough like business facilitators. As a result, permit applications are often rejected for insignificant reasons. Moreover, staff at government agencies are often not aware of the necessary steps and processes for obtaining permits. Often they require the submission of documents and the acquisition of permits that according to the law are not really necessary.

CUSTOMS PRACTICES

Jordan's customs practices are a major deterrent to the efficient conduct of business, and dealing with the bureaucracy of the Customs Department is a nightmare for businessmen. This department is responsible for collecting duties, which constitute a major source of government revenue. The common complaint by businessmen concerns the delays in clearing goods and the tendency of officials to exercise any discretion that they have in the interpretation of the customs bylaws in order to overcharge the rates and the fines.

Delays are often the result of inefficiencies in the system. Overlapping areas of authority are prevalent. Clearance procedures are onerous. The incidence of goods selected for checking is unnecessarily high. While no single procedure may seem burdensome or illogical, the aggregate process of clearing the goods through customs is cumbersome. The current bureaucratic practice is oblivious of the fact that competitiveness is now often built on very small (2 or 3 percent) profit margins, and that having to keep the goods in customs an extra day can fatally damage the margin that sustains the business.

Inconsistent application of customs rules is also a problem. Businesses complain that conflicting and unclear regulations allow officials to make discretionary decisions about tariff rates and applications. Inconsistencies also arise out of inadequate equipment or insufficiently educated staff. A pharmaceutical company, for example, claims that composition tests for the same imported chemicals will often yield different results at the customs laboratories, resulting in different duties being charged.

There is a tendency for customs officials to levy unnecessary fees. They are prone to search for minute irregularities, often on matters beyond the control of importers (for example, errors on bills of lading) and fine the importer accordingly. The incentive system used by the Customs Department to reward good performance has much to do with this tendency. Of the fees collected by the Customs Department, 25 percent are placed in a common pool to reward officials according to the fines they generate. Recently, this system was reformed, with bonuses capped at a percentage of the salary of the official. However, it is admitted that many officials do not meet their caps, and therefore are still liable to be overzealous.

A recent significant measure for reform was put into effect, namely the green line for accredited importers. According to this new procedure reputable importers are allowed to clear their imports to their warehouses expeditiously on the basis of their own declarations. The department of course reserves the right of spot-checking from time to time.

TAX PRACTICES

While the rates of taxation have considerably improved, the procedures for tax assessment are perceived to be damaging to business incentives and the investment climate. This is basically attributed to the wide latitude given to the officials of the Income Tax Department in assessing and confirming amounts of taxes falling due, which results in encouragement of tax evasion and causes companies to spend significant amounts of time and resources on the tax assessment process.

The tax assessment process for company X starts with the company filing its tax declaration with the department. Next, an assessor from the department is put in charge of reviewing the filing. As per Article 29 of the Income Tax Law, the assessor has the discretion to make changes in what he or she believes to be the true amount of income and tax liabilities, and the right to make his or her own estimates about income and expenses. Businesses who have toiled with this process report that assessors feel little restraint in revising companies' tax liabilities, even in the absence of evidence. While the company in question has the right to appeal the initial assessment at the Income Tax Court of Appeals, Article 34 of the law stipulates that the burden of proof that the assessed tax is excessive rests with the appellant. In short, the assessors, probably encouraged by the department culture, see themselves as performing a public service duty in their endeavor to maximize government revenue.

The system creates a dynamic in which the tax assessment is the outcome of a negotiation process, with companies starting out with a low figure on the expectation that the assessment made by the auditor will be much higher, and the court of appeals will finally arrive at an amount somewhere in between. As a result, a vicious circle is created: If the tax assessor tendency is to overestimate a company's tax liabilities, the company will assume that state of affairs and falsify their tax liabilities.

The Business Environment from Private Sector Perspective

Interestingly, the private sector perception of the investment environment has been the subject of professional monitoring in at least two studies separated by about eight years.

The earlier study was done in 1988 by the consulting arm of Stanford Research Institute (SRI) International, commonly referred to as SRII. Researchers of SRII were assigned the task of assessing "the attractiveness of Jordan as an investment site from the point of view of private investors. For this purpose, they interviewed "dozens of business people in the United States with Jordanian subsidiaries, in Jordan itself, and in competitor countries." Their findings are summarized below (SRII 1988, pp. 35–39).

To start with, business executives interviewed agreed that companies seeking to sell to the Middle Eastern markets should establish either a regional headquarters or a production site within the Middle East. The issue was whether

Jordan qualified as the best candidate to host such regional headquarters or production sites.

Customs delays were singled out for intensive criticism by most.

One main problem was the requirement to get approval by the Ministry of Industry and Trade of the investment to be undertaken. Concern was almost unanimously expressed that the ministry's personnel assigned to evaluate proposals and give approvals had an insufficient understanding of their industries, markets, products, and technologies. Thus, investors are faced with the greatest degree of hassle in precisely those areas in which the government is seeking to make progress. While the incentives that Jordan offers appear to be generous, obstacles in the application process seriously erode their value to investors.

Another main problem was that the criteria used in evaluating investments for approval of incentives were far from being transparent.

One important development since the time of that study was the government decision to abolish prior substantive conditions on the issue of investment licenses from the Ministry of Industry and Trade. The ministry's approvals became limited only to industries seeking the exemptions and concessions granted to investments that satisfy conditions specified in the Encouragement of Investment Law.

The more recent empirical study on the business environment from a private sector perspective was conducted in 1995 by a research team of the Center for Strategic Studies at Jordan University (Al Jomard 1996). It was based on a sample of 151 firms (companies, corporations) chosen at random from the largest 500 firms in the productive sector. The latter is defined to exclude commercial, banking, and financial concerns. It included 116 firms in the manufacturing industry together with 35 firms in other sectors covering energy, transport, construction, storage, real estate, tourism and other services. The questionnaires were conducted in person with CEOs of the firms with adequate preparation beforehand and subsequent verification and scrutiny. The survey aimed at exploring four main themes:

(1) The general environment for investment;

(2) Interaction of businesses with the investment environment;

(3) Impediments and disincentives to investment; and

(4) Expectations for the future.

The following are main elements in the investment perceptions of the firms surveyed:

Rate of return on investment (RR). Firms that engaged in investment both in the domestic economy and abroad estimated that the realized RR on investment abroad averaged at 18.6 percent, compared with an average realized RR on local investment of 7.3 percent, and compared with an acceptable (desired) RR of 16.6 percent.

Political stability. Percentage of respondents who perceived Jordan as politically stable was 65.6 percent, compared with 26.5 who did not think so, and 7.9 percent who were indecisive. Of those who thought that Jordan was politically unstable, 80 percent attributed the perceived instability to external factors (regional, peace process, and so on).

Exchange rate stability. Percentage of respondents who expressed worry about exchange rate stability of the JD was 52.3 percent, compared with 35.8 percent who felt assured, and 11.9 percent who were indecisive. In explaining their reasons for worry, only 30 percent of the respondents gave specific substantive reasons—such as level of reserves, indebtedness, budget and trade deficits, and so on. The majority referred to general internal and external political and economic reasons.

Coefficient of association. Coefficient of association between perceptions of political stability and exchange rate stability was weak (0.39).

Impediments and Disincentives to Investment

The survey pre-defined the possible impediments to investment in six categories. Those were bureaucratic (and civil service–related) impediments; legislative and legal impediments; impediments related to skills and education; costs of operation; impediments to marketing (in the local market and in foreign markets); and finally, financial impediments. The following are highlights of the survey findings concerning each category:

BUREAUCRATIC IMPEDIMENTS

About 83 percent of respondents thought that this category was "very important," and gave the following weights to its different aspects:

- Delays and slowness in bureaucratic action on an application: 35 percent.
- Lack of understanding by the civil servant(s) concerned of the specific details of an application: 30 percent.
- Corruption: 30 percent.
- Other: 5 percent.

LEGISLATIVE AND LEGAL IMPEDIMENTS

About 68 percent of respondents thought that this category was very important, and gave the following weights to its different ramifications:

- Multiplicity of laws and by-laws: 27 percent.
- Too many changes and amendments to laws: 27 percent.
- Corruption in the application of laws: 18 percent.

- Legal problems with labor: 6 percent.
- Legal problems with competitors: 6 percent.
- Legal problems with partners: 2 percent.
- Other: 14 percent.

IMPEDIMENTS RELATED TO SKILLS AND EDUCATION

About 75 percent of respondents in the industrial sector and 83 percent of respondents in the services and other sectors thought that lack of skills and education in a wide variety of areas constituted important impediments for their investment. A weight of 58 percent was given to shortcomings in the level of experience, compared with a weight of 39 percent given to shortcomings in the level of education and training.

COSTS OF OPERATION

About 72 percent of respondents thought that elements of cost that are too high were among the impediments to investment in Jordan. The following weights were given to the importance of the different cost elements as impediments:

- Imported inputs: 38 percent.
- Local inputs: 13.2 percent.
- Communications: 9.9 percent.
- Transport: 10.8 percent.
- Technology: 9 percent.
- Labor wages: 8.4 percent.
- Rental of premises: 4.5 percent.
- Other: 6.3 percent.

IMPEDIMENTS TO MARKETING IN THE LOCAL MARKET

The following impediments to marketing in the local market and their relative weights, were recognized:

- Smallness of the local market: 35.5 percent.
- Price competition: 19.5.
- Foreign competition: 17.4.
- Cost of production: 11.7.
- Promotion and advertising: 3.2.
- Distribution costs and problems: 3.2 percent.
- Other: 9.8 percent.

IMPEDIMENTS TO MARKETING IN FOREIGN MARKETS

The following impediments to marketing in foreign markets and their relative weights, were recognized:

- Problems in political relations with other countries: 20 percent.

- Product quality: 13.5 percent.
- Costs of production: 17 percent.
- Custom duties of other countries: 13 percent.
- Suitability of trade agreements: 11 percent.
- Promotion and advertisement: 9 percent.
- Export credit insurance: 7 percent.

FINANCIAL IMPEDIMENTS

About 40 percent of the firms surveyed reported that they faced financing problems. Financing difficulties appeared highest among construction firms (50 percent), and lowest among food manufacturing firms (20 percent). The following problems of financing and their relative weight have been identified:

- High interest rates and cost of borrowing: 33 percent.
- Lack of acceptable collateral: 15 percent.
- Inadequate credit ceilings: 15 percent.
- Shortage of specialized financing schemes: 17 percent.
- Indifference to feasibility studies of projects: 9 percent.
- Other: 11 percent.

In comparison, the actual sources of finance for the surveyed firms and their relative weight were reported to be the following:

- Bank overdrafts: 38 percent.
- Capital increase: 17 percent.
- Commercial banks' term loans: 15 percent.
- Undistributed profits: 11 percent.
- Industrial bank term loans: 9 percent.
- Foreign loans: 2 percent.
- Other: 8 percent.

EXPECTATIONS FOR THE FUTURE

Each of the surveyed CEOs was asked about his or her expectations for the future over the next three years, as it would affect his or her firm with respect to the following:

Local demand and size of market for the firm's products: In this respect, 52 percent of the firms expected an expansion of the local market, 22 percent expected contraction of the local market, and 26 percent expected no change.

External demand and size of market for the firm's products: In this respect, 65 percent of the firms expected an expansion of the external market, 13 percent expected contraction of this market, and 22 percent expected no change.

Sources of finance. In this respect, 38 percent expected improvement in sources of finance, 16 percent expected a decline, while the majority, 42 percent, expected no change.

Size of investment. In this respect, 61 percent expected that there would be investment in the expansion of their business, 11 percent expected contraction of their business, and 27 percent expected no change.

Conclusions and Recommendations

An up-to-date study on "Making Jordan the Best Place to Do Business in the Middle East" was completed by SRI International in February 1998, 10 years after their first study of the same subject. The new study was conducted from the perspective of SRII's Commercial Policy Model. This model and database are diagnostic and benchmarking tools to explore the degree to which a nation's policies are "business friendly." Information based on examination of the country's relevant policy variables is translated into "scores," which can be compared to those of regional and competitor countries as well as to international best practices (SRII 1998b).

According to this model, Jordan attained the highest overall score (along with Lebanon) of Middle Eastern countries used as benchmarks. Its overall score in the commercial policy matrix was 77 out of a maximum of 100, representing a strongly business-friendly policy environment. "Jordan's import policies (level of protection) are the best in the region, while its tax and labor policies are among the most business friendly in the world."

This very favorable evaluation left SRII with a big challenge to answer the compelling question: Why then is Jordan not teaming with investors, both domestic and foreign, seeking to start new enterprises or expand their existing businesses?

Explanations, which SRII provided to clear this apparent paradox, were the following:

(a) Jordan's investment environment is constrained by the limited size of the domestic market, and more important, it is adversely affected by regional political instability, which deters investors throughout the region.

(b) It takes time for policy reforms to generate changes in investment behavior.

(c) Investors may not be sufficiently aware of reforms.

(d) The Commercial Policy Model does not cover all relevant policies and procedures. Problems can arise owing to bureaucratic red tape or restrictions in areas not covered.

All four reasons cited above for the nonresponsiveness of investors to what is at first look a very attractive investment environment are valid. However, the last explanation seems to be the most relevant for future policy actions. A *de jure* legislative and policy *framework* is a necessary but not sufficient condition for assuring investors of a *de facto* level playing field, maximal labor efficiency and productivity, and minimal transactions cost.

The following sentiments of the respondents to the Institute of Strategic Studies Survey are very pertinent and illuminating:

Bureaucratic impediments were categorized as "very important" by 83 percent of respondents. This supports the evaluation of "transactions costs" presented in the section on the business environment above.

Lack of skills and lack of education in a wide variety of areas were categorized as "important impediments" by 75 percent and 83 percent of respondents in the industrial and service sectors, respectively.

Improvements to minimize the costs of production need to be further pursued, particularly with regard to imported inputs, and with regard to financial facilities—in the form of long-term finance, and lending based on modern cash flow analysis of the borrower rather than on blind real-estate collateral.

References

The word *processed* describes informally reproduced works that may not be commonly available through libraries.

Al-Jomard, Atheel Abdul-Jabbar. 1996. *Variables Affecting Private Sector Investment in Jordan*. Amman: Institute of Strategic Studies, Jordan University.

Hashemite Kingdom of Jordan, 1998. Department of Statistics, Amman.

Kanaan, Taher H. 1996. *The State-Owned Enterprise in Jordan, An Evaluation.* Cairo: Economic Research Forum (ERF) for the Arab Countries, Iran & Turkey.

Kanaan, Taher H. 1998. "The State and thePrivate Sector in Jordan." In Nemat Shafik, *Economic Challenges Facing Middle Eastern and North African Countries, Alternative Futures*. London: Macmillan Press Ltd.

SRII (Stanford Research Institute [SRI] International). 1988. "Comparative Assessment of Investment Incentives in Jordan." The Ministry of Planning and USAID/Jordan, Amman.

SRII (Stanford Research Institute [SRI] International). 1998a. "Jordan Commercial Policy Assessment." Investment Promotion Corporation and USAID/Jordan. Amman.

SRII (Stanford Research Institute [SRI] International). 1998b. "Making Jordan the Best Place to do Business in the Middle East." Investment Promotion Corporation and USAID/Jordan. Amman.

World Bank, Hashemite Kingdom of Jordan. 1997. "Economic Reform and Development Loan III, Initiating Memorandum." World Bank: Washington, D.C. (processed, November).

PART II
Privatization

CHAPTER 5

The Results of Privatization:
Evidence from International Experience

John Nellis

Does ownership matter? Does the type of ownership—public or private—affect the performance of a firm? This question has long been of interest to economists, politicians, policy analysts, and various segments of the public in many countries.[1]

In the 1970s and early 1980s, a fair number of studies tried to analyze the relationship between ownership and enterprise performance by looking at roughly comparable sets of firms, in which some were publicly owned, others private. This "with and without" form of analysis yielded mixed results. That is, a small percentage of these studies concluded that state-owned firms performed better than privately owned, similar companies. A larger and significant, but still minority percentage of these studies could find no differences between public and private ownership, or the results were so ambiguous that no definitive conclusion could be reached. Even though the clear majority of these early studies pronounced in favor of private ownership (Megginson and Netter 1998),[2] the mixture of results led many reasonable people and analysts to conclude that ownership was a less important determinant of enterprise performance than market structure and the degree of competition faced by a firm.

From the late 1980s to the present, the number of studies on the effects of ownership has expanded greatly, and their nature has changed considerably. "With and without" examinations are still undertaken, but the field of inquiry has shifted far beyond the industrialized, OECD countries in which almost all the earlier studies were conducted, to examine privatization's effects in Asia, Africa, Latin

America and the "transition," or formerly planned economies. Some recent "with and without" studies, in industrialized settings and in India, conclude clearly that private firms perform better than public firms (Dewenter and Malatesta 1998; Majumdar 1998, pp. 1–24). Just as important, the "with and without" approach has been supplemented by "before and after" analyses. These look at the operations of firms in the period prior to their privatization, and contrast this to performance in the post-privatization period. The vast majority of these more recent studies show superior performance by the privatized firms in the post-sale period, as measured by a variety of financial, operational and efficiency measures.

The purpose of this note is to review some of these recent studies and present their prime findings. It will then briefly interpret the findings in an effort to show what they say, and do not say, for privatization policy and practice in settings in which divestiture has generally not yet been subjected to rigorous assessment—and that includes most of the Middle East and North Africa.

The Recent Record on Privatization

What follows does not pretend to be an exhaustive survey of the literature on the effects of privatization; rather, the intention is to present a sample of the findings of the most recent (post-1994, with most of the studies conducted in 1997 and 1998), careful, and important analyses of the issue.

I begin with a path-breaking study carried out in the early 1990s, but not formally published until 1995: *Welfare Consequences of Selling Public Enterprises,* by Galal and others (1995). The study analyzed in detail 12 privatizations in 4 countries—Chile, Great Britain, Malaysia, and Mexico. The firms reviewed were large, and included telecommunications companies, airlines, and an electricity generator. The study found improved financial and operating performance in 11 of the 12 cases. It revealed in addition that 11 of the 12 privatizations led to an increase of welfare in the economy. That is, the sales resulted not just in improvement of the firms' financial performance, but added to the aggregate level of resources in the economy as a whole. These welfare gains were quite large, resulting from increased investment, increased efficiency, and increased prices charged by the privatized firms (many state-owned firms lose money because government holds their output prices below cost-covering levels; this usually adds to inefficiency and is economically harmful, regardless of what those benefiting from these low prices think). The increased investment is very important, since so many state-owned firms—especially infrastructure enterprises—in developing and transition economies are starved for investment capital to expand their networks to meet unsatisfied demand and modernize their production lines.

Among the many innovative aspects of this important study was an effort to determine who in society gained and lost from the transactions. The authors concluded that almost all buyers, domestic and foreign, did very well. Consumers gained or came out even in a majority of cases, though in a few cases they ended up paying much higher prices. Surprisingly, workers did not appear to lose in any case examined; and in several cases were big winners, owing to their obtaining valuable shares in the privatized firms, or even because of generous severance payments. The selling governments often did not receive as much as they might have, probably because they tended to underprice the offerings in order to ensure the sales would be well-received in the financial and political market.

This study made a strong case for the view that ownership matters, that private ownership in and of itself is a powerful determinant of enterprise performance. But the study also showed, and quite clearly, that ownership is not the only item of importance. The study demonstrated that decent policy and well-functioning institutions, especially in the field of regulation, matter greatly as well. The acknowledged limitation of the study was that it dealt with a small number of cases, in middle- or high-income countries.

In their 1994 article, "Financial and Operating Performance of Newly Privatized Companies," Megginson, Nash, and van Randenborgh (1994, pp. 403–452) looked at 61 privatized firms, from 18 countries and 32 different industrial sectors, for a 6-year period—three before and three after sale. They found highly positive results of privatization—on average, substantial increases in output, profitability, operating efficiency, capital investment spending, and dividends, as well as decreases in leverage. This study found that employment levels were maintained or even increased slightly in the average privatized firm.

Most of the cases examined were from OECD countries, though divestitures from several middle-income developing countries were reviewed. Moreover, the method of privatization was through the issuing of shares on the local stock exchange (often referred to as an "initial public offering," or IPO). One could argue that since most of the cases reviewed came from industrialized settings, and that the IPO method is usually applied to high-quality candidates, then the positive findings might not apply in non-industrialized countries, or to firms divested by methods other than share issuing.

A World Bank study of infrastructure privatizations in Argentina concluded that the fiscal impact of the five examined sales was large and positive, that financial performance improved in all five cases, that productivity increased in four of the five, that service quantity and quality improved, and the government seller and the buyers and investors were better off after the transactions (Shaikh 1996). The study reported more mixed results for the workers, many of whom lost their jobs, either as part of the preparations for privatization, or after the new owners came on board.

C.A.F. Dowlah (1997) looked at the results of 10 privatizations in the difficult economic environment of Bangladesh. All of the firms were large, and all had been registering serious losses in the period prior to the sale. Within a few years following privatization, 7 of the 10 became profitable, showing increases in output, sales, capacity utilization, and labor productivity. Unit and labor costs fell, on average, by 21 and 18 percent, respectively, in the firms turned around. True, the study showed that 3 of the 10 had not succeeded in halting the losses, but a 70 percent success rate is nonetheless remarkable. Moreover, it is possible (the issue is not discussed in the study) that the new private owners of the failing firms will eventually have to declare bankruptcy. This is not necessarily, as is sometimes argued, a sign that privatization has failed. On the contrary, it is likely that had these firms stayed in public hands they would have continued to be subsidized and kept alive artificially by the state, at the expense of the public at large. Having chronically nonperforming companies undergo bankruptcy can be seen as a way to give a second, and it is hoped, more productive life to the assets. Privatization in Bangladesh was thus doubly positive; in putting most of the firms back to profitable work, and in finding a way to stop the flood of government resources into chronic loss-making firms.

Pohl and others (1997) looked at financial and operating information for 6,300 public and privatized firms in seven Eastern European transition economies.[3] They analyzed data from 1990 through 1995 and found "on average, in a firm that has been privatized for four years, productivity increases three to five times more than in a similar state-owned enterprise." They also found that investment per worker in privatized firms was 5 to 10 times higher than in state-owned firms in their sample. They concluded that privatization was the crucial and necessary key to restructuring in transition economies. A controversial conclusion of this study was that almost any form or method of privatization—save that of handing over ownership to the workers—produced positive results. This finding has been contested by other studies and analysts; we shall return to this issue below.

A second analysis of privatization's effects in transition economies was made by Frydman and others (1997). This careful study reviewed performance in 188 medium-size firms, roughly half state-owned and half privately owned, in the Czech Republic, Hungary, and Poland, and concluded that the privatized companies in their sample performed far better than state firms in terms of generating new investment and maintaining and creating jobs. The principal conclusion was that "private ownership, except for worker ownership, dramatically improves corporate performance." The authors were so impressed by the ability of privatized firms to create jobs that they concluded that privatization was the single best policy in transition countries to generate employment.

Two important features of this study were its attention to the question of "selection bias," and its analysis of the differences in performance attributable to different types of owners. The idea behind "selection bias" is straightforward: improved performance in privatized firms does not necessarily show that private owners are better; the improvements may rather indicate that it is the better firms that were privatized. This possibility has particularly haunted the studies of privatization in transition economies, with their thousands of transactions, the tendency to reward insiders (who might be thought to possess good information on the firm's prospects), and the lack of constraints on insider trading. Frydman and others deal with this question by looking at performance before and after privatization. They conclude that "selection bias" does not explain good performance in privatized firms, that there are qualities in private ownership itself that lead to improved operations.

In contrast to the findings of Pohl and others, Frydman and his colleagues find that different methods of privatization do produce different outcomes. Their study indicates that some types of private owners are better than others—in terms of how quickly and effectively they restructure the firm to increase its capability to survive and thrive in competitive market operations. They found that external owners tend to do better than "insiders," that is, former managers who became owners.

The rigor of this study is exemplary, but it must be admitted that the sample size is small and the performance data—which end in 1994, just before many economic changes took place in this region—a bit dated.

La Porta and Lopez-de-Silanes (1997) reviewed the results of 218 privatizations in Mexico, and found highly positive results. They calculated, on average, "a 24 percentage point increase in the ratio of operating income to sales," significant increases in profitability and output, and substantial decreases in unit costs and employment levels (though the blue-collar workers who retained their jobs received large salary increases).

David Newbery and Michael Politt (1997, pp. 77–80) looked at the privatization of electricity supply in the United Kingdom. The sale yielded enormous financial benefits to the firm, amounting to "an extra 40 percent return on assets." Because of investments in new and cleaner technology, pollution was substantially reduced. Wholesale prices declined, though not as fast as costs, which led to savings for the consumer—and very large profits for the shareholders in the firm. This case is interesting because, despite the lowered real costs of the service, and the clearly beneficial environmental effects, many British citizens have nonetheless concluded that this privatization should not have been carried out. Why? Mainly, it would seem, because of the very large windfall profits earned by the shareholders, and the vast increases in salaries to managers, who just a few years before had earned modest public sector salaries. Technically, this privatization was beneficial to the British economy (though Newbery and Politt show that it could have been structured to yield even higher welfare gains), but the widespread perception of "unfair" and unjustified gains on the part of a few led to heavy criticism. The lesson is that privatization is always and everywhere an intensely political process; the management of public perceptions is as important as the financial and technical arrangements.

Boubakri and Cosset (1998) extended the analysis by looking at privatizations carried out in developing countries. Moreover, they examined transactions carried out by various methods, not just IPOs. Reviewing 79 transactions in 21 developing countries—mainly middle income, but including Bangladesh, Jamaica, Nigeria, Pakistan, and the Philippines—they found that the privatized firms in their sample, on average, "showed significant increases in profitability, operating efficiency, capital investment spending, output... and employment, and a decline in leverage and an increase in dividends" (p. 1081). Contrary to expectations, they found that two-thirds of the privatized firms increased employment after sale. This study is quite encouraging for proponents of privatization, since it shows positive results in non-industrialized settings, arising from a variety of sales methods. However, Boubakri and Cosset also document an important fact: the number, and degree of success, of privatizations is significantly associated with a country's level of income. The lower the income level of a country, the more difficult it will be to start privatization, and the more likely it will be that results will be modest.

D'Souza and Megginson (forthcoming) studied a set of privatizations carried out in the 1990s; 78 different transactions in 25 countries around the world. Once again, they found "significant increases" in mean and median levels of profitability, real sales, operating efficiency, and dividend payments, plus lower leverage ratios. Unlike several earlier studies, this review found more or less unchanged levels of investment and employment in the privatized firms. The authors conclude that "privatization yields significant performance improvements in divested firms."

Not all studies show positive results from privatization. Djankov and Kreacic (1998) looked at 92 state and private firms in the Republic of Georgia (formerly part of the Soviet Union). They could not attribute what restructuring they found to private ownership. Rather, firms exposed to competition and financial discipline were restructuring; those not facing competition and a "hard budget constraint" were not—regardless of ownership form. In neighboring Armenia, an assessment of 50 firms one year after their privatization concluded that only 3 had generated any new investment; for the others the "prognosis was for continuing decline and ultimate bankruptcy."[4] A study on Mongolia provides evidence that partially state-owned firms perform better than privatized firms (Anderson, Lee, and Murrell 1999). Early surveys in Russia showed few differences in performance between privatized and state firms, or modestly positive differences in privatized firms.[5]

What these studies reveal is that a country's policies and institutional make-up strongly affect both the way in which privatization is designed and carried out, and the outcomes that one can expect from the process. They confirm that country conditions are important, and that private ownership has to be placed in an enabling environment of proper policy and institutions for it to produce the benefits of which it is so clearly capable. We shall return to this issue in the final section.

Conclusions

The majority of studies, carried out in a range of countries, examining a wide variety of industries and approaches, and using a number of methods, show that privatization results in improved performance at the level of the firm. The majority of privatized companies work better, by a variety of measures, after the sale than before. This is true of both infrastructure and manufacturing enterprises. In addition, most macroeconomic and efficiency changes are also positive. Ownership matters.

However, as noted, policy and institutions matter as well. While it can be argued that proper policies are relatively easy to adopt, there is not much dispute that longer-term, more complex historical, geographical and social forces affect the evolution and operation of the institutional arrangements required to put new and good policies in place and enforce them. The issue becomes intricate, since both opponents and proponents of privatization can thus argue in favor of delaying a change of ownership until institutional conditions are "right." The weight of experience argues in favor of privatizing rapidly any firm that operates in competitive markets, but of not privatizing infrastructure enterprises possessing a "natural monopoly" component until the essential market structure enhancing competitive forces and regulatory elements are in place. In practice, ownership and regulatory reform frequently proceed in parallel.

On a more practical level, some operational lessons of experience emerge:

- Share issues sales, or IPOs, are more suitable for large, good firms, in countries with effective equities markets (or with access to such markets in other countries).

- Asset sales—negotiated transactions between seller and buyer—are more likely to be the norm in lower-income countries, which tend to have an embryonic (or no) equities market.

- "Outsiders"—investors and managers external to the historic company—tend to be better owners than insiders.

- Concentrated owners tend to be better than dispersed; that is, a single or core group of owners is associated with better performance than a large number of fragmented owners.

- In particular, there is a poor record of workers as owners.

- The greater the number of the bidders, the better the final transaction and the higher the return to the seller.

- The costs of new physical investments made just prior to the sale are usually not recovered by the seller.

Clearly, we now know a great deal about privatization and its likely effects on firms. What is it that we do not yet know, or at least not know sufficiently well?

Not enough is known about the macroeconomic and fiscal impacts of privatization.

More work needs to be done on privatization's effects on income distribution.

Some information is available on the effects of privatization on labor (see Kikeri 1998), but there is a need to follow up on these beginnings to determine the medium-run impact of divestiture on workers. The expectation is that over time the positive stimulating effects of more efficient and productive privatized firms will contribute to economic growth and greater job creation. While some of the studies reviewed above indicate that this is happening, others do not. The matter merits follow-up.

As seen in the case of British electricity, how the public perceives and reacts to privatization is most important. What information the public (and specialized segments of the public intensely concerned with the issue) receives, how it receives it, how it matches the reality on the ground—these are questions recently receiving attention, but much more needs to be known.

Perhaps of greatest importance is the question of whether, and how, to privatize in institutionally weak settings—which are usually, but not always, low-income countries.

Notes

1. Note that some of the examples and phrases in this note are drawn from an earlier paper, "Time to Rethink Privatization in Transition Economies?" IFC Discussion Paper No. 38, May, 1999.

2. Nemat Shafik of the World Bank is presently working on a similar review and has produced a draft, unpublished paper titled, "The Evidence: Does Privitization Work?" which lists and reviews the range of studies published on this question.

3. Bulgaria, Czech Republic, Hungary, Poland, Romania, Slovakia and Slovenia.

4. Center for Economic Policy and Analysis 1997, p. 1. Note that while bankruptcy of 30 percent of a group of privatized firms might be considered as tolerable in Bangladesh, bankruptcy of 93 percent of a set is more difficult to accept blithely.

5. "[O]wnership changes are generally rather weakly associated with most indicators of performance, including sales, wages and employment." From the "Introduction" to Commander, Fan, and Schaffer 1996, p. 8; the data in this study run to mid-1994.

References

The word *processed* describes informally reproduced works that may not be commonly available through libraries.

Anderson, James H., Young Lee, and Peter Murrell. 1999. "Do Competition and Ownership Affect Enterprise Efficiency in the Absence of Market Institutions? Evidence after Privatization in Mongolia." Working Paper (forthcoming). Department of Economics and IRIS Center, University of Maryland, College Park, Maryland.

Boubakri, Narjess, and Jean-Claude Cosset. 1998. "The Financial and Operating Performance of Newly Privatized Firms: Evidence from Developing Countries." *Journal of Finance* 53(3): 1081–1110.

Center for Economic Policy and Analysis. 1997. "Mass Privatisation of Enterprises in the Republic of Armenia: An Early Assessment." Assessment prepared for USAID. Yerevan, Armenia. Processed. November.

Commander, Simon, Qimiao Fan, and Mark Schaffer. 1996. *Enterprise Restructuring and Economic Policy in Russia*. Washington, D.C.: World Bank, EDI Development Series.

D'Souza, Juliet, and William L. Megginson. 1999. "The Financial and Operating Performance of Privatized Firms During the 1990s." Forthcoming in *Journal of Finance* 54(4).

Dewenter, Kathryn, and Paul Malatesta. 1998. "State-Owned and Privately-Owned Firms: An Empirical Analysis of Profitability, Leverage and Labor Intensity." Working Paper. School of Business, University of Washington, Seattle.

Djankov, Simeon, and Vladimir Kreacic. 1998. "Restructuring of Manufacturing Enterprises in Georgia: Four Case Studies and a Survey." World Bank, Processed.

Dowlah, C. A. F. 1997. "Privatization Experience in Bangladesh, 1991–96." Dacca, Bangladesh. Processed. (Unpublished paper submitted to the World Bank, Washington, D.C.)

Frydman, Roman, Cheryl Gray, Marek Hessel, and Andrzej Rapacynski. 1997. "Private Ownership and Corporate Performance: Some Lessons from Transition Economies." Policy Research Working Paper No. 1830.

Galal, Ahmed, Leroy Jones, Pankaj Tandon, and Ingo Vogelsang. 1995. *Welfare Consequences of Selling Public Enterprises*. New York: Oxford University Press.

Kikeri, Sunita. 1998. *Privatization and Labor: What Happens to Workers When Governments Divest?* Technical Paper No. 396.

La Porta, Rafael, and Florencio Lopez-de-Silanes. 1997. "The Benefits of Privatization: Evidence from Mexico." *Viewpoint* 117: 1–4. World Bank, Washington, D.C.

Majumdar, Sumit. 1998. "Assessing Comparative Efficiency of the State-Owned, Mixed and Private Sectors in Indian Industry," *Public Choice* 96: 1–24.

Megginson, William, and Jeffrey Netter. 1998. "From State to Market: A Survey of Empirical Studies on Privatization." Paper presented to the Global Equity Markets conference, Paris. December.

Megginson, William, Robert C. Nash, and Matthias van Randenborgh. 1994. "The Financial and Operating Performance of Newly Privatized Firms: An International Empirical Analysis." *Journal of Finance* 49(3): 403–52.

Nellis, John. 1999. "Time to Rethink Privatization in Transition Economies?" International Finance Corporation (IFC) Discussion Paper No. 38. World Bank, Washington, D.C.

Newbery, David M., and Michael G. Politt. 1997. "The Restructuring and Privatization of the U.K. Electricity Supply—Was It Worth It?" In Suzanne Smith, ed., *The Private Sector in Infrastructure: Strategy, Regulation and Risk*. Washington, D.C.: World Bank.

Pohl, Gerhard, Robert Anderson, Constantijn Claessens, and Simeon Djankov. 1997. "Privatization and Restructuring in Central and Eastern Europe—Evidence and Policy Options." Technical Paper No. 368. Washington, D.C.: World Bank.

Shafik, Nemat. 1998. "The Evidence: Does Privatization Work?" Washington, D.C.: World Bank. Processed.

Shaikh, Hafeez. 1996. *Argentina Privatization Program: A Review of Five Cases*. Washington, D.C.: World Bank.

CHAPTER 6

Privatization in Egypt:
Constraints and Resolutions

Mokhtar Khattab

The sale of state-owned enterprises (SOEs) to the private sector (privatization) is considered a key component of Egypt's economic reform program, which the country started in 1991. However, the implementation of privatization was complicated by several factors. First, public opinion was not conducive to carrying out the process. Second, implementation required important legal and legislative changes. Third, there were technical difficulties, especially with respect to such a debatable issue as the evaluation of enterprises for sale.

Egypt was able to overcome most of these constraints. This paper addresses the question of how policymakers in Egypt overcame the constraints to privatization, and what lessons can be drawn from the Egyptian experience for other countries. To give a quick overview, the process started by preparing the public opinion and the legislative framework for privatization. To increase public awareness of the benefits of privatization and capitalize on the experience of other countries, there was a series of seminars and workshops attended by international experts. On the legal side, Law 203 was passed in 1991, rendering the public sector companies independent economic units, and setting forth a framework for their management as private sector entities. It also detached them from the state budget and other Government of Egypt (GOE) entities. Furthermore, the Capital Market Law 95 was issued in 1992, introducing the framework in which trading could take place. Finally, the government published the Guidelines for Privatization. The program gained momentum in recent years. Privatization was carried out across many enterprises, using several techniques.

The rest of the paper is organized as follows. The first main section below presents the evidence of progress on privatization to date. This is followed by a section that deals with the political and legislative constraints and their resolutions, then a section on the constraints encountered in implementation and how they were addressed, and finally, a conclusion.

Progress to Date

Privatization in Egypt went through two distinct stages. The achievements of the first stage, which lasted from 1991 to 1996, were modest. The government sold only three companies to strategic investors using direct negotiations: Coca Cola, Pepsi, and Al Nasr Boilers. It floated minority shares, ranging from 5 to 20 percent, of 16 companies in the stock market. And, it sold a majority stake in 10 companies to their employees.

Starting in April 1996, the privatization program gained momentum, helped by the continuous improvement in the macroeconomic environment, increased public receptivity to privatization, and a boost in investors' confidence in government policies.

Both stages of the privatization program produced an impressive record of the sale of 91 enterprises for £E63.8 billion or US$18.8 billion (table 6.1). This amounts to one-third of all SOEs, or 35 percent of the book value of total assets. The percentage is somewhat more modest (14 percent) when the ratio is measured in terms of the market value of the assets.

TABLE 6.1 PRIVATIZATION TO DATE

Description	All state-owned enterprises	Privatized companies	Percentage privatized
Number of companies	314	91	29
Book value £E billion	12.01	4.2	35
Market value £E billion	63.8	9.1	14

Source: Public Enterprise Office (PEO).

Privatization was carried out as follows: flotation of majority stake of 38 companies through the stock market, majority sale of 9 companies to strategic investors, total sale of 17 companies to their employees, and total sale of assets of 27 companies to private investors.

Moreover, tranches representing a stake of less than 50 percent were sold in 20 enterprises (flour mills and pharmaceutical companies). This means that the privatization program has affected 111 companies so far.

Political and Legislative Constraints and Resolutions

The political and legislative constraints on privatization originated from the opposition of some within the executive branch, the public, the press, and the People's Assembly. The positions of these actors are discussed below, along with the way they were dealt with in Egypt.

The Executive Branch

Until 1988, no one in Egypt dared discuss the sale of public enterprises. However, the second half of the 1980s witnessed important changes, including the end of the Soviet Empire, the revolution in communications and information, the prevalence of free trade (Uruguay Round), heightened international competition, and the formation of regional economic blocks based on free trade areas (for example, countries that are party to the North American Free Trade Agreement [NAFTA], the European Union, and others). These changes coincided with the inability of the Egyptian economy to honor its debt obligations in 1987 and later in 1991. In light of these changes, it was well recognized that the country needed to move toward trade liberalization, structural fiscal reform, deepening of the financial sector, measures to improve private sector incentives and last, but not least, privatization and public sector reform.

The response of government entities to the required changes, especially with respect to privatization, was not uniform. The entities responsible for the management and implementation of the program were more motivated and convinced of the validity of reforms than others. This gap manifested itself in the less-than-full support expressed by some parts of the government with respect to such issues as valuation, notarization of land belonging to the companies slated for privatization, and granting needed licenses.

This challenge was addressed in three ways. First, the heads and staff of different government entities were invited to seminars and workshops, focusing on privatization. Second, the leaders of these entities were included in the committees entrusted with the formulation of privatization policies, for example, the Ministry of Power Supply, Maritime Transport, the Ministry of Finance, the Central Auditing Agency, and others. Third, consensus was further built through the formation of the Higher Ministerial Committee, which is headed by the Prime Minister and has 22 ministers as members. Beyond building consensus, the committee provided a forum for removing obstacles to implementation across different ministries.

The Public

For several decades, the Egyptian government intervened in almost all aspects of the economy. Even in the agricultural sector, which was dominated by private ownership (97 percent), the government had full control over the supply of inputs, the marketing of output, and finance. Moreover, the government dictated what crops should be cultivated and where all over the Egyptian countryside.

State domination led several groups in Egyptian society (workers, students, intellectuals, and think tanks in universities and media institutions) to believe that government intervention was essential to guarantee fair distribution, protect the poor and, hence, maintain social stability. To them, returning to a market economy meant reverting to the system that existed before 1952, which had been attacked furiously in every respect for four decades. The prevailing motto was that the public sector is the backbone of the economy, its strong base, and the driving force for growth, in addition to being the protector of Egypt from poverty and starvation at times of war. Those views were publicized widely, making SOEs seem like untouchable taboos.

At the same time, the debt crisis of the late 1980s made it clear to the government that a comprehensive reform of the economy was inevitable. Partial reforms of the early 1980s and the debt rescheduling of 1987 had been insufficient. Moreover, some members of the government recognized that the comprehensive reform would have to turn SOEs into market-driven units by transferring their ownership and management to private hands. There was also recognition of the importance of starting to work on preparing public opinion to accept SOE reform and privatization.

To this end, it became apparent that the best way to start was through a discussion of the privatization experience of other countries. The expectation was that this would lead gradually to a discussion of the situation of SOEs in Egypt, yielding a list of suggestions at the top of which should be the privatization option. This would provide the seeds for forming a public opinion supportive of reform, eventually growing to be a trend that flourishes with the success of the transformation.

Accordingly, privatization experts were invited from several countries that had undertaken successful programs as early as 1990. The discussions and workshops were attended by intellectuals, journalists, university professors, government officials, and SOEs' top management. On several occasions, those experts were invited to meet the concerned ministers for informal discussions. Over a period of three years (1990–92), the workshops and seminars covered the experiences of countries such as Britain, France (two events), Italy, Germany, Mexico, Chile, Argentina, Korea, Thailand, Russia, Turkey, and others. These events created awareness among influential opinion-makers, who in turn carried the message to the public at large through the press and mass media.

Many intellectuals as well as leaders of the Egyptian society shifted positions in less than two years from the discussion of other experiences to that of the necessity of privatization in Egypt. Actual privatization took off, albeit modestly, with the successful sale of 3 companies to strategic investors and the flotation of 5–20 percent of the shares of 16 SOEs on the stock market in 1994 and 1995.

The awareness campaign continued during the program to attract new supporters and win or at least neutralize the effect of opponents. This campaign utilized all available mass media and public communication channels. It is worth mentioning that the creation of a supportive public opinion is a continuous process, since there are always issues that could be used by opponents to derail the process and erode public opinion.

The Press

The Egyptian press comprises 300 daily, weekly, and monthly newspapers and magazines, which employ more than 4,000 journalists and reporters, representing various parties in the Egyptian political and cultural landscape. Freedom of speech and expression, and abolishing censorship on the Egyptian press progressed in parallel with economic reform and the move toward market economy. This environment gave a forum for journalists, writers, and intellectuals of various schools of thought and ideologies to express themselves freely.

On the one hand, the press exposed the public to the privatization experience of other countries. It communicated to the public the fruits of discussions, and provided an important forum for open dialogue about the problems of the public sector in Egypt. On the other hand, a few newspapers and magazines contributed to the emergence of a trend opposing privatization. These newspapers are mainly those expressing the views of the opposition parties or those that stand against a free market economy. They doubted the ability of markets to realize economic growth and fair distribution, and criticized the process and measures taken to implement the program. They used provocation techniques to increase distribution, relying on young, hasty, and economically and politically inexperienced reporters. With the commencement of the take-off stage of the program in mid-1996, these reporters misused the information they received. Their efforts started to undermine the image of the public enterprise sector, its leaders, and some sale transactions that had taken place.

This led the holding companies (HC) chairmen and officials from the Public Enterprise (PE) Ministry and the Public Enterprise Office (PEO) to restrict information giveaway, which created a big, discomforting chasm between information providers and reporters. This situation worsened, turning into a vicious circle, when some of reporters published untrue information about companies whose shares were being offered for public subscription in the stock market, causing the coverage rates for the shares offered in some companies to decline.

In response to this challenge, the Minister of PE took two initiatives. First, he began to hold a daily meeting with representatives and correspondents from the major newspapers to provide them with accurate information regarding, among other things, the policies that would be followed in the program. This approach improved the accuracy of reporting, although some opposition newspapers still manipulated the information. Second, he created the "Cairo Center for Economic Information," in collaboration with the IMF. The center holds high-level scientific seminars regularly for journalists. The objective of these events is to provide a forum for journalists to acquire accurate and in-depth information about the topics of the seminar, and to get answers to their inquiries from high-ranking government officials and experts.

The People's Assembly

The People's Assembly (PA) is the main legislative body of Egypt, with the authority to issue legislation and monitor government performance. It is made up of 454
members, of which 435 represent the National Democratic Party (NDP), 6 members represent the opposition party "Al-Wafd," 5 members represent the leftist party
"Al-Tagamoa," 1 member represents "Al-Ahrar Party," 1 member represents the
"Labor Party," and 6 members are independent. Through the outstanding majority
of the government party—NDP—and the highly effective participation of the opposition parties and independents, the Assembly has played a supportive role by issuing the necessary legislation and offering constructive criticism. Because this paper
is concerned with the constraints on privatization, the focus will be on the monitoring role played by the Assembly. This involved questionnaires and inquiry requests
in the various subcommittees of the Assembly.

In a period of two years, two questionnaires were submitted by one opposition
member representing Labor. The subject of the inquiry was the implementation procedures and the policy behind the appointment of the Board's Chairmen. Also, 18 inquiry
requests were submitted regarding SOE losses and efficiency of management. In addition, 19 questions came from majority representatives concerning: the remuneration and
bonuses to top management, the valuation and privatization process, the sale proceeds
and their allocation, and the situation of the textile sector.

Four mechanisms were employed in dealing with these requests. First, regular
meetings were arranged between the Minister of Public Enterprises and the officials of the Ministry and holding companies and members of the concerned
committees in the Assembly to discuss relevant issues. Second, comprehensive
databases were established, including hard copies and electronic files for each
company. These were used to prepare a White Book for every case, with the
objective of disclosing all the measures and procedures taken, and how these
were in compliance with the relevant laws. A copy of each White Book was sent
to each member of the Assembly.

The third mechanism was the establishment of Management Information
Systems (MIS) and Decision Support Systems (DSS) to help in the preparation
of answers to the questionnaires and inquiries, in addition to supporting the
decision-maker in the privatization process. Finally, support was given to the
defense bureau in those lawsuits that were filed by some opposition members of
the Assembly claiming that the privatization process under the umbrella of Law
203 was against the constitution.

Legal Constraints

Any political-economic system functions on the basis of a set of laws, decrees and
regulations within a specified constitutional framework. The system could be changed
into another via a legislative process to render the new system legal. This means that
the transformation of the Egyptian economy from relying on semi-central planning
to relying on market forces could not take place without the necessary legislative

changes. Privatization is one area that could not be undertaken without appropriate legal changes.

Several legal constraints stood in the way of privatization. First, some argued about the constitutional legality of privatization. In their argument, they relied on article 24 of the Constitution, which asserts that public ownership belongs to all people, and that the public sector is entrusted with the responsibility of leading development in all sectors and the implementation of the national plan. On these grounds, a few members of the People's Assembly, including heads of the opposition parties and a number of intellectuals and lawyers, filed a lawsuit before the Higher Constitutional Court, asking the Court to render Law 203 of 1991 and, in turn, the entire privatization program unconstitutional.

The second constraint concerns the laws and regulations that governed the operation and management of SOEs until 1991. These laws and regulations effectively meant that SOEs were run like government departments or socioeconomic entities, not as commercial entities. SOEs were organized under 37 government organizations, each of which fell under the domain of the Minister of its sector or field of activity. About 14 ministers intervened in the day-to-day management of these organizations. The boards of SOEs did not have managerial autonomy, and investment decisions were mostly dictated by the National Investment Bank. SOEs were forced to employ a number of new graduates, and had to live with government intervention in the price-setting of purchases and sales. This led to cross arrears, operational losses, and eventually a burden on the state budget. From the perspective of privatization, this also meant that it was difficult to evaluate these companies for privatization because their value could change following decisions taken by the government affecting the size of investment, labor, or any other variable. This would render the valuation made obsolete, and would bring the privatization transaction to a halt.

The third constraint relates to the stock market, which until the late 1980s was not ready to entertain privatization transactions. In 1990, the value of transactions in the markets of Cairo and Alexandria Stock Exchanges totaled only £E342 million, averaging around £E1 million per day, which is extremely low. The limited size of the market was coupled by weak operating institutions, which were confined to a limited number of brokerage and portfolio management companies. How, then, was the stock market expected to absorb the shares of privatization, which might amount to several billion Egyptian pounds? Clearly, a new legislation was needed to pave the road for the creation of capital market institutions capable of undertaking the various privatization functions.

The constitutional constraint was difficult to deal with, given that changing one provision to permit privatization would have opened the door for many other changes in the constitution. That was not considered desirable at this stage. Ironically, the way out came from the opponents of privatization themselves. They did the supporters of privatization a big favor by appealing to the Higher Constitutional Court claiming that Law 203 and other privatization measures were not constitutional.

The Court decision was not in their favor, declaring Law 203 and privatization measures constitutional and legal.[1]

As for the legal constraints concerning the organization and management of SOEs, these were all addressed through the issuance of Law 203 for 1991. In addition to treating SOEs as business establishments, this law permitted privatization. It reorganized the 314 companies under 17 HCs managing diversified portfolios instead of 27 HCs, each of them specializing in a specified sector or activity. All SOEs were subjected to one Minister for Public Enterprises, hence abolishing multiple interventions by different government entities. The law also specified that the Board of Directors of these HCs—elected by and responsible before the General Assembly—would set forth the policies for the affiliated companies and monitor their implementation under the supervision and monitoring of the General Assembly. The General Assembly of the HC is currently responsible for taking decisions related to the sale of a stake greater than 50 percent of its affiliates' shares.

Finally, Law 95 and its Executive Regulations were issued in 1992 to introduce new types of institutions not known previously to the Egyptian capital market, regulating its operations and control. The law regulated the establishment and regulation of investment funds for the first time. These funds represent institutions that invest its shareholders' money in portfolio investment (shares and bonds). The law regulated the establishment, operations, and monitoring of brokerage firms by the Capital Market Authority (CMA). Law 95 also regulated the operations of portfolio management, share promotion companies and underwriting firms, all of which are necessary for the success of privatization. For the first time, the law also introduced the notion of Employee Shareholders Associations (ESAs), and their establishment as independent entities. Through these ESAs, workers could buy their companies' shares and repay using annual dividend yield.

In conclusion, starting in 1992 the legal environment was complete for undertaking privatization transactions. Thereafter, the program acquired strong momentum and capital market institutions increased from 7 by the end of the 1980s to 204 firms by the end of 1997 (table 6.2).

Implementation Constraints

Four major constraints or issues were encountered in the implementation of privatization. These are excess labor, enterprise valuation, capita market absorptive capacity, and selling money-losing companies. Each of these constraints is analyzed below, along with the solutions adopted in Egypt.

Excess Labor
A major characteristic of the Egyptian economy for several decades has been the domination of social considerations over economic efficiency in policy formulation. This orientation manifested itself in various practices, the most important of which was an attempt to absorb the inflow of labor into government entities and

TABLE 6.2 CAPITAL MARKET INSTITUTIONS, END OF 1997

Type of institution	Number	
Brokerage firms	132	firms
Underwriters and portfolio managers	36	firms
Investment funds	18	funds
Investment fund management	9	firms
Depository institutions	4	institutions
Records management	3	firms
Clearance houses	1	firm
Securities valuation and rating	1	firm
Total	204	firms

Source: Capital Market Authority (CMA), Internal Reports (April 1993).

public sector companies and enterprises irrespective of actual needs. This policy led to overstaffing, leaving SOEs under Law 203 with close to one million employees during 1995–96 (table 6.3).

To date, there is no study that specifies accurately the size of redundant workers in SOEs. However, estimates by the management of troubled companies indicate that the figure hovers around 180,000 redundant workers in these SOEs.

TABLE 6.3 NUMBER OF WORKERS IN SOEs UNDER LAW 203/1991, 1995–96

Holding company	Number of workers	Total salaries (£E million)	Average salary per worker (£E)
Spinning and weaving	96,524	534	5,532
Textile manufacturing and trade	96,762	492	5,085
Cotton and foreign trade	49,156	290	5,900
Engineering industries	62,178	478	7,688
Metallurgical industries	72,827	680	9,337
Mining and refractors	61,826	559	9,042
Chemical industries	47,400	369	7,785
Pharmaceutical industries	29,145	221	7,583
Food industries	94,616	413	4,365
Mills and silos	56,505	218	3,858
Agricultural development	40,082	122	3,044
National construction	57,061	389	6,817
Electrical construction	90,741	496	5,466
Housing, tourism, and cinema	19,918	126	6,326
Maritime transport	24,187	229	9,468
Transport	33,476	231	6,900
Total for PEs	932,404	5,847	6,271

Source: The Ministry of Public Enterprise Sector.

Redundant workers are mostly white-collar employees (dealing with finance, administration, and services). The number could be higher if we take into account the need in these companies for restructuring and modernization, both technically and managerially (in other words, organizationally).

Including the troubled enterprises, the estimate of redundant workers can be as high as 300,000 (table 6.4). This amounts to around 33 percent of the total labor force in those companies. The problems emerging from this huge size of excess labor constitute a serious constraint and a real challenge facing the Egyptian privatization program. This challenge causes serious worries among labor regarding privatization, and even resistance to it. Making things more difficult is the expectation that at least half of the retired 300,000 workers would search for jobs in a market that is still unable to provide jobs for nearly 1.6 million unemployed individuals who are of the same type of skill as those to be declared redundant.

TABLE 6.4 ESTIMATION OF EXCESS LABOR IN SOEs

Category of companies	Number of excess laborers
More than 20 unprofitable companies	60,000
More than 60 other unprofitable companies	100,000
140 companies realizing modest profit	140,000
Total excess laborers	300,000

Source: The Ministry of Public Enterprise Sector.

Early retirement would also be costly. For an estimated compensation package averaging £E25,000 per worker, the cost of retiring excess labor would be £E7.5 billion over a period of three to four years, or £E2.5 billion annually. This figure exceeds available funds, which is estimated to total around £E4 billion, or one-sixth of the sale proceeds forecasted for the coming three to four years.

In light of the above, it is apparent that the concerns of workers, the high rate of unemployment and the scarcity of resources needed to pay compensation packages represent critical constraints on privatization.

Egyptian policymakers have followed several approaches in dealing with this problem.

Negotiations and Dialogue with Labor Unions and the Formation of Committees on Issues Related to Labor
The Ministry of Public Enterprise and HCs do not take any decisions prior to negotiations with labor unions of various sectors, the Ministry of Manpower, and the General Union for Egyptian Workers to reach a joint decision. Labor committees in SOEs are represented in the early stages of the diagnostic study regarding the status

of the unprofitable companies, and in the discussions on management proposals for dealing with excess labor.

This process has helped union representatives become aware of the need for reform, reduced opposition only to those groups with political ideologies that reject the process of transformation to a free market economy, and neutralized the majority of workers, winning their mandatory support for the reform efforts.

OFFERING WORKERS SPECIAL PRIVILEGES THROUGH THE PRIVATIZATION PROGRAM

Workers of SOEs, through their ESAs, can buy 10 percent of the shares of any of their companies, whether the company is sold to strategic investors or on the stock market. Their share is taken before any prorating is applied to the offered shares, with a discount of 20 percent on the selling price. ESAs are also granted credit facilities for the term of repayment of the purchased stake in 8 to 10 years in annual installments, enabling them to repay out of their dividends.

These privileges provide an opportunity to acquaint workers with the privatization program and elicit their support, by enabling them to observe the positive impact of privatization and feel loyal to their company even under the umbrella of the private sector.

POSSIBILITY OF SELLING MAJORITY STAKE OF COMPANIES TO ESAS

In some cases, it is possible that SOEs could be sold in full to ESAs, who represent their workers. The idea is to reduce workers' suspicion that privatization would hurt their interests. By the end of May 1998, 17 SOEs had been sold to ESAs. Of these companies, 10 were in the public works and land reclamation sectors, 5 were inland transport companies, 1 was a rice milling and animal feed and pasta production company, and 1 a marine supplies company.

These companies were sold for reasonable prices (normally the book value with repayment over 8–10 years). Moreover, the HC provided technical and financial support in the form of soft loans bearing only 5 percent simple interest. These loans enabled the companies to improve and grow so that they could preserve their operations and employees.

IMPLEMENTING THE EARLY RETIREMENT SYSTEM (OPTIONAL)

The optional early retirement system has been implemented in SOEs suffering from excess labor. The system was designed in collaboration with the union committees, the Ministry of Manpower and the General Union for Egyptian workers. It was approved by the higher Ministerial Committee for privatization. The system allows workers to request early retirement optionally in return for a termination bonus of at least £E15,000, subject to a ceiling of £E35,000.

The following conditions should be met for the worker to be eligible:

(a) The request should be made by the worker;

(b) The worker's age must range from 50 to 58 for males, and from 45 to 58 for females; and

(c) The worker should have accumulated a minimum of 20 years in service, and subscribed to social insurance during this period, to be eligible for the monthly pension from the company after retirement.[2]

The system was applied in its first stage to unprofitable companies under liquidation or companies sold as assets or separate units—and to unprofitable companies under restructuring prior to the sale. By March 1998, this system had been applied to 60,000 workers. A few HCs rehabilitate younger workers through the Social Fund for Development by training them to meet the requirements of the labor market. Despite the appeal of this technique for dealing with the excess labor problem, it was applied in Egypt only on a very limited scale.

As regards the financing of the early retirement plan for excess labor, the country opted for a specific way of allocating the sales proceeds of shares and assets. Namely, the rule is that the HCs retain one-third of these proceeds, whereas two-thirds go to the Ministry of Finance. The share of the HC is used normally to finance the retirement compensations for those who have chosen early retirement, along with settlement of the debts of affiliated companies. The remainder two-thirds given to the Ministry of Finance are used to settle public debt.

The HCs have already used the one-third allocated to them in the payment of £E1.5 billion in compensation to 60,000 early retirees. So far, there is a good match between the resource inflows from privatization proceeds and the outflows in compensation for excess labor. The reason behind this is that the sale of profitable companies has occurred simultaneously with and parallel to the restructuring of companies with financial and labor difficulties, enabling their transformation into viable and profitable units ready for sale in successive stages. Hence, as long as there are profitable companies, not burdened with excess labor, that could be sold, the labor restructuring for unprofitable companies could be financed by what becomes available from privatization proceeds. But with the decline in the remaining profitable companies, and the start of preparations for the sale of unprofitable or modestly profitable companies—which suffer from excess labor to varying degrees—the issue of financing early retirement will become a pressing issue.

The HCs today have 80,000 requests for early retirement, equivalent to £E2 billion. The Ministry of Public Enterprise is considering different alternatives for financing these retirements and the ones expected in the future. These include:

• Raising a syndicated loan with banks in foreign or local currency using either unutilized land (real estate collateral) or shares held by the HCs as collateral.

- Selling a portion of the excess real estate bearing high values and hence utilizing the proceeds through a "Pool of Finance," out of which the other HCs could be loaned funds to settle dues related to early retirements.

- Issuance of "privatization bonds" with three to five years maturity to finance early retirement, amortizing the balance from the HCs' share in privatization proceeds.

Although privatization in Egypt can, based on the above account, be said to enjoy the support of labor, it is important to note that the problem of excess labor could be a problem in the future. In particular, two worrisome phenomena could possibly occur. First, a huge number of retiring workers, especially the younger ones, could stay jobless for an extended period of time. There is the fear that the compensations could be spent on consumption, with workers eventually returning to knock on the doors of the government and the public sector for jobs. Second, the process could transform important groups in society—most important among them labor—to oppose privatization. This might happen if the first phenomenon takes hold.

To deal with this eventuality, it is recommended that the government expand the retraining program and establish the necessary institutions to finance and facilitate development of small and medium industries development so that these can absorb the portion of the excess labor force that is under the age of 50. Also, it would be desirable to devise new incentives for early retirement of the younger workers, in addition to the system already in place, which awards cash compensation to whomever chooses to retire early.

Enterprise Valuation

Valuation is a key step in the process of preparing SOEs for sale. Its importance lies partly in the fact that the main after-sale criticism is related to valuation in most cases. And the problem is that valuation is a mix of both science and art, since it involves the application of various well-known techniques and principles, in combination with special skills and knowledge related to each case separately. To illustrate the artistic part of valuation, it is indeed possible to increase the sale value by selling a few unutilized or unprofitable assets separately prior to the sale of the company as an ongoing concern.

The first problem with valuation stems from the fact that available valuation techniques are likely to produce different results. To elaborate on this point, the following major techniques will be explained.

THE NET BOOK VALUE OF THE COMPANY

This technique reflects the historical worth of the company, and is represented by the book value of net equity (paid-up capital, reserves, retained earnings, and provisions that do not cover real risks). This value is also equal to the total value of assets after deducting liabilities and provisions against possible risks.

THE ADJUSTED BOOK VALUE METHOD

This technique is applied to obtain a figure that is closer to the market value of the company. It relies on applying the relevant inflation to each asset type, for the relevant period since the acquisition of the asset, in addition to accounting for the change in exchange rates of the country of origin of the asset.

THE REPLACEMENT VALUE

This is an asset-based valuation technique that yields a net asset value that should reflect the cost of acquiring or building a similar project or plant. There are three approaches for applying this technique:

- Replacement as is: The value of the asset is based on its current condition and remaining useful life. This approach is appropriate for privatization purposes.

- Replacement anew: The value of a similar asset in terms of the cost of acquiring it new. The asset's current condition is disregarded.

- Replacement with state-of-the-art technology: The value of, for example, a similar plant but with the current technology.

THE DISCOUNTED CASH FLOW (DCF) MODEL

This is one of those models that describe the value of the company as an ongoing concern that is based on its ability to generate future cash. The model takes into account the time value of money, and the various levels of risks associated with this activity.

PRICE-TO-EARNINGS MULTIPLIER

This method could be viewed as a benchmark against which investors compare various securities, using the reciprocal of the rate of return by measuring the price as a multiple of the earnings per share (EPS). It is taken into consideration in privatization prior to the sale, since it reflects the forecasted market reception for the share.

EVALUATING THE TECHNIQUES

These techniques are likely to yield values that are not far apart if the size of the company is optimal, and if it possesses technological, administrative, and marketing abilities that reflect its capacity to generate revenue and, hence, its profitability. In this case, all the company's assets are fully utilized, and the current and future revenue-generation ability is at its peak. As a result, the value according to the "Price-to-Earnings" multiplier will not differ much from the "Replacement Value" of assets or the value obtained using the "Discounted Cash Flow" method. Unfortunately, these conditions are rarely met, especially in the case of SOEs. Moreover, significant variations are always found in practice.

The following example illustrates the problem by presenting the valuation results of one of several cases encountered in Egypt. The example is that of "Kaha Co. for Preserved Food," which was sold in March 1998.

Market value of net assets (using market value of land)	£E	218.6 million.
Market value of net assets (using new cities prices for land)	£E	179.2 million.
Adjusted book value (using new cities prices for land)	£E	62.4 million.
Book value of the company	£E	37.8 million.
Valuation according to the DCF model:		
Discount rate 13 percent	£E	19.8 million.
Discount rate 12 percent	£E	22.6 million.
Discount rate 10 percent	£E	29.9 million.

The second problem in the valuation process is the cost attached to it, which averages £E200 thousand per company. This implies that the cost of valuation of all SOEs in Egypt could reach £E62 million. The cost could be higher if the company is not sold within the six months following the valuation, since new updates would become necessary after the end of that period.

A third problem relates to the nationality of the evaluators. In Egypt, national expertise was limited at the beginning of the privatization program. In addition, available expertise was appropriate for handling only a few types of companies. Relying on foreign expertise, along with local consultants, was by necessity. Moreover, it also followed for practical reasons—namely, foreign funds were made available to support the program. This situation made it only logical to use part of these funds to hire consultants from the donor countries—but it led some intellectuals to assume that those foreign experts were directed by their countries to set unfair values to enable their investors and foreign or local private sector to buy companies at below-market value.

Egyptian policymakers have followed two principles in dealing with these problems. First, individual officials are not allowed to take decisions on their own. Instead, decisions are taken by one of seven committees or institutions: the company's Board of Directors, the company's general assembly, the HC's Board of Directors, the HC's general assembly, the Quadripartite Committee, the Central Auditing Agency, and the Higher Ministerial Committee for privatization (chaired by the Prime Minister). Second, decisions are taken by consensus. These arrangements have enabled those in charge of privatization to avoid any embarrassment.

Egypt overcame the bottleneck of scarcity of funds to conclude the transactions by accepting grants from the World Bank ($600,000), USAID ($35 million), the European Economic Community (ECU) (43 million), and UNDP ($3 million). This approach reduced the financial drain on the GOE to such an extent that its contribution did not exceed $2.5 million since the beginning of the program.

The problem of assigning valuation to foreigners was addressed by forming a joint committee from the HC and the enterprise in question with the objective of conducting their own valuation. Moreover, several foreign consultants as well as local committees were asked to prepare valuations in cases in which the SOE was considered critical to the success of the program or was known to have special problems. These arrangements demonstrated to those keeping an eye on the program and to the public at large that the aim was, and is, to obtain a fair price. They also helped avoid overvaluation, which could have derailed the program.

The Quadripartite Committee, comprising representatives of the sellers (namely, the HC, the SOE, and the Ministry of Public Enterprise), together with representatives from the CMA, the Stock Market, and the Central Auditing Agency[3] review all valuations for each company, choosing the best offer based on the stock market's prevailing conditions. As such, the valuations by foreigners are only used as guidelines for decisionmaking to reach a justifiable decision not based on subjectivity.

Absorptive Capacity of the Stock Market

In the early stages of the privatization program, there was a remarkable success in public offerings. From May 1996 to the end of 1997, not one single offering failed. Oversubscription covered the companies' shares many times over. Hence the problem before the PEO and the HCs was to prepare more companies for further offerings. The pace of privatization was constrained by supply, given that demand seemed almost guaranteed.

Naturally the stock exchange was not the only vehicle used in privatization. The sale technique for each privatization transaction was determined on the basis of the profitability and size of the firm, and the need for better technology and equipment, and managerial and marketing know-how. But the main reason the program gained momentum and developed a good reputation was because it relied mainly on the sale through the stock market. This point is illustrated by the following schedule, which shows the privatization transactions completed during the period from May 1996 to December 1997:

Number of companies sold (minority or majority) through stock market:	42
Number of companies sold to employees' associations:	5
Number of companies sold as assets:	20
Number of companies sold to a strategic investor:	5
Total number of companies:	72

The momentum of the privatization program encouraged local and foreign investors, individuals and institutions, to invest in portfolios. The increase in demand led to an inflow of portfolio investment (buying the privatization shares in the stock market), which facilitated the sale of any company without substantial promotion. The share prices of privatized companies appreciated owing to the increase in demand and to the relative scarcity of the supply of shares on a wider scale other than those of Law 203 companies. Consequently, the price-to-earnings multiplier of these shares went up (table 6.5), which boosted the price-to-earnings ratio of the initial valuation of new offerings.

TABLE 6.5 PRICE-TO-EARNINGS RATIO IN JUNE–JULY 1996 VERSUS JUNE–JULY 1997

Company	Date offered	P/E	Company	Date offered	P/E
Starch and Glucose	6/96	8.3	Simo for Paper	6/97	10.6
Kafr Zayat Pesticides	7/96	6.9	Alex Flour Mills	7/97	9.3
Nile Matches	7/96	7.9	Al Saiid Contract	7/97	11
Misr Oil and Soap	7/96	8	Giza Contract	7/97	9.8
Average		7.775	Average		10.175

Source: PEO.

The attraction of the Egyptian stock market to investors began to fade away, and prices started appearing too high, yielding only modest gains. The situation went from being favorable to selling on the stock market to the point at which it appeared that the government would not be able to meet its plans. Several factors influenced the stock market (supply, demand, and prices) in the last quarter of 1997.

The fall in prices of shares coincided with two major events. The first is the beginning of the economic crisis in East Asia, starting in Thailand in July 1997 and spreading later to Indonesia, Korea, and then to Japan's stock market, among others during the second half of 1997—its impact is still being felt. The second was the terrorist attack on tourists, which took place in Luxor in November 1997. Both events had their negative effects on investment and capital inflows to Egypt. The net demand from foreigners on Egyptian shares declined. Table 6.6 shows the trend of foreign net demand during the last 16 months in the stock market (March–October 1997 versus November 1997–June 1998).

TABLE 6.6 NET DEMAND BY FOREIGNERS

March 1997–October 1997		November 1997–June 1998	
Month	Net demand	Month	Net demand
March	148	Nov. 1997	−8
April	−2	Dec. 1997	45
May	39	Jan. 1998	−19
June	512	Feb. 1998	−110
July	131	March 1998	−80
August	162	April 1998	−16
September	271	May 1998	11
October	444	June 1998	15
Total (cumulative)	1705	Total (cumulative)	−162

Source: PEO.

In addition, a new type of supply of shares appeared on the stock market, with the offering of the Mobile Phone Co. in March 1998, and that of joint ventures and private sector family-based companies. These offerings absorbed part of the liquidity available in the market, and affected negatively the demand for privatization shares. For the first time, the problem of undersubscribed companies was seen in September 1997, recurring in March, April, May, and June 1998. The inability of the stock market to absorb new offerings became a critical constraint on privatization. It thus became clear that new policies and measures were needed to restore pace to the privatization process and meet the government's commitments.

The first measure introduced starting December 1997 was the more extensive use of sale techniques other than IPOs. Although the sale of SOEs to Employee Shareholders Associations (ESAs) is only adopted when appropriate, the first quarter of 1998 saw the sale of five inland transport companies using this approach. The process was also initiated to sell three more companies to ESAs in the second quarter (Maritime Works Co., or Martrans, General Marine Supplies, and Sharkeya Rice Mills). Finalization of these sales is under way.

Another measure was in the form of extending the application of the assets sales technique for troubled companies in the form of separate assets or units. The last quarter of 1997 through the first half of 1998 witnessed the sale of seven companies adopting this technique. Emphasis was made on selling to strategic investors through the stock market or direct negotiations.[4] Currently, preparation of another batch of companies for sale during the second half of 1998 through 1999 is being finalized.

The approach of promoting candidate companies was also revised, and the decision was made to rely on professional promoters by involving underwriters. This entailed modifying the valuation mechanism. In response to the prevailing price levels in the stock market, the price-to-earnings ratio for new offerings was lowered. This was applied to the case of Misr Food Co. (Bisco Misr). It was decided that a price-to-earnings ratio of 7.2 times would be used in pricing the shares, based on the Price Discovery Mechanism, allowing for 10 percent fluctuation in the price instead of the 5 percent range used previously.

Collectively, the above measures made it possible to overcome the obstacles and bottlenecks stemming from the weak absorptive capacity of the stock market. They are expected to enable the government to meet its plan of privatizing 10 companies each quarter.

Selling Companies with Heavy Losses to Strategic Investors

According to the financial statements of SOEs for fiscal 1996–97, 82 companies posted losses. Sixty of these SOEs can be helped, given the imbalances they suffer in their financial structure and labor force. Modest investment in them would rapidly make them profitable and ready for sale at a higher price. The problem lies in the remaining 20 SOEs, which are in serious trouble. These SOEs have losses from operations before deducting interest expense or taxes. While they need financial and labor restructuring, their real problems stem from the need for sizable invest-ment to renew their equipment and machinery. They also need organizational and managerial restructuring, in addition to enhancement of marketing capacity, and training for technicians and workers.

It is possible of course to continue for a while to sell the profitable SOE units, but this strategy would deteriorate the performance of the sector. This situation will impose a burden on society in the form of borrowing from banks to cover the losses, thereby crowding out the private sector. At the same time, keeping these companies in the hands of the state means that the leakage of funds will continue to finance the losses. What is the solution in such cases?

In my opinion, it is undesirable economically or socially to liquidate many of these companies, especially if there is a way to privatize them and to make them profitable and growing entities. To this end, I would propose the following:[5]

- The sale of 51–61 percent of those SOEs to local private industrial groups for no immediate price, with the state retaining 39–49 percent stake of their equity. The company would be offered in a public tender, seeking bids after a period for due diligence. The bids would have to include the bidder's business plan, within the range of the allowable percentage of ownership of 51–61 percent. The ranking of proposals should be based on the volume of new investment, the adequacy of the plan for improving the business, and finally, the percentage of ownership claimed (between 51 and 61 percent).

- The winning local investors would then be allowed to sell a stake of up to 49 percent of their share in the company to foreign partners, with the aim of bringing in technical know-how and new technology. The proceeds from the sale of a stake to foreigners would have to be turned over back into the company.

- Finally, as the economy grows and the company improves its performance, the state can sell its shares in the stock market to the public or to investors for a higher value.[6]

To bring this proposal into effect, it would have to pass through a chain of approvals, starting with the Ministerial Committee for Privatization, the Cabinet, and the President. After that, the proposal would have to be submitted to the People's Assembly as legislation.

Concluding Remarks

The success of privatization is measured by the degree to which its objectives are achieved. These objectives are certainly not confined to the sale of a few units, although the number of companies sold is one of the measures. Rather, the goal is to reduce the state monopoly, encourage competition, and put the market mechanisms in place, with the ultimate objective of increasing the efficiency of SOEs in private hands. Against this yardstick, a survey has been undertaken of 28 privatized companies, operating in 10 sectors (the most important of which are textiles, cotton, flour mills, cement, chemicals, electrical devices, contracting, and food industries). This survey reveals the following:

- Sales increased in 20 companies, or in 71 percent of the sample.

- Earnings before interest and taxes (EBIT) increased in 19 companies, or in 68 percent of the sample.

- Average salary per worker increased in 27 companies, or in 96 percent of the sample.

- The balance of loans to banks, including short- and long-term, declined in 23 cases, or in 82 percent of the sample.

These indicators and the actual sale of some 111 SOEs suggest that Egyptian policymakers were able to successfully meet the challenges of implementing privatization and generate the necessary public support for the program. However, privatization involves a radical change in the role of government, which provokes political, ideological, economic and social concerns. Although these concerns have been addressed well in the past, public opinion could still deteriorate if drawbacks appear in the implementation of the program and become the basis of criticism by intellectuals and writers.

In part, criticism could mount for failing to abide by the main objectives of the program in implementation. The main objective is to enable the enterprises to operate under market conditions, striving under competition to enhance profitability. This requires adherence to the transfer of ownership to private hands, abolishing any influence from the HCs that retain a minority share in a sold company, and giving preference to investors who present good business plans even if they do not offer the highest price in their bid.

Criticism could also intensify if labor problems are not resolved preserving the workers' rights and eliminating their fears. Excess labor must be addressed prior to the sale, and should not be left to the private sector. Any early retirement of workers under private sector will be misinterpreted and could provide a basis for criticism and attack. Also, the concerned organizations should undertake the retraining and small-enterprises financing needed for the youth who retire from unprofitable companies, since early retirement schemes are not enough, and would be best for the older workers. At the early stages, the number of early retired workers is relatively modest, but this number could soar when unprofitable companies suffering from excess labor start being sold. A substantial number of those would be from the younger generations.

Another reason for possible criticism may be the sale of profitable companies, while delaying and hesitating in selling unprofitable companies. This could occur because unprofitable companies typically suffer more from excess debt and excess labor. Their valuation is also more problematic.

Furthermore, criticism could arise from the government's not abiding by the principle of transparency and adequate disclosures in all stages of privatization. Experience shows that public opinion, capital market institutions and investors stress the need for transparency. The public has to know the facts related to sold companies, as well as the uses of the proceeds from privatization transactions.

Lack of understanding, expediency, and cordiality on the part of the government agencies involved in the process could also affect the credibility of the program. In the past, some investors gained expertise and experience in dealing with the government agencies involved in the process. But others accumulated negative experiences in their interaction with some authorities, especially with respect to the slow response and overvaluation in a few unsuccessful transactions. This negative experience could lead those investors to be reluctant to bid for offered companies in the future, thus slowing down the pace of the program.

Notes

1. The Higher Constitutional Court ussued the following justification to its verdict:
   The abuse of the articles of the Constitution to subjugate it to a certain philosophy contradicts its adaptability to serve new horizons sought by the public. The Constitution must not be viewed as presenting final and everlasting solutions to the economic conditions that were surpassed by contemporary evolution. Rather, it should be understood in light of higher values aiming at liberating the national and the citizens politically and economically. The Constitution is a progressive document, its texture being in harmony with the spirit of this era. The Constitution, in spite of guaranteeing through article 59 the so-called "socialist privileges" (its support and preservation perceived as a patriotic obligation), presented no definitions for socialism.

2. Nonviable companies that must be liquidated could apply the system to workers who do not meet the above conditions, jointly with the union committees, especially for those who fall below the required age and who are not entitled to a monthly pension.

3. The Central Auditing Agency plays an important role in reviewing the valuation studies and their methodology. The agency has the option of rejecting the study altogether or providing comments that have to be addressed.

4. The transactions that were concluded between December 1997 and the end of June 1998 covered the following companies: Alexandria Spinning and Weaving, Delta Industrial-IDEAL, Kaha Preserved Food, Al Nasr Civil Works, San Stefano Hotel, Al Wady Agricultural Exports, Gianaklis Beverages, and Distillation Factory. As of June 1998, a number of transactions were under way. These are: Nile Hotel, Nobaseed for Seeds Production, Steelco, Metalco, Al Nasr Glass & Crystal, Beni Sweif Cement, and Abou Zaabal Fertilizers.

5. This is the author's personal view on how to deal with firms that are heavily losing money.

6. Under this scheme, the same to foreigners is kept at a ceiling of 37.24–39.64 percent of the shares as follows:
    a maximum of 49 percent of the 51–61 percent initially held by local investors;
    plus a maximum of 25 percent of the 49 percent initially retained by the state;
    equals a total maximum of 37.24–39.64 percent.

CHAPTER 7

Constraints of Privatization in Turkey

Özer Ertuna

Over the last two decades, privatization has attracted the attention of policymakers in developed and developing economies as a means to improving the efficiency of public sector companies. The privatization wave started as early as 1974 in Chile under the military government of General Augusto Pinochet, but received its popularity under Margaret Thatcher's administration in Britain. The subsequent failure of the socialist economies gave privatization an added momentum as a means to create private ownership and free market structures.

Turkey started its privatization programs as early as 1986. However, progress has been limited until recently. The purpose of this paper is to assess past attempts at privatization in Turkey, analyze the constraints on the process, and make recommendations accordingly.

While it is accepted that privatization must be used to achieve the specific objectives of the country in which it is implemented, these objectives should include an improvement in efficiency, in management techniques, and of the competitive position of the companies

Improving the competitive position of the companies may deserve an explanation. In global markets, "critical success factors" have changed significantly. For many industries and companies, technology, image, and quality have become as important as lower costs. In this regard, privatization can be seen as an opportunity to acquire such "critical success factors," especially if it entails forging new strategic alliances with domestic or foreign firms that possess these factors.

The rest of the chapter is organized as follows. The next section assesses progress on privatization to date. This is followed by a section analyzing the constraints on privatization, and finally, a conclusion.

Progress to Date

The creation of State Economic Enterprises (SEEs) in Turkey dates back to the formation of the Republic in 1924. At that time, the country hardly had any industry or entrepreneurial skills. Incomes were below subsistence levels, thus savings were also low. The population was 12.6 million and per capita income was only $45, in contrast to a population today of about 63.7 million and per capita income of more than $3,000. Facing these limitations, SEEs were created to boost economic development. In that sense, establishing SEEs was not a choice but a necessity.

The "etatist" policies pursued since the formation of the Republic persisted to varying degrees until 1980. Attempts to reinstitute liberal economic policies and private initiative in the 1950s did not succeed despite changes in the government's polity. Instead, the public sector grew even more. In the period 1960–80, the Turkish economy became a "mixed economy," but the shift came in 1980, when Turkey began to follow liberal economic policies and a competitive free market economy in pursuit of greater integration with the rest of the world. Privatization was considered an important part of this process.

State Economic Enterprises in Turkey

Evidence of the slow progress on privatization can be seen from the relatively stable contribution of SEEs to GNP, which stayed constant around 11 percent between 1985 and 1991 (table 7.1) (TOBB 1993). During this period, SEEs dominated the mining sector and maintained significant presence in all other sectors of the economy, save agriculture. Their contribution to the public sector borrowing requirement (PSBR) was also substantial, with Turkish Electricity Administration (TEK) and Turkish Postal and Telecom Administration (PTT) being the most notable. SEEs' borrowing requirements amounted to 3.1 percent of GNP in 1985 and increased to 5.2 percent in 1991. Since high PSBR is believed to be the main cause of inflation in Turkey, reducing PSBR became one of the objectives of privatization.

TABLE 7.1 SEEs' CONTRIBUTION TO GNP
(percentage)

Sector	1985	1991
Agriculture	0.3	0.5
Mining	74.5	72.7
Industrial production	16.5	16.9
Energy	46.5	34.5
Transport. and communications	27.0	33.9
Commerce and others	1.9	2.5
Total contribution	11.5	11.6

Source: TOBB p. 92 (1993).

An additional motivation for privatization was that SEEs performed less well than private sector companies. A study of the 500 biggest firms in Turkey over 1983–93 indicated that SEEs' operating productivity was on average 21 percent lower than the productivity of private companies (table 7.2 and figure 7.1). This finding applies both to capital and labor productivity, more so to the latter. The financial position of SEEs was also weak and deteriorating, as they had to borrow at high interest rates to finance their losses and long-term investment.

TABLE 7.2 RELATIVE FACTOR PRODUCTIVITY
(Private Sector = 100)

Year	Capital	Labor
1983	59.1	53.4
1984	76.3	78.0
1985	65.7	64.1
1986	61.2	55.9
1987	62.9	58.1
1988	96.0	90.7
1989	94.3	69.9
1990	62.2	49.5
1991	62.5	48.6
1992	73.0	50.9
1993	54.2	36.4

Source: Ertuna (1994).

FIGURE 7.1 RELATIVE FACTOR PRODUCTIVITY
(Private Sector = 100)

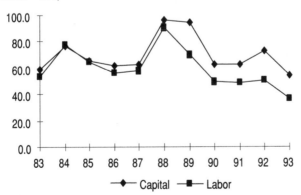

Source: Ertuna (1994).

Privatization

Privatization was initiated in 1984, but it only intensified in the last couple of years. The total proceeds from selling SEEs over a period of over 12 years were $4.5 billion (table 7.3). The government used a wide spectrum of privatization methods, including direct sale to strategic investors, IPOs, transfer of ownership to employees, giveaway, and allowing private sector entry into monopoly markets (T. C. Başbakanlık Özelleştirme İdaresi Başkanlığı 1998). The government transferred 153 establishments to the Privatization Administration between 1986 and 1998, of which the shares or assets of 129 were sold (with 111 of them in full). As a result, SEEs no longer operate in the cement, animal food, milk, meat, and fish sectors.

While the privatization process has gained momentum in recent years, the overall record of privatization in Turkey up until now compares less favorably with the programs in such comparable countries as Argentina, Mexico, and Chile. Progress also remains modest relative to the size of the SEE sector in Turkey and the SEEs' domination of key sectors of the economy.

TABLE 7.3 PRIVATIZATION REVENUES IN TURKEY, 1986–98

Method of privatization	US$ million	Percentage
Block sales	2,002.1	44.9
Property and asset sales	531.7	11.9
Public offer	672.1	15.1
Sales to international investors	719.0	16.1
Sales at Istanbul Stock Exchange	526.6	11.8
Sale of incomplete plants	4.1	0.1
Total	4,455.7	100.0

Source: T.C. Basbakanlik Özellestirme Idaresi Baskanligi (1998).

The government plan for 1998 is ambitious, targeting the generating of $12.2 billion in revenue. Implementation of this plan could not be fully documented at the time of writing this paper. But the Privatization Administration was to sell enterprises worth $4.6 billion, with two transactions accounting for half of this target. The first involves the sale of 12.3 percent of the shares of İş Bank.[2] The second involves the sale of 51 percent of the state-owned petroleum company (POAŞ) to a strategic buyer or consortium for $1.2 billion.[3] The government was also to sell 34 percent of Turkish Telecom for an estimated price of $3 billion.[4] Finally, the Ministry of Energy was to privatize 8 energy-producing plants and 20 distribution establishments for an estimated revenue of $3.6 billion.

Whether the plan is fully implemented or not, some insights can be gained from reviewing the main features of past privatization. Some of these features are elaborated on below.

BLOCK SALES AND COMPETITION
More than half of the privatization revenues came from sales to strategic investors, especially in the cement industry. The cement industry in Turkey is fast-growing and profitable. The industry is composed of private, public, and mixed companies, but each company is able to exercise some monopoly power in its geographical location because of transportation costs. This power could be diminished to some degree if privatization is handled with care. But that does not seem to have happened in Turkey (Tallant 1993). The initial sale of five cement companies was made to SCF (Société Ciment Française), and another eight were sold to a single Turkish holding group. But this conclusion is not universal. One study shows that privatization has improved competition in the cement market in some regions, while leaving the semi-monopolistic conditions preserved in other less developed regions, where transportation is not well-developed (Dernek 1994).

CONTRIBUTION TO THE DEVELOPMENT OF CAPITAL MARKETS
Privatization efforts in Turkey contributed to the broadening of ownership and the development of the Istanbul Stock Exchange and the capital markets. These objectives ranked high on the list of objectives set for privatization in Turkey in 1986.

The first major privatization through a public offering was in 1988. In this transaction, 42,000 small investors bought shares in TELETAŞ, a company that produced telephones and telecommunication switches. The offer was oversubscribed. Having sold 22 percent of the shares to the public, the government sold its remaining shares in the company (18 percent) to Alcatel in 1993. Now, Alcatel owns and controls the company.

Major public offerings (about 18 of them) took place between 1990 and 1991. Most of these offerings represented the sale of government minority interests in some well-known private companies, such as ARÇELIK, TOFAŞ (a car manufacturer with Fiat's participation), and MIGROS (the biggest supermarket chain in Turkey). They also included some giant SEEs, although the percentage of shares offered was very small. For example, the government sold only 8.08 percent of the shares of PETKIM (in 1990), 1.66 percent of the shares of TÜPRAŞ (1991), both petrochemical complexes, and 1.55 percent of Turkish Airlines (1990). All stocks were registered in the Istanbul Stock Exchange and are actively traded. The total revenues obtained from privatization through IPOs were $433 million, roughly 10 percent of market capitalization. The total number of people who purchased stock in these public offerings amounted to 292,000.

TRANSFER OF OWNERSHIP TO EMPLOYEES
A chain of stores belonging to Sümer Holding Company (SHC) was privatized at the end of 1993 by transferring ownership to the employees of these stores. Out of 433 retail outlets of SHC, 291 were successfully privatized. These outlets had been posting losses for more than five consecutive years prior to

privatization. They were located mostly in small towns all around Turkey, selling textiles, ready-to-wear clothing, and leather products mostly produced by SHC. One of the objectives of privatization was to create new entrepreneurs in these communities. Through this scheme 330 employees of these outlets became successful entrepreneurs.

A survey was conducted among the new owners, shortly after privatization. The respondents believe that privatization has been beneficial to most of the parties involved and Turkey as a whole (Ertuna 1993). About 76 percent of them expected to gain, 50 percent indicated that the government would also gain, and 36 percent thought that SHC would gain. It is interesting to note that 35 percent of the respondents indicated that customers would benefit as well. They admitted that they were not treating their customers properly. Another survey was conducted a year later. It showed that most of the outlets made a profit, expanded their business and were making plans for further growth. Some were considering establishing chain stores; others were planning to enter new production lines (Geneer 1995).

In November 1995, 88 outlets were privatized by transferring their ownership to 292 former employees. In 1996, 11 more of the outlets were privatized. Now SHC runs a small number of outlets, which require a different kind of privatization method, since they are big department stores, located in big cities. The privatization of SHC retail outlets has been planned and executed by the management of the company from start to finish. This experiment suggests that, if they are properly guided and authorized, the managers of SEEs can successfully design creative privatization schemes and implement them.

PLANT GIVEAWAY

In 1994 Turkey privatized one of its steel plants by giving it away. Karabük Steel Plant was established in 1937. It is an integrated steel plant using domestic ore and coal in its production with a capacity of 600,000 tons per year. The plant was carrying heavy losses because of redundant labor, extremely high interest burden, delayed renovations, and unfavorable market conditions. In 1994 Turkey faced an economic crisis, which led the government, in its austerity measures of April 5, to decide to privatize or liquidate the company. By the end of 1994, the plant was privatized by transferring the ownership free of charge to its employees, members of the local chamber of industry and commerce and artisans associations, and citizens in the community. The government also assumed the debts of the plant, paid severance indemnities to employees, and provided working capital and funds needed to complete the current renovation program. The total cost of the transaction to the government was $358 million.

This experiment is considered successful. In 1994, the company lost $231 million; in 1995, it was able to break-even; in 1996, it made a profit of $26 million, and in 1997, $44 million. The total number of employees declined from 5,890 in 1994 to 5,125 at the end of 1997. But the reduction represents only 13 percent of the total, and fell mostly on white-collar employees.

ALLOWING PRIVATE ENTRY

Beyond the sale of enterprises, significant steps have been taken to allow private sector entry into markets dominated by government monopolies. The airlines industry is a good example; a number of successful private airline companies now operate in Turkey. Another example is the market for cigarette production, which now includes a Turkish–American joint venture company. Recently, the government has been considering the breaking up of "raki" production, a well-known Turkish drink.

Constraints to Privatization

It is difficult to claim that the reason for the Turkish privatization program advancing slowly until recently was lack of political will. Over this period, almost all successive governments seemed determined to accelerate privatization. Each government made promises to speed up the process. They set highly optimistic revenue objectives every year during the budget discussions. But, accomplishments were never even close to these targets.

The record is even more puzzling because Turkey seems to have approached privatization in a rational manner as early as 1984. The government commissioned Morgan Guaranty Bank, Industrial Development Bank of Turkey, Industrial Investment and Credit Bank, Muhas Audit Company, and the Investment and Finance Corporation to prepare a "Master Plan." Morgan, in a short period of time, prepared the study, which specified the privatization objectives and strategy, classified SEEs into three categories in order of priority for privatization, and spelled the course of action necessary in each case. Unfortunately, Turkey could not benefit fully from this plan.

The following sections attempt to explain why. Although the explanations are presented separately, they are interdependent in nature.

Political and Legal Constraints

The Master Plan studied the Turkish legal system to determine if any changes were necessary. It concluded that the Turkish constitution and relevant laws did not outlaw privatization. However, it pointed out that privatization could be complicated by two constitutional provisions. The first relates to the requirement that SEEs be audited by the High Audit Council ("Yüksek Denetleme Kurulu"). The second related to the requirement that SEEs be run by government civil servants.

Unfortunately, the government did not think that it had the time to make the necessary changes in the relevant laws to facilitate privatization. It attempted to carry out privatization without making the necessary changes in constitution and related laws. This strengthened the position of those who were against privatization in principle. Many of the transactions were challenged at the Constitutional Court, leading to the reversal of decisions.

To be sure, the government made some legal changes. But these changes did not address the concerns stated above. In 1984, a law was passed authorizing the government to securitize the revenues of hydroelectric dams and toll bridges by issuing "revenue sharing certificates." And Mass Housing and the Public Participation Administration (PPA) were established to implement the privatization decisions made by the Public Participation High Council. This law was modified in June 1986 to empower the Council of Ministers with the decision to privatize SEEs. The law allowed free-of-charge transfer of ownership of SEEs to the PPA. Although the law provided for the corporate status of SEEs transferred to PPA, it did not provide sufficient legal details to implement privatization and resolve problems related to labor, managerial and financial restructuring.

In 1992, the government recognized that it needed a comprehensive legal basis to accelerate privatization. However, instead of passing a comprehensive detailed law for privatization, a much simpler law was passed by Parliament in 1994 empowering the council of ministers to pass the necessary decrees to speed up the process. Various decrees were issued thereafter, but once again, the law empowering the government to pass these decrees was challenged in the Constitutional Court. Both the law and the decrees passed accordingly were overturned by the Constitutional Court.

In November 24, 1994, the current privatization law was enacted. The law was welcome as if it would solve all privatization problems. Expectations were elevated with intensive propaganda. SEEs were declared to be the cause of all ills in Turkey, including inflation. It was claimed that this law was to solve all the problems Turkey had. The law did not, in principle, bring anything new. The PPA was renamed Privatization Administration. The authority to make privatization decisions, including decisions to determine the companies to be privatized, means and methods of privatization and finalizing the sale, was granted to High Council of Privatization. The High Council of Privatization was to be composed of Prime Minister, a State Minister, Minister in charge of Privatization, Minister of Finance and Minister of Industry and Commerce.

Another legal constraint on privatization relates to the protection of public interest from anticompetitive behavior or monopolistic exploitation in natural monopoly markets. This protection requires regulatory rules and regulatory agencies for privatization to be beneficial to society (Kikeri, Nellis, and Shirley 1992). In Turkey, a Competition Board ("Rekabet Kurulu") was established only recently. And, although Turkey is making plans to privatize its telecommunications services, it has not designed a system, such as OFTEL of England, to protect the interests of the public.

The lack of sufficient attention to the legal framework of privatization has been the most important reason for the limited success of privatization in Turkey. The lesson to be learned is that it is better to take the time needed to formulate the legal framework before privatization than after.

Labor Constraints
Good and reliable estimates of labor redundancy in SEEs are lacking, but the problem is not uniform across companies. In some cases, redundancy is about 10 per-

cent, while reaching as much as 300 percent in others. Turkish Coal Enterprises (TKİ, located in Zonguldak) is a good example of the second variety. It employed about 32,000 in 1994, while available estimates indicate that the company only needed 12,500 employees to be profitable. This case led many to argue that the government would be better off paying labor full wages, letting them stay at home and closing the company.

The number of SEE employees in Turkey is not very high, which suggests that labor should not be a problem for privatization. In 1985, SEEs employed 635,000, or about 4.1 percent of the total labor force. This figure remained fairly constant through 1991, but privatization and early retirement plans brought it down to 463,000 in 1997 (SPO 1998). But this assertion may not hold because SEEs employees are often well-organized and can mount serious opposition to privatization.

An added problem in the case of Turkey is that labor redundancy is extremely high in the relatively underdeveloped regions of the country. In spite of the fact that Turkey has accomplished much in its economic development and in integrating its economy with the rest of the world, the country has not been as successful in distributing the benefits of development to all regions. Many SEEs operate in such regions, providing jobs and income for the local community.

The current privatization law, which was enacted in 1994, provided solutions to the labor redundancy problem. These solutions can be summarized as follows:

- If an employee loses his or her job during or after privatization, he or she will be entitled to a supplementary unemployment indemnity in addition to the severance pay and termination indemnity will be paid in accordance with the current laws.

- Personnel of SEEs under the privatization program who are subject to a Government Pension plan may receive their retirement benefits with a 30 percent premium if they apply to retire within two months following their acquisition of the right to retire.

- Civil servants or personnel working under special contracts with SEEs who lose their positions owing to privatization will be transferred to other public institutions in which positions are available.

Constraints in Implementation
The slow takeoff of privatization created some problems of its own. Overselling the program along with failure to deliver eroded public support. The change of the privatization objective over time had a similar effect. Finally, the long time following the transfer of SEEs to the Privatization Administration without actual privatization deteriorated morale, the financial position, and the technology of enterprises slated for privatization. These issues are elaborated on below.

CHANGING OBJECTIVES AND UNDUE EMPHASIS ON CASH GAINS

The Privatization Master Plan compiled a list of privatization objectives on the basis of the opinions of ministers, undersecretaries, directors in the public sector, gathered through a questionnaire. The list included 14 objectives, listed according to their importance. These objectives included improving the functioning of markets, improving efficiency, contributing to the development of capital markets, broadening ownership, and reducing the burden of SEEs on the Treasury. Other efficiency objectives included attracting modern technology and management techniques. The list even included strengthening the economic and political alliances internationally. The least emphasized objective was generating revenue for the government (Kilci 1994).

Unfortunately, as time passed, the objective of revenue generation became the main objective of privatization in Turkey. The main reason for this was the desire to reduce public sector borrowing requirements (PSBRs) in order to control inflation. While justified in part, this shift led to overemphasis on cash generation and less emphasis on increasing competition, improving management, and gaining strategic advantages.

OVERPROMOTING THE RESULTS OF PRIVATIZATION

The government conducted successful public campaigns to improve the climate for privatization. The problem is that this effort was overdone and may have created a backlash.

Starting in 1986, SEEs were blamed in Turkey as the "cause of all ills." They were declared "a burden on the economy," "bleeding wounds of the economy," and "misery for all." This propaganda was so successful that common people on the street expected wonders from privatization. When privatization did not produce miracles, the public was disillusioned. A small minority of opponents to privatization on ideological grounds had an opportunity to make the counter case. They were able to point out that PSBR had not gone down; and inflation was still high.

DETERIORATION IN FINANCIAL POSITION, MORALE, AND TECHNOLOGY OF THE SEES

Since the privatization took much longer than expected, the financial position, morale, and technology of SEEs deteriorated fast. In some cases deterioration was so significant that some of the privatization options were eliminated altogether.

The Master Plan made some recommendations of crucial importance, which were not adopted. It was recommended that (a) privatization should not impair the investment plans of SEEs, and (b) since privatization was likely to take quite a long time, public sector reforms needed to continue at an accelerated pace. Unfortunately, the investment plans of the SEEs that were transferred to the Privatization Agency were cancelled. These investments included investment in growth, technology, and human resources. Canceling the investment plans would have been understandable if privatization had been implemented quickly. Since the pace was slow, the plant, technology, and human capital of SEEs deteriorated fast, however, reducing their marketability.

Conclusions

Although Turkey started its privatization program more than 12 years ago, it has accomplished much less than its potential. Perhaps the major lesson to draw from this experience is that privatization is more complicated than a simple "sale" of government assets. The objectives of privatization have to be articulated clearly and adhered to. These objectives, while possibly varying from one country to another, should focus on improving competition and management techniques, and on helping enterprises gain strategic advantages.

Privatization could benefit from early "success stories." Success should mean that all the parties involved and the country at large gain from privatization. Success stories can then be explained to the public at large, without overpromising. Successful propaganda campaigns are not substitutes for real success.

At the beginning of the privatization effort, time and care is needed to make the necessary changes in the legal environment. If the legal environment is not suitable for successful privatization, implementation cannot proceed just by using better privatization techniques. Improving the legal structure can also help by getting parliament involved in the process and building consensus.

Given that SEEs are often overstaffed, programs must be devised for job creation, especially in the less-developed regions of the countries where alternative job opportunities are not available. Unemployment benefits and similar financial compensation schemes may not be sufficient to make up for lost jobs.

A realistic timetable for privatization is needed. At the same time, it is important to engage the management of SEEs in the process and carry it out fast. Otherwise, the financial position, morale, and technology of enterprises will deteriorate fast. In cases in which privatization is expected to take time, public investment complementary to private investment should not be delayed. Management of SEEs must improve their performance independent of the privatization timetable. This requires a "public sector reform" program to be conducted in tandem with privatization.

Notes

1. The study defines the value added as a function of labor and total assets (capital). A total of 101 private companies and 12 SEEs are included in the study. Therefore the number of observations amounts to 1,243. All the parameters of the equations were significant at a 95 percent level (Ertuna 1994).

2. The shares have already been offered to the public (38.85 percent domestically and 60.15 percent in international markets); 80,798 buyers were involved and $596 million in revenue has been raised.

3. In July offers from strategic buyers were received. Through continuous bidding a strategic buyer was selected. The Privatization Administration had not received the opinion of the Competition Board of Turkey yet. Now the privatization is awaiting the opinion of the Board.

4. The sale of two GSM licenses to private companies was already concluded in 1998, resulting in $1 billion in revenue.

References

The word *processed* describes informally reproduced works that may not be commonly available through libraries.

Dernek, Ismail. 1994. "Performance Analysis of the Privatized Cement Companies in Turkey." MBA Thesis. Bogaziçi University, Istanbul, Turkey.

Ertuna, Özer. 1993. "An Experience in Privatization, Transfer of the Retail Outlets of Sümer Holding Company to its Employees." *Bogaziçi Journal, Review of Social, Economic and Administrative Studies* 7(1–2):105–23.

Ertuna, Özer. 1994. Working Paper. Bogaziçi University, Istanbul, Turkey. Processed.

Gencer, Gaye. 1995. "A Case in Privatization." Master Thesis. Bogaziçi University, Istanbul, Turkey.

Kikeri, Sunita, John Nellis, and Mary Shirley. 1992. *Privatization: The Lessons of Experience*. Washington, D.C.: World Bank.

Kilci, Metin. 1994. *Bugune Yurkie' de Ozellestirme (1984–94), Devlet Planlama, Temmuz*. (A publication of the State Planning Organization of Turkey.)

State Planning Organization (SPO). 1998. *Main Economic Indicators*. March.

T.C. Basbakanlik Özellestirme Idaresi Baskanligi. 1998. *Türkiye'de Özellestirme*. July 6.

Tallant, Drury. 1993. "Relative Efficiency of Public Sector Ownership and the Privatization of the Turkish Cement Industry." *Bogaziçi Journal, Review of Social, Economic and Administrative Studies* 7(1–2):102.

TOBB (Türkiye Odalar ve Borsalar) (Union of Chambers and Exchanges of Turkey). 1993. "Özellestirme Özel Ihtisas Komisyonu Raporu." Ankara. August.

PART III

The Role of Government and the Private Sector in Infrastructure

CHAPTER 8

Welfare Impact of Telecom Reform in Egypt: An Ex Ante Analysis

Ahmed Galal

There is a general consensus that the provision of efficient and universal telecommunication services is critical for growing economies (Wellenius and Stern 1994; World Bank 1994). Yet there is no consensus among policymakers about how to achieve this objective. Since the mid-1980s, only a handful of developing countries (for example, Chile, Mexico, Argentina, and Venezuela) have chosen to rely fully on private ownership, competition, and incentive regulation of the monopolistic segment of their telecom markets. Despite the evidence showing the positive effects of these liberal policies, the majority of developing countries still prefer state ownership and exclusive monopoly, combined with overlapping ownership and regulatory functions.

The preference for state ownership and its associated policies can be traced to a number of factors. One of these factors is insufficient knowledge about the future impact of reform on different economic actors, especially with respect to workers and consumers. Another factor is the fear among producers that their assets could be expropriated through underpricing of output, taxation of profit, or outright nationalization. This fear is particularly prevalent in countries in which government has a history of failing to develop, commit to, and enforce appropriate regulatory regimes (Levy and Spiller 1993). Finally, the lack of experience regulating private monopolies and the reliance on bureaucratic solutions may be an additional factor reinforcing this preference for state ownership.

This chapter explores whether developing countries benefit most by adhering to state ownership of telecommunications, exclusive monopoly and bureaucratic solutions to regulatory problems, or by moving to a new regime of competition, incentive regulation and private ownership.[1] The first main section examines the performance of Telecom Egypt, a state-owned company that is exclusively responsible for providing all telecom services in Egypt. This is followed by a section that attempts to explain observed performance, focusing on the market and the institutional structure of the sector rather than the internal workings of the company. Then the section on potential winners and losers looks ahead by estimating the welfare implications of reforming the environment in which Telecom Egypt operates. In conclusion, the paper outlines the key reforms ahead.

This paper complements the literature concerned with the ex post effects of reforming telecom (Vickers and Yarow 1998; Galal and others 1994). But it differs in two main respects. First, the paper deals with the effects of reforms ex ante, rather than ex post. Second, it deals with the impact of a comprehensive reform package, including competition, incentive regulation and privatization, on all important economic actors, rather than the impact of privatization alone on these actors.

The Performance of Telecom Egypt

The saying, "If it isn't broken, don't fix it," is not an appropriate yardstick to judge the performance of a company or a sector. From society's standpoint, it is important to explore whether performance is satisfactory compared with best practices elsewhere. In other words, an improvement in performance over time is certainly good, but measuring performance against an appropriate benchmark is also important. From this perspective we assess the performance of Telecom Egypt, after providing a brief background of the sector.

Background

Telephone services were first introduced in Egypt in the late 19th century. Since then, several institutional landmark events have taken place. In 1918, the Egyptian Telephone and Telegraph Administration was established and operated until the founding of the Egyptian Telecommunications Organization in 1957. The Arab Republic of Egypt National Telecommunications Organization (ARENTO) was created in 1980 as an autonomous public utility and was recently renamed Telecom Egypt. According to Law 153, Telecom Egypt operates under the supervision of the Minister of Transport and Communications as the sole provider of telecommunication services in Egypt.

Until the early 1980s, telecom services in Egypt were scarce, inefficient, and costly. The installed capacity was approximately half a million lines, and telephone density was less than one per 100 inhabitants. The waiting period for a phone line approached 10 years, and the rate of completed calls was low. It was not unusual for businesspeople in Cairo to send messengers rather than make telephone calls. Customers were offered a narrow range of services at a time when the sector was witnessing a technological revolution abroad.

Great strides have been made in Egypt since then. Telecom Egypt invested heavily and made a noticeable difference in the quantity and quality of telecommunication services. As shown in table 8.1, the number of installed lines is now more than 4 million, and there are five phones per 100 inhabitants. The waiting period for a phone line is declining, and telephone services to rural areas, reclaimed land and industrial developments have been expanded. The quality of service has also improved with the replacement of semiautomatic with automatic exchanges and the addition of digital exchanges and automatic exchange connections to the national long-distance network. In 1996, GSM and VSAT networks were introduced.

TABLE 8.1 TELECOM EGYPT: SELECTED GROWTH INDICATORS
in thousands, unless specified otherwise

Indicators	1987–88	1991–92	1992–93	1993–94	1994–95	1995–96
Installed lines	1,562	2,530	2,738	3,151	3,526	4,104
Lines in service	1,200	2,022	2,234	2,456	2,716	3,024
Telephones per 100 inhabitants (TD)	2.27	3.48	3.77	4.06	4.60	5.02
Pay phones per 1,000 inhabitants	0.03	0.055	0.062	0.068	0.070	0.075
Waiting period (years)	—	—	6.1	—	5.8	5.7

— Not available.
Source: All indicators except waiting period: Telecom Egypt; Waiting period: ITU, World Telecommunication Development Report, various issues.

In view of these favorable developments, one might question the need for reform. Answering this question requires further analysis of Telecom Egypt's performance and its potential. These issues are taken up next.

Performance of Telecom Egypt over the Past Decade

By all indicators, the performance of Telecom Egypt improved significantly over the period 1986–96. As figure 8.1 indicates, the company's public profits increased 7 times and private profits increased 17 times over the period analyzed.[2] Over the last four years, profits increased at an unprecedented rate.

In principle, the surge in private and public profits in absolute terms can be attributed to an increase in prices or an improvement in productivity. To distinguish one factor from the other, a number of additional performance indicators are calculated. One such indicator is public profit in constant prices, according to which Telecom Egypt has improved its performance steadily throughout the period analyzed (figure 8.2).[3] In other words, while the company did benefit from favorable price changes, it was able to increase the quantity of output more than the corresponding increase in the quantity of inputs, including wages, factor rentals and intermediate inputs.

The disproportionate increase in output was also due to a significant increase in fixed-capital formation. While this expansion was financed largely by internal funds (figure 8.3), it raises the question of whether Telecom Egypt's performance is as good if we look at relative indicators of performance, such as public and private profitability.[4] That is, can we still say that Telecom Egypt improved performance if profits in absolute terms are divided by net worth or revalued assets?

FIGURE 8.1 PUBLIC AND PRIVATE PROFITS OF TELECOM EGYPT AT CURRENT
MARKET PRICES, FROM 1986–87 TO 1995–96

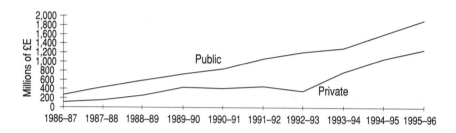

Source: Calculated from Telecom Egypt data.

FIGURE 8.2 PUBLIC PROFIT AT CONSTANT MARKET PRICES, TELECOM EGYPT,
FROM 1986–87 TO 1995–96

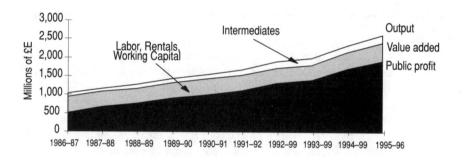

Source: Calculated from Telecom Egypt data.

According to these indicators, Telecom Egypt did well. Figure 8.4 shows that
private profitability in relation to net worth averaged 13.7 percent per annum during
the period from 1986–87 to 1995–96, higher than the prevailing 10.4 percent interest on a 3–6 month deposit in 1996. In addition, public profitability in current prices
in relation to revalued capital averaged 8.5 percent. Turning to productivity, the
results still show that Telecom Egypt improved over time (figure 8.5).[5] Labor productivity rose over the period 1986–96, and total factor productivity (TFP) improved
at a compound annual growth rate (CAGR) of 1.94 percent over the same period.

In large measure, improved productivity can be traced to the expansion of capital without a significant increase in labor. Expansion brought the latest technology
and enabled the company to realize substantial economies of scope and scale. The
new technology was provided by such well-known companies as AT&T, Siemens,

FIGURE 8.3 SOURCES OF FUNDS, TELECOM EGYPT, FROM 1986–87 TO 1995–96

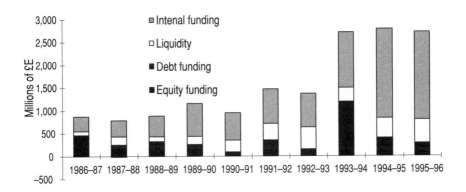

Source: Calculated from Telecom Egypt data.

FIGURE 8.4 PROFITABILITY, TELECOM EGYPT, FROM 1986–87 TO 1995–96

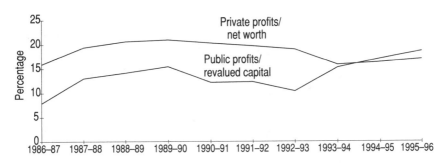

Source: Calculated from Telecom Egypt data.

CIT Alcatel, Ericsson, and NEC. Many of the trunk-cables are now made of fiber-optic technology, which offers an almost unlimited bandwidth; manual exchanges have been replaced largely by semiautomatic and automatic switches; several international links have also been installed, most of fiber-optic cable; and coaxial submarine cables connect Egypt with Italy, Greece, Southeast Asia, and Western Europe, providing greater capacity, reliability and speed.

Performance of Telecom Egypt Compared to Other Countries
While Telecom Egypt has improved over time, its services do not compare to telecommunications in most countries in the region. As table 8.2 indicates, telecom

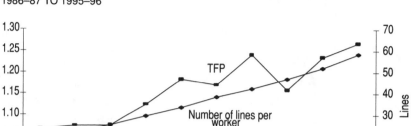

138   PARTNERS FOR DEVELOPMENT

FIGURE 8.5 LABOR AND TOTAL FACTOR PRODUCTIVITY, TELECOM EGYPT, FROM
1986–87 TO 1995–96

Source: Calculated from Telecom Egypt data.

services in Egypt lag behind oil- and non-oil-producing countries on most counts, including teledensity, demand satisfaction, and waiting period for a phone line. Egypt also scores low on two efficiency indicators: the number of lines per worker and revenue per line. If Egypt is to compete with these countries in the world market, Telecom Egypt must make a dramatic improvement.

A similar conclusion is reached when we compare Egypt with seven developing countries that adopted competition in the markets for value added services, cellular and other telecom services, incentive regulation for the market of basic telephony, and private, rather than public, ownership of all telecommunication services (table 8.3). The performance of telecom in these countries is clearly superior to that of Telecom Egypt by most measures. With the exception of the Philippines, the remaining countries did better in terms of the number of telephone lines per 100 inhabitants, demand satisfaction and pending applications for a phone. Of course, these countries have higher per capita incomes than Egypt, thus they are capable of providing more telephone services per person. However, there is no reason why they should have greater labor productivity or revenue per line than Egypt.

In summary, Telecom Egypt has shown significant progress in the quality and efficiency of services offered. Expansion and new technology were the main forces behind this improvement in performance. However, Egypt's telecom sector still does not compare favorably with other developing countries, especially those that reformed their telecom sectors. This suggests that Telecom Egypt could do much better. The next section addresses why Egypt's telecommunications are lagging behind other developing countries.

TABLE 8.2 TELECOMMUNICATIONS IN EGYPT COMPARED WITH SELECTED ARAB COUNTRIES, 1994

| | Egypt | Lower-middle-income Arab countries | | | | | | Upper-middle-income Arab countries | | | High-income Arab countries | | |
		Lebanon	Tunisia	Algeria	Morocco	Syria	Jordan	Saudi Arabia	Libya	Oman	Kuwait	Qatar	UAE
Service availability													
Overall country TD	3.92	9.26	5.38	4.11	3.07	4.85	7.24	9.58	4.84	7.61	22.57	21.74	32.11
TD outside largest cities	2.95	4.71	4.96	3.62	2.39	4.12	3.18	8.54	6.23	5.32	59.02	34.27	24.3
Pay phones per 1,000 inhabitants	0.06	0.03	0.64	0.25	0.23	0.13	0.05	0.43	—	1.54	0.28	0.83	4.28
Waiting period (years)	5.8	>10	2.8	8.1	0.7	>10	8.9	>10	>10	0.2	0.2	0.1	0
Satisfied demand (%)	65	59.3	79	63.4	90.2	19.3	71.8	58.5	50.9	98.4	99.3	99.4	99.8
Efficiency indicators													
Lines per worker	45	78	62	61	74	41	79	84	27	65	51	69	121
Revenue per line ($)	322	133	460	206	643	293	718	1,056	1,188	1,261	716	1,327	1,282

— Not available.
Note: TD = teledensity.
Source: ITU (1995).

TABLE 8.3 TELECOM EGYPT COMPARED WITH A SAMPLE OF REFORMING
ECONOMIES, 1994

	Egypt	Argentina	Chile	Jamaica	Malaysia	Mexico	Philippines	Venezuela
Service availability								
Overall country TD	3.92	14.14	11.01	8.63	14.69	7.95	1.68	10.92
TD outside largest cities	2.95	10.31	8.01	5.75	14.73	6.74	0.57	8.29
Pay phones per 1,000 inhabitants	0.06	1.66	1.32	0.69	3.28	2.36	0.09	2.57
Waiting period (years)	5.8	0.9	1.2	4.3	0.3	0.2	5.5	3.7
Satisfied demand (%)	65	90.7	88.6	59.6	95.9	97.7	56.7	71.8
Efficiency indicators								
Lines per worker	45	155	153	59	97	174	55	119
Revenue per line ($)	322	1,023	775	1,067	598	1,019	759	445

Note: TD= teledensity.
Source: ITU (1995).

Explaining the Performance of Telecom Egypt

The primary obstacle to improved telecom services in Egypt seems to be the nature
of the implicit contract governing the operation, entry to and management of the
sector. The most critical deficiency is that Telecom Egypt does not face competition
or even the threat of competition. In the monopolistic segment of the market, the
regulatory contract is also not designed to provide incentives for efficient operation
or consumption. Finally, the operation, ownership and regulatory functions are not
well defined, and several elements of commitment are not in place, such as conflict
resolution mechanisms and insulation of regulatory reform from politics. These features of the implicit contract are elaborated on below.

Lack of Competition or Threat of Competition
Telecom Egypt monopolizes the market for local, national and international long-
distance service. It also monopolizes the market for complementary services, including cellular telephones, facsimile, telex, telegraph and data transmission. The
market domination of Telecom Egypt, its sheer size and sunk cost give the company
a favorable position relative to potential competitors.

Recently, there have been cases of private sector participation in Internet and
VSAT service, and the private sector is licensed to sell subscriber terminal equipment for GSM and paging services. But Telecom Egypt independently owns the
Egyptian Telephone Company (ETC), which manufactures under license telephone
sets, boxes, and small switches. It also works with Siemens in a joint venture called
EGTI to provide manufacturing facilities. Clearly, private participation, free entry
and competition are lacking in Egypt's telecommunications sector.

In contrast, Argentina, Chile, and Mexico liberalized their telecom sectors by
allowing competition in the value added, and in some cases, in the market, for

long-distance services. Competition in these markets is forcing firms to operate efficiently without costly regulation. These countries also auctioned off new licenses, inducing competition for the markets themselves and the selection of more qualified and efficient suppliers. Finally, when these countries privatized their basic networks, they introduced regulation first, which in Chile preceded privatization by some five years. To ensure that the private operator meets pending and growing demand, they committed the buyers to specific quantity and quality targets, retaining the right to revoke the concession in case of failure to meet these targets. These reforms collectively imposed pressure on firms to be efficient, kept them from taking full advantage of their information privilege and reduced the burden of regulation.

Lack of Incentives for Efficient Operation and Consumption

The prevailing tariff structure in Egypt involves cross-subsidization of local users at the expense of national and international users. Telecom Egypt also charges new subscribers a significant allocation fee. The company does not pay taxes and, ironically, funds the expansion of the Cairo Metro. While the funds earmarked for the metro almost match the taxes Telecom Egypt would have had to pay on profit, this practice has the effect of reducing transparency. Finally, tariffs are cost-plus-based and are revised on an ad hoc basis. These features of the incentive regime are not conducive to efficiency in consumption or in production. Users of telecom services tend to consume more local services and less national and international services than desired by society. At the same time, Telecom Egypt is not motivated to improve efficiency, given that higher costs can be passed on to consumers.

Contrast this system with the price cap regulation (or RPI–X) adopted, for example, by Argentina, Mexico, Venezuela, and Malaysia. According to this scheme, a ceiling is imposed on the average tariff increase for a prespecified basket of services in which the firm has a monopoly. The average price increases do not exceed the Retail Price Index minus X factor, which is predetermined for a given period of time. A positive X factor at the time of revising tariffs simply means that some of the benefits of technological progress and improved productivity are transferred to the consumer. Because prices are set independent of costs, there is no incentive for the firm to distort its cost data or shift the costs of competitive services onto its monopoly activities. Instead, the firm is motivated to minimize costs because it can retain any savings until tariffs are revised next.

In further contrast, Chile follows benchmark regulation, according to which tariffs are calculated to allow the firm a fair rate of return, based on the cost of an "efficient" firm.[6] This method of calculating tariffs ensures that the firm has no incentive to inflate its costs. Meanwhile, because tariffs are revised only periodically (every five years), benchmark regulation has cost-saving properties similar to price cap regulation.

Overlapping Functions and Lack of Commitment

Telecom Egypt plays a dual role operating and regulating the sector. By law, Telecom Egypt has the exclusive right to provide telecom services, subcontract services, provide concessions, manage the spectrum, and establish joint ventures. The company proposes tariff revisions, which are approved initially by the Minister of Transport and Communications and finally by an interministerial committee. In other words, tariffs are not decided by an independent regulatory agency. Under the current regulatory regime, disputes are resolved administratively. Complicating matters is the fact that the ownership rights are exercised by the Ministry of Finance and the Ministry of Transport and Telecommunications.

In 1994, the government began a process of separating the regulatory and operating functions of Telecom Egypt by creating a five-member independent regulatory commission. But this was only a partial reform. It was not accompanied by regulatory reforms, leaving the commission with no clear mandate; and it was not accompanied by allowing entry into different telecom markets. As a result, the implicit contract governing the sector has remained effectively unchanged.

The contrast between Egypt's approach and the approach adopted by reformers of telecom is again apparent. Countries such as Chile and Argentina created independent regulatory bodies and introduced competition and privatized their telecom sectors. These reforms led to the separation of different functions, stimulated competition and generated significant benefit to the public at large. The independence and neutrality of the regulatory agencies were enhanced by separating them from the bureaucracy, giving them the power to request information from firms and endowing them with the financial resources to retain or hire needed skills. In most cases new regulations were introduced a few years prior to privatization.

To strengthen the credibility of government commitment, reformers of telecom also defined conflict resolution mechanisms and selected the most appropriate institutions to settle these disputes efficiently and fairly. In Chile, for example, disputes over pricing are resolved by a three-member arbitration committee, with one member selected by each party and the third by mutual agreement. The antitrust commissions resolve disputes over entry, with possible appeal to Supreme Court. Disputes over interconnection are subject to binding arbitration. Finally, they protected their regulation from arbitrary changes following political turnovers. Chile enacted its regulation in a detailed law that is difficult to change given the country's long history of split legislature. Jamaica, on the other hand, incorporated its regulatory regime in an explicit license that stipulates a specific rate of return and other terms of operations, as well as the conditions under which the parties can change the license. To make reneging costly for the government, any rulings by the Supreme Court in Jamaica are subject to review by the Commonwealth Privy Council in London (Spiller and Sampson 1993).

In summary, Telecom Egypt operates in an institutional and policy environment that does not promote efficiency in production or consumption. International experience suggests that reforming the policy and institutional environment is beneficial to society, although such reforms are often resisted by those whose interests are threatened. To make reforms politically acceptable it is important to identify who is likely to win and lose in the process. This question is taken up next.

Potential Winners and Losers from Reforming Telecom Egypt

The potential gains and losses from reforming Telecom Egypt depend on the changes following reform. This section first highlights the likely changes if Egypt moves towards enhanced competition, incentive regulation and private sector participation. It then summarizes how these changes are modeled to estimate the welfare gains or losses. Finally, it presents an estimate of the impact of reforms on the main economic actors (consumers, workers, government, and buyers).

Likely Changes Following Reform

The experiences of countries that followed a telecom reform strategy relying on competition, incentive regulation, and private ownership suggest that three changes are likely to follow:

Tariff Rebalancing. Following reform, prices of local services often go up, while those of national and international services go down. This is because the initial tariff structure typically favors consumers of local services at the expense of consumers of national and international services. Reforming countries correct this imbalance in relative prices to ensure that they reflect the economic scarcity of resources. This phenomenon has been observed in almost all countries that introduced telecom reforms, ranging from the United Kingdom to Mexico. Egypt should be no exception.

Increased Investment. Typically, developing countries undergoing fiscal reform find it necessary to reduce public expenditure on telecom services in favor of social services such as health and education. To maintain sufficient telecom services, governments seek private sector participation, either through outright privatization or BOTs. When privatization is pursued, governments typically commit new buyers to meet pending demand within a few years and demand growth thereafter. This commitment has been required of the private sector in Mexico, Chile, and other countries. If Egypt were to privatize Telecom Egypt this commitment should be expected as well.

Improved Productivity. This is due in part to faster growth in investment than in employment. It is also attributed to the fact that the private sector tends to introduce internal incentive regimes that link labor productivity with effort. The two factors reinforce each other, creating a surge in labor productivity, sometimes in excess of 3 percent per year, as in Mexico and Chile. In the Egyptian case, similar results can be anticipated.

Modeling the Impact of Reform

Assuming that reform brings these changes, how can their impact on welfare be assessed? The methodology applied below follows Galal and others (1994) closely. It is a partial equilibrium methodology, but takes into account the impact on the welfare of all important economic actors: buyers, sellers, workers, and consumers. Welfare effects are derived by subtracting the net present value (NPV) of the firm under two scenarios: the factual scenario (the no-reform scenario) and the counterfactual scenario (the reform scenario). In each case, the NPV of the firm is the sum of expected benefits to consumers, workers, government, and the private sector.[7]

In applying this methodology to Telecom Egypt, the performance of the company, and thus the sector, is projected with and without reform. The key differences between the two scenarios relate to the tariff structure, investment level, and productivity. Under the counterfactual scenario, it is assumed that incentive regulation will result in higher prices of local services and lower prices of national and international services. Second, investment is assumed to increase to meet pending demand over a period of 10 years. Finally, it is assumed that the number of lines in service per workers will increase progressively to match the average for other countries that reformed their telecom sectors. More specifically, it is assumed that labor productivity will increase at a compound annual growth rate (CAGR) of 0.8 percent under the factual scenario and at 4.5 percent under the counterfactual scenario. With the exception of these three differences, all other variables, regarding demand and cost, are the same in both scenarios.

Potential Winners and Losers

Based on these assumptions, reforming Telecom Egypt should bring net gains in national welfare of 96 percent of the company's sales during 1995–96. This is the difference between the social value of Telecom Egypt with reform (Vsp) and its social value without reform (Vsg). Given the magnitude of the potential gains, Egypt is better off reforming its telecom sector with competitive markets, efficiency-inducing incentives, and private sector participation.

There is a chance that the country will benefit while consumers and workers do not—that is, the gains may accrue to the private sector and possibly the government, leaving consumers and workers worse off than before. This, however, is not the distribution pattern likely to emerge on the basis of the stated assumptions (table 8.4). Rather, consumers are expected to benefit the most, realizing 70 percent of the improvement in domestic welfare.

Consumer gains will come from reduced prices and more services. While users of local telephone services will lose, users of international services will win. But both will benefit from expansion and provision of a variety of value added services.[8] Similarly, workers as a group will also gain approximately 4 percent of the annual sales of Telecom Egypt, assuming that they buy 10 percent of the shares. One reason workers are expected to be benefit is the assumption that laid-off workers will be compensated adequately. As for workers that stay with the firm, experience elsewhere suggests that they typically gain from receiving a percentage of the shares at a discount. In addition to consumers and workers, reform is expected to benefit the buyers of Telecom Egypt, at an estimated gain of 32 percent of the company's annual sales, for purchasing 90 percent of the company. These gains will be split between foreign and domestic buyers in proportion to their share in equity, which is assumed to be 51 percent foreign and 39 percent domestic.

As for government, it is assumed that it will just break even by accepting a price equal to what the Treasury would have received (in dividends, retained earnings, and taxes) if it were to retain the ownership of Telecom Egypt and what it is

TABLE 8.4 TELECOM EGYPT: POTENTIAL WINNERS AND LOSERS
1995–96 present values; millions of pounds

	Private (Vsp)	Public (Vsg)	Gains from reform (Vsp – Vsg)	Perpetual annuity/ 1995–96 sales (percent)
Government				
Taxes	19,952	15,844	4,108	—
Net quasi-rents	870	23,559	(22,689)	—
Net sale proceeds	18,581	—	18,581	—
Total government	39,403	39,403	0	0
Private shareholders				
Employees	967	—	967	4
Private domestic shareholders	5,585	—	5,585	21
Foreign shareholders	2,977	—	2,977	11
Total private shareholders	9,529	—	9,529	—
Consumers	141,699	126,072	15,627	60
Grand total	190,632	165,475	25,156	96

— Not applicable.
Source: Author's estimates.

expected to receive if it sells the company (in the form of taxes and sale price). This floor price is estimated at £E18.6 billion. However, the government could do better. The private sector's maximum willingness to pay for the company is estimated at £E28.1 billion. As such, it is possible that the bidding process could generate a price between £E18.6 and £E28.1 (billion). In that event, the fiscal impact of selling Telecom Egypt will be positive. Additional gains to the government will reduce the private sector's gains, leaving the estimated welfare effect of reform unchanged.

Where will the improvement in welfare come from? Table 8.5 shows that the expansion of the basic network and price rebalancing will contribute almost equally to the improvement in welfare. Labor productivity contributes modestly, because the industry is relatively capital-intensive. Both the estimated changes in welfare and their distribution clearly depend on the assumptions made. For this reason, it is useful to think of these estimates as orders of magnitude. Moreover, the results can be seen as a point of departure for policymakers in their attempt to design reforms that are politically acceptable, while ensuring that the country is better off. The endogenous quality of reforms raises a question about the policy and institutional reforms most likely to maximize gains. This question is taken up next.

The Reform Agenda

What then needs to be done to achieve these substantial gains? The key to maximizing the benefits of reform in Egypt is to forge a new contract whose main features

TABLE 8.5 TELECOM EGYPT: ORIGIN OF THE CHANGE IN WELFARE

Behavioral difference	Contribution (£E billion)	Relative contribution (percentage)
Investment	11.6	46
Price rebalancing	10.6	42
Labor productivity	1.9	7
Interaction effect	1.1	4
Total	25.2	100

Source: Author's estimates.

are competition, incentive regulation, and privatization. The reform process takes two to three years to implement—thus there is a premium on starting now.

While some actions may be taken simultaneously, the most appropriate sequence of reform seems to be first to introduce competition and a new regulatory regime, followed by the creation of an independent regulatory body and the commercialization of the operation of Telecom Egypt, and finally, privatization. The key features of this reform are elaborated on below.

Regulation and Competition
The experiences of successful telecom reformers suggest that the new regulation should allow free entry into all markets, competition among existing and future entrants, and the transparent bidding of new concessions (see Galal and Nauryal 1995). Based on technological progress thus far, competition is now possible in the markets for long-distance phone service, cellular phones and a variety of other value added services. Competition is also now possible to some degree in the market for local services, which was once a natural monopoly. However, given that segments of the market remain monopolistic, the protection of consumers and investors requires that the regulation include explicit provisions regarding price setting, interconnection, and conflict resolution mechanisms. The price rules could be based on the price cap or benchmark regulation.

Commercializing Telecom Egypt and Creating a Regulatory Agency
Following the adoption of a new regulatory regime and the introduction of competition, Telecom Egypt will face a new and more competitive market structure. It may therefore be necessary to restructure the company legally, organizationally, and financially. At the same time, the conflict of interest inherent in assigning Telecom Egypt the operational and regulatory functions demands the creation of a neutral regulatory agency to implement the new regime fairly and efficiently among the multiple players. To ensure its neutrality, it may be necessary to separate the agency from the bureaucracy and give it quasi-judicial status.

Privatization

Once experience implementing the new regulation is gained, the rules of the system well understood, and the policy and institutional framework of investment and operation in the sector clarified, privatization becomes a viable option with significant potential gains to society. An important dimension of privatization is committing the new players to meet pending and growing demand, subject to specified quality standards.

With this reform package, there is an opportunity for policymakers to create a positive-sum game in which all economic actors can benefit from reforming Egypt's telecom sector. Reforms will relax the resource constraint facing Telecom Egypt and mobilize foreign capital. They can restore balance to the pricing regime with built-in incentives for firms to operate efficiently. And they can provide consumers—residential and business—with the variety of services that will enable Egypt to be more competitive in an increasingly globalized world.

Notes

1. The author would like to thank Amal Rifaat for superb research assistance, Clemencia Torres for help with the computational program used in this paper and Suilin Ling for valuable input. All remaining errors or misinterpretations remain the responsibility of the author. Neither ECES nor its Board of Directors is responsible for the views expressed herein.

2. Public profit is the same as quasi-rent, or the return to all investors, owners and lenders. It is defined as:

$$\text{public profit} = X - II - W - R - rK^w,$$

where X is the value of output, II is the value of intermediate inputs, W is employment compensation, R is factor rentals, and rK^w is the opportunity cost of working capital. Private profit is the return to equity holders alone. It can be defined as profit before or after taxes, or retained earnings plus dividends.

3. Constant prices are derived from detailed information supplied by Telecom Egypt in which major outputs and inputs are decomposed into their price and quantity components.

4. Public profitability is public profit divided by revalued capital. Revalued capital is estimated using the perpetual inventory methodology, or:

$$K_t = K_{t-1} * (1 + \text{inflation rate}_t) * (1 - \text{depreciation rate}) + I_t,$$

where K_t is capital stock in year t, K_{t-1} is capital stock in the previous year, and I_t is investment this year. Private profitability is profit after tax divided by net worth.

5. Total factor productivity is obtained by dividing the value of total output by the value of total costs, both expressed in constant prices. That is,

$$\text{TFP} = \text{benefits/costs} = X / (II + W + R + rK^w + rK^f),$$

where all variables are as defined before, and rK^f is the opportunity cost of fixed capital.

6.   More specifically, tariffs are set for each regulated service on the basis of the incremental costs of an "efficient" firm. The resulting prices are adjusted to ensure that the firms can earn a fair rate of return on revalued assets, using the capital asset pricing model. That is,

$$R_i = R_{rf} + {}_i (R_p - R_{rf}),$$

where R_i is the rate of return on revalued capital of firm i, R_{rf} is the rate of return on risk-free assets, ${}_i$ is firm i's systematic risk, and R_p is the rate of return on a diversified investment portfolio (which can be drawn from international data).

7.   More formally, the change in welfare is estimated using the following formula:

$$\Delta W = \Delta s + \Delta \Pi + \Delta L,$$ where ΔW is the change in welfare, or the difference between the social value of the firm with and without reform, ΔS is the change in consumer surplus, $\Delta \Pi$ is the change in profit, which is shared by the buyer and seller through the payment of a price for the firm, and ΔL is the change in the welfare of workers.

8.   Expansion to value added services is particularly important because the telecommunications business is increasingly marked by contraction in "POTS," or the Plain Old Telephone Service, and expansion into "VANS" or value-added network services (see *The Economist* 1991 for details).

References

The Economist. 1991. "A Survey of Telecommunications." October 5.

Galal, Ahmed, and Bharat Nauryal. 1995. "Regulation of Telecom in Developing Countries: Outcomes, Incentives and Commitment." *Revista de Analisis Economico* 10(2): 41–62.

Galal, Ahmed, Leroy Jones, Pankaj Tandon, and Ingo Vogelsang. 1994. *Welfare Consequences of Selling Public Enterprises: An Empirical Analysis.* New York: Oxford University Press.

International Telecommunications Union (ITU). World Telecommunication Development Report, various issues. Geneva.

Levy, Brian, and Pablo Spiller. 1993. "Regulation, Institutions, and Commitment in Telecommunications: A Comparative Analysis of Five Country Studies." Paper presented at the World Bank Annual Conference on Development Economics, May 3–4. World Bank, Washington, D.C.

Spiller, Pablo and Cezley Sampson. 1993. "Regulation, Institutions and Commitment: The Jamaican Telecommunications Sector." Paper presented at the World Bank "Conference on Institutional Foundations of Utility Regulation," April 16. World Bank, Washington, D.C.

Vickers, J., and G. Yarrow. 1988. *Privatization: An Economic Analysis*. Cambridge, Mass: MIT Press.

Wellenius, Bjorn, and Peter A. Stern, eds. 1994. *Implementing Reforms in the Telecommunications Sector: Lessons from Experience*. Washington, D.C.: Regional and Sectoral Studies, World Bank.

Williamson, Oliver. 1989. "Transaction Cost Economics." In Richard Schmalensee and Robert Willig, eds., *Handbook of Industrial Organization*. Amsterdam: North Holland.

World Bank. 1994. *World Development Report, Infrastructure for Development*. World Bank, Washington, D.C.

CHAPTER 9

The Debate over Sequencing Private Sector Participation in Infrastructure[1]

Edmund O'Sullivan

A policy logjam over the role of the private sector is delaying essential investment in infrastructure across the region and there is an urgent need to advance from debate to action if the chronic inadequacy of basic utilities is to be cured.

Middle East and North African countries will have to invest up to $370,000 million in infrastructure in the years to 2006, according to new World Bank estimates. Government and aid agencies will be able to finance no more than 85 percent of this huge bill. The rest, about $45,000 million to $60,000 million, will have to come from somewhere else. In other words, from the private sector. (See box 9.1 for a description of the extent of the problem.)

The figure is a daunting one for those who have followed the twists and turns of government efforts to develop private power projects in the region over the past 15 years. Between 1984 and 1997, says the World Bank, more than 1,350 private infrastructure projects were completed in 128 countries with a combined value of $650,000 million. The Middle East accounted for just $9,000 million worth of those projects: barely more than 1 percent of the total (see figure 9.1).

The price paid for the striking failure to attract capital and know-how into power, water, telecommunications, and transport networks in those 14 years is evident in most countries in the region. With government finances under pressure during the whole of that period, essential investment has simply not happened.

"The public sector in Middle East and North African countries has done a poor job in managing infrastructure," says World Bank Middle East infrastructure devel-

---

BOX 9.1 THE DAMAGE DONE IN THE MIDDLE EAST

- Up to 60 million people lack access to safe water.

- 80 million people lack access to adequate sanitation.

- Water losses in Jordan, Lebanon, Yemen, and the West Bank and Gaza are 50–55 percent of total supplies.

- 20 percent of urban wastewater is treated compared with 60–70 percent in the United States and Europe.

- Electricity and telephone connections per capita are below the average for comparative countries.

FIGURE 9.1 VALUE OF PRIVATE INFRASTRUCTURE PROJECTS, 1984–97

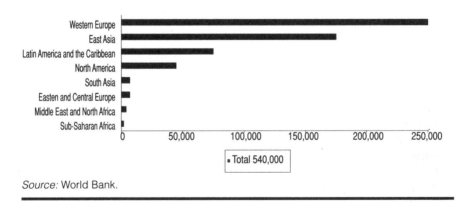

Source: World Bank.

---

opment group leader Jamal Saghir. "With the exception of the Gulf States, the region is seriously lacking in quality and quantity of services. Up to 60 million people do not have access to safe water and 80 million people lack access to adequate sanitation."

Water networks in several countries are so dilapidated; more than half of the supplies are lost. If you want a telephone in Yemen, you have to wait six years. Unlucky new subscribers in Algeria will not get their phone connections until after 2005 on present trends.

The logic seems compelling. Rapid population growth and the need to repair aging infrastructure means there has to be huge investment across the Middle East. Governments, incapable of financing the needs of the past, have no chance of paying for the demands of the future. International development agencies have other priorities, so attracting private capital is the only option.

So why are there so few private infrastructure initiatives in the region? And why are the ones under way taking so long to bear fruit?

Saghir is clear. "Obstacles to private infrastructure investment can be found in every single country," he says. "There are problems with infrastructure service pricing, poor regulatory environments, high infrastructure costs and domestic financing weaknesses."

Middle East governments that have accepted the principle of privatizing at least some infrastructure services have got bogged down in a host of issues. How to manage the introduction of cost-based tariffs for water and electricity is the most sensitive one. Most countries in the region have also yet to decide what the most acceptable form and extent of private involvement in infrastructure is. Is a private sector monopoly acceptable in some services, even for a temporary period? What is the right regulatory system? And how do you direct the inevitable debate about private infrastructure policy?

The result is policy logjams right across the Middle East. Practically no one is going very far. And those that are moving are going slowly.

Attention is now shifting from pressing the argument for infrastructure privatization, which finds little open resistance among Middle East policymakers. The challenge is getting projects moving to meet the desperate needs of the future.

Abderrahmane Saaidi, Moroccan privatization minister until March this year and probably the most convinced advocate of speedy privatization in the Arab world, says the Middle East infrastructure system is like an elephant. "And you have to have a mouse to make an elephant dance." In other words, too much time has been spent fretting about the policy framework. What is needed is action—a successful project that creates a model for others to follow.

He points to Lyonnaise des Eaux's monopoly contract to provide power, water and sewage services to Casablanca, awarded in 1997, as an example. Much maligned by critics in Morocco, it nevertheless has provided a model for a similar initiative in Rabat.

Managing director of Patricof Emerging Markets of New York, Roger Leeds, who has worked on private infrastructure financing across the developing world, says government obsession with getting policy in place before promoting projects is damaging. "From my private sector perspective, the issue of sequencing is really a euphemism for delay," he says. No one would dispute the importance of having an effective policy and regulatory framework. Every private sector participant would prefer to have a strong framework. But this is not a central issue, especially because it is 15 years since this process of privatization in emerging markets started. There is enough experience and knowledge in the world to provide all the rules you need."

The delays will be costly. "Focusing the debate on sequencing sends a negative signal to investors," Leeds adds. "You may be placing this region at a competitive disadvantage for finance and know-how. The world is no longer awash with liquidity. I believe that if countries focus on sequencing and get hung up on it, they send a signal that will create a competitive disadvantage in global markets."

Leeds says the key factor is the quality of the privatization transaction. "The most important issue is the valuation of the asset being sold and what price the buyer is prepared to pay," he says. "This market is no longer very arbitrary. Companies are very large players. They know about valuation. They know what industry norms are. There is not much mystery in privatization anymore."

"The good thing is that companies will come to this region—even with the financial turmoil—provided agreements can be reached on asset valuation and they feel comfortable that the enabling environment is competitive with what they see elsewhere in the world."

Ahmed Galal of the World Bank's Private Sector Development program argues that policy must always come first. "Doing transactions before policy is like playing soccer without rules," he says. "Of course, the balance between theory and practice has to be right. This is not a perfect world. But East Asia went on a transaction-first road. Where did they end up? All contracts concerning power stations are being renegotiated. Governments there are going to carry liabilities of $10,000 million. In contrast, in Latin America, where they had policy reform, there were transactions and investment as well." "Without rules, you are getting the private sector, but not the proper private sector," Galal adds. "It is a private sector that is not carrying risk. So even if it takes longer, it is better to travel on the right rather than the wrong road."

Lawyers specializing in infrastructure financing are uniformly adamant. Unless a basic policy framework is established by the government, private infrastructure deals are not bankable. Governments that do deals first hinder rather than help an economy by giving a country a reputation for playing without rules. Says a senior partner in an international law firm: "I would find it very difficult to do a deal without some basic rules. The present financial turbulence provides even more reasons for having policy and rules."

Guy Pfeffermann of the International Finance Corporation (IFC) says the rules versus action debate is a false one. "This is a dialogue process," he says. "Of course, you need a minimum of policies. But it is not a matter of black and white. In my opinion, there are some countries that could do with a little bit of a push. It is time they got deals on the table."

The Middle East, still grappling with the first principles of infrastructure privatization, is one area where the message is still not getting through. The elephant still sleeps. And there is no mouse in sight.

Note

1. Cover Story, MEED, September 15, 1998, with a variation in title.

PART IV

Transaction Costs in Government–Private Interaction

CHAPTER 10

Tax Administration and Transaction Costs in Egypt

Sahar Tohamy

As Egypt becomes a more private sector-led economy, the need to study the principles underlying tax collection becomes apparent. Tax collection methods that were suitable for an economy dominated by public sector firms are inadequate for the current and future stages of economic development. Further evidence of the need to modify Egypt's tax collection process is the general perception that taxpayers are increasingly evading accurate and prompt tax payment. The fact that 250,000 tax cases are pending in Egyptian courts, and a recently passed Reconciliation Law that allows taxpayers and the tax authority yet one more avenue to settle their disputes, serve as evidence of the need for reform. Meanwhile, over 70 percent of documented taxpayers do not file taxes by the deadline.

Two issues raise heated debate on tax administration in Egypt: tax evasion, and the difficulty taxpayers face in dealing with the tax authority. Depending on whom one asks, one of the two issues will be declared as the primary weakness behind the poor performance in tax collection. Each side when pressed, however, will acknowledge the other party's complaints.[1]

The purpose of this paper is to analyze tax administration problems from a contracting perspective.[2] This analysis argues that both extensive tax evasion and the discretionary nature of the tax authority's interaction with the business community are symptoms of a relationship, or "contract," that does not clearly define the rules, roles and consequences of different parties' types of behavior. This results in uncertainty, discretion, disputes, and negotiations. This negative relationship raises the transaction costs of tax collection and payment. Using the contracting literature

157

on tax administration, reform must focus on aligning the incentives of various par ties instead of "policing" parties every step of the way.

At the beginning, it is necessary to define the concepts: "contract" and "transaction costs." Contract, in economics, refers to an agreement that parties enter into to change their behavior in ways that are mutually beneficial. These agreements may encompass the sort of actions each is to take, payments from one party to another, the rules and procedures they will use to decide matters in the future, and the behavior that each can expect from the other (Milgrom and Roberts 1992, p.127). A contract does not have to be a formal legal document; it can be represented by tradition, a verbal agreement, or even norms that define the rights and responsibilities of the parties involved. Hence, a contracting perspective on analyzing tax administration in Egypt looks at the terms of the relationship between the tax authority and taxpayers. It identifies the legal incentives to behave in a specific manner and this contracting perspective evaluates whether the incentives are compatible with the efficiency and effectiveness of the government's tax collection function.

Second, the textbook definition of transaction costs, describes these as the costs that relate to the time, effort and other resources needed to search out, negotiate and consummate an exchange. This definition, however, neglects the rich interaction between the concept of transaction costs and the contract literature. Variations in organizational structure and institutions represent different contracts, which in turn have an impact on the efficiency of any economic transaction. Although the origin of transaction costs has been related to examining economic efficiency in the zero-transaction costs state (Coase 1960), a growing argument of the empirical literature in this area focuses on the real world of positive transaction costs. This recent literature examines organizational structure within a public or private body, or institutional structure outside an organization—including political institutions, laws, customs, and norms—and how various structures are associated with different levels of positive transaction costs.[3] Coase (1984, 1992) argues that this approach focuses legitimate attention on the study of feasible organizational alternatives. This paper takes this comparative approach.

Based on this perspective, the paper poses four specific questions to analyze tax evasion and the business sector's complaints of high transaction costs in tax payment:

(1) How does tax evasion in Egypt compare with other countries?

(2) Are taxpayers' transaction costs higher in Egypt than in other countries?

Answers to these two questions give a sense of the magnitude of these two problems, as perceived by both taxpayers and the tax authority in Egypt. The discussion then addresses the following two questions:

(3) What are the main sources of transaction costs in tax administration?

(4) How can transaction costs in tax administration be reduced?

These questions help to identify possible weaknesses in the tax payment–collection relationship and to explore remedies for the current system.

This paper is organized as follows: The next section estimates the magnitude of the tax evasion problem in Egypt. This is followed by a section that discusses the business community's perspective on tax administration issues as a major institutional obstacle to private sector activity in Egypt. Next is a section that uses the literature on contracting to give insights into the main sources of transaction costs in tax administration, both for the business community and the tax authority, and identifies various "contractual" weaknesses in Egypt's tax administration system. The final two sections consider policy recommendations to reduce transaction costs in Egypt's tax administration, and summarize the discussion, respectively.

How Does Tax Evasion in Egypt Compare with other Countries?

Estimates of tax evasion abound in the media, government circles and the business community. These estimates vary widely; some sources indicate that tax evasion amounted to £E3.6 billion during 1988–89,[4] others argue that it was £E8 billion,[5] while still others estimate that it reached £E80 billion[6] in 1996 (*Al-Ahram Al-Iktisadi* 1997). It is difficult to judge the accuracy of these figures, therefore this paper's analysis evaluates the magnitude of tax evasion in Egypt by comparing it with tax evasion in other countries.[7]

Descriptive Statistics

To evaluate the extent of tax evasion in Egypt it is necessary to look first at the size of tax revenue. Limited tax revenue can be a preliminary sign of prevalent tax evasion. Tax revenue, however, must be relative to some measure of the country's size, usually GDP. Table 10.1 shows Egypt's tax revenue-to-GDP ratio in comparison with other countries.

In Egypt, tax revenue was 17 percent of GDP in 1995, while it ranged from 4 percent for Zaire to 45 percent for Israel. Member states of the Association of Southeast Asian Nations (ASEAN), to whom Egypt is often compared, exhibit a narrower range for tax revenue-to-GDP ratio (from 13 percent for Indonesia to 20 percent in Malaysia, with a median of 16 percent). These preliminary figures suggest that Egypt's tax revenue relative to GDP is comparable with similar countries. If this evidence were enough, it might be concluded that Egypt does not have a tax evasion problem, but that is not the case. A country's tax revenue is not only a function of how many people evade taxes; tax revenue is also a function of a country's level of development and its economic structure—among other factors. Therefore, in order to determine whether Egypt has a tax evasion problem or not—and its extent if it does—it is necessary to exclude the effect of these other variables. The following section includes a measurement that does this.

Tax Effort Index

The literature on tax evasion indicates that a country's ability to collect taxes can be limited by its general level of development and the structure of its tax base. GDP per capita may be a proxy for a country's level of development. The shares of various

TABLE 10.1 DISTRIBUTION OF TAX REVENUE: CROSS-COUNTRY COMPARISON
percentage of GDP

Country	Year	Tax revenue	Taxes on income, profits, and capital gains of which: Total	Corporate	Individual	Taxes on goods and services (total)	Taxes on international trade
Mediterranean countries							
Egypt	1995–96	17.10	7.50	6.80	0.70	6.00	3.50
Cyprus	1995	26.50	6.30	1.80	4.10	9.20	2.60
Israel	1995	35.40	15.90	3.10	11.40	13.80	0.20
Lebanon	1995	15.00	2.50	n.a.	n.a.	2.20	8.80
Morocco	1995	22.00	5.80	1.90	2.80	10.90	4.30
Jordan	1995	16.50	3.30	2.00	1.30	7.10	6.10
Turkey	1995	14.20	5.70	1.40	4.30	7.20	0.70
Tunisia	1995	25.10	4.80	n.a.	n.a.	6.90	7.70
ASEAN member countries							
Korea	1995	17.70	6.40	2.50	3.90	6.50	1.30
Indonesia	1994–95	12.60	7.40	6.10	1.00	4.00	0.80
Malaysia	1995	20.30	9.40	6.50	2.90	6.60	3.00
Philippines	1994	16.00	5.40	2.30	2.20	4.90	4.60
Singapore	1995	16.20	6.60	4.60	2.00	5.70	0.70
Thailand	1995	17.70	6.00	3.90	2.10	7.60	3.20
Selected Latin American countries							
Argentina	1995	12.90	1.30	0.90	0.40	4.70	0.67
Bolivia	1996	10.40	0.40	0.40	n.a.	6.20	1.04
Brazil	1993	30.30	3.89	0.93	n.a.	4.80	0.45
Chile	1996	22.40	4.14	n.a.	n.a.	10.34	2.10
Colombia	1993	14.60	5.47	n.a.	n.a.	6.11	1.24
Mexico	1995	15.70	4.25	n.a.	n.a.	8.52	0.63
Peru	1996	13.50	2.60	n.a.	n.a.	7.50	1.50
Uruguay	1996	37.30	5.30	2.80	2.35	13.10	1.40
Venezuela	1996	20.50	7.84	n.a.	n.a.	5.70	1.42
Selected Sub-Saharan African countries							
Cameroon	1995	10.62	1.43	1.43	0.00	2.82	2.75
Côte d'Ivoire	1995	17.83	4.02	1.81	1.37	7.54	6.28
Ghana	1995	15.03	3.63	2.07	1.07	6.65	4.75
Nigeria	1995	7.00	1.40	0.00	1.40	5.60	n.a.
Senegal	1995	13.59	3.09	0.85	1.97	3.44	6.41
South Africa	1995	24.86	13.67	3.42	10.24	9.61	1.26
Zaire	1995	4.06	0.97	0.32	0.31	0.96	1.20
Zambia	1995	15.50	4.90	1.09	3.81	5.46	4.63
Industrialized European countries							
Austria	1995	32.73	6.94	1.31	5.63	8.34	0.14
Belgium	1992	41.96	14.38	1.78	12.60	10.69	n.a.
Denmark	1995	35.24	14.72	1.81	12.91	16.43	0.02
Finland	1995	27.61	8.98	1.37	7.61	13.38	0.05
France	1995	38.00	7.12	1.63	5.50	11.44	0.00
Germany	1993	32.79	5.25	0.92	4.34	8.58	n.a.
Greece	1994	19.94	5.24	1.99	3.25	13.29	0.01
Ireland	1994	36.04	15.18	3.39	11.79	12.18	1.82
Italy	1992	38.85	14.63	2.07	12.57	11.89	0.00
Netherlands	1995	44.88	12.10	3.43	8.67	10.96	n.a.

Country	Year	Tax revenue	Taxes on income, profits, and capital gains of which:			Taxes on goods and services (total)	Taxes on interna- tional trade
			Total	Corporate	Individual		
Sweden	1995	36.42	4.90	3.31	1.59	13.04	0.29
United Kingdom	1995	33.53	13.05	3.35	9.70	11.84	0.02
Pacific countries							
Japan	1993	17.99	7.75	2.67	5.08	3.09	0.27
Australia	1995	22.37	15.53	3.88	11.65	5.26	0.76
New Zealand	1991	33.26	19.79	2.41	17.38	9.67	0.72

n.a. = Not available.
Sources: IMF, Selected Latin American countries; IMF (1997a), Selected Latin American countries; Stotsky and Woldemariam (1997), Selected Sub-Saharan countries; Abdel-Rahman (1998), Mediterranean countries and ASEAN member countries.

economic sectors in GDP are usually used as proxies for the structure of the tax base. Some sectors of the economy are easier to tax than others. Mining, for example, is assumed to be a highly concentrated sector, with import and export links that provide checks and balances on tax payment. Similarly, the relationship between the share of imports and exports in GDP is assumed to be positive. Therefore, if there are two countries with the same level of income, but one has a larger international sector (imports and exports), the country with the larger international sector will have a larger capacity to raise tax revenues relative to GDP. By contrast, agriculture in developing countries usually has a large subsistence component and is fairly small-scale, hence the potential for extensive tax evasion. Based on these relationships, it is possible to produce a predicted tax revenue-to-GDP ratio that can be used to construct the tax effort index.

$$Tax\ Effort\ Index = \frac{actual\ tax\ revenue/GDP}{predicted\ tax\ revenue/GDP}$$

A tax effort index that is less than 1 indicates that the country's actual collected tax revenue is lower than its potential tax revenue. By contrast, a country with a tax effort index greater than or equal to 1 is controlling tax evasion better than comparable countries. The results of earlier research using this method are summarized in table 10.2.[8]

This paper's analysis, however, adds two sets of variables to economic structure and GDP per capita: institutional variables that can impact the effectiveness of any tax administration system, and statutory corporate and income tax rates.[9] Institutional differences play a role in taxpayers' willingness to voluntarily pay taxes and the ability of tax authorities to enforce prompt and accurate tax payment. For example, if corruption is perceived as a prevalent phenomenon, a country's tax rev-

enue-to-GDP ratio falls. Inadequate law enforcement or slow justice can also limit a
country's ability to collect taxes even when the structure of the economy is conducive to effective tax collection. Statutory income and corporate tax rates are also
variables that influence the tax revenue-to-GDP ratio. If two countries have similar
levels of tax evasion, but one has higher statutory income and corporate tax rates,
that country should have a higher tax revenue-to-GDP ratio.[10] Therefore, the relationship between each of the tax variables and the tax revenue-to-GDP ratio is expected to be positive (table 10.6).

TABLE 10.2 RESULTS OF PREVIOUS EMPIRICAL STUDIES

	Previous studies				
Variables	Chelliah, Baas, and Kelly (1975)	Tait, Gratz, and Eichengreen (1979)	Tanzi (1992)	Leuthold (1991)	Stotsky and Woldemariam (1997)
Agricultural share	−	Insignificant	−	−	−
Mining share	+	+			−
Manufacturing share					
Export share					+
Import share			+		
Per capita income					Insignificant
Non-mineral export share	Insignificant	+			
Non-export income per capita					
Foreign debt share			+		
Foreign trade share				+	
Sample size	47 developing countries	47 developing countries	83 developing countries	8 Sub-Saharan countries	30 Sub-Saharan countries
Period	1969–71	1972–76	1978–88	1973–81	1990–95
Analysis type	(averages)	(averages)	(panel)	(panel)	(panel)

Notes: (−) Negative, significant; (+) Positive, significant.
Source: Stotsky and Woldemariam (1997).

The empirical analysis uses panel data from 60 countries for the period between 1990 and 1995, which translates into 301 observations, to estimate the predicted tax revenue-to-GDP ratio.[11] As usual in cross-country analysis, variables
unaccounted for can be significant. Therefore, both fixed- and random-effect regression analyses are used to reduce the influence of the exogenous variables—not
included in the model—on the dependent variable.[12] Economic explanatory variables are the following: constant 1990 dollar GDP per capita; the shares of agriculture, manufacturing and mining in GDP; and an openness index that relates the
share of imports and exports to GDP. The relationship is expected to be positive for
GDP per capita, manufacturing, mining, and openness, and negative for agriculture.

For institutional variables three indexes are used from *International Country Risk Guide* (Political Risk Services 1995) produced for the period between 1982 and 1995. These variables are: bureaucratic quality, rule of law, and corruption. The bureaucratic quality index reflects the degree of bureaucracy's autonomy from political pressure and its strength and expertise to govern without drastic changes in policy or government services (0 to 6, with 6 representing the most independent). Similarly, the rule of law index reflects citizens' willingness to accept established institutions that make and implement laws and adjudicate disputes (0 to 6, with 6 representing the greatest acceptance). Finally, the corruption index reflects the pervasiveness of unofficial payment (0 to 6, with 0 representing the highest possible level of corruption and 6 representing virtually no corruption). The expected relationship between the tax revenue-to-GDP ratio and all three indexes is positive.[13] As expected, the correlation between the three institutional variables is high; therefore, regressions were run for each of these variables together with economic variables. Only the regressions with corruption are reported. Regressions with rule of law and quality of bureaucracy produced similar but weaker results. Results of regressions that do not include tax rates are reported in table 10.3; these utilize the larger sample. Adding statutory income and corporate tax rates reduces the sample to 28 countries and 134 observations. Those results appear in table 10.4.

TABLE 10.3 FIXED AND RANDOM EFFECTS, INCLUDING OPENNESS INDEX

Variables	OLS, including fixed effects	OLS, including random effects
Constant		14.473[a]
		(5.069)
Openness/GDP	0.0007	0.0570[a]
	(0.03)	(2.947)
Corruption	0.6600[a]	0.9851[a]
	(2.53)	(4.055)
GDP per capita	0.0002[a]	0.0004[a]
	(2.28)	(5.316)
Agriculture sector/GDP	−0.0090	0.1456[a]
	(−0.12)	(−2.382)
Mining sector/GDP	0.1300[a]	0.0288
	(2.09)	(0.526)
Manufacturing sector/GDP	−0.0060	−0.0125
	(−0.08)	(−0.189)
Adjusted R-squared	0.97	0.590
Hausman test	34.81[a]	
Number of observations	238	238

Note: t-statistics are in parentheses.
a. Significant at 5 percent level.
Source: Author's estimates.

TABLE 10.4 REGRESSION RESULTS, INCLUDING CORPORATE AND INCOME TAX
RATES

Variables	AR(1)
Constant	14.7441[a]
	(2.479)
Openness	0.0832[a]
	(4.080)
Corruption index	−0.5078
	(−1.072)
GDP per capita	0.0001
	(1.165)
Agriculture sector/GDP	−0.0462
	(−0.430)
Mining sector/GDP	−0.0866
	(−0.755)
Manufacturing sector/GDP	−0.1127
	(−1.388)
Corporate tax	0.1128
	(1.471)
Income tax	0.2970[a]
	(4.591)
Rho	0.8590a
	(19.354)
Likelihood ratio test	
χ^2	58[a]
Number of observations	134

Note: t-statistics are in parentheses.
OLS=ordinary least squares.
a. Significant at 5 percent level.
Source: Author's estimates.

Results of both regressions—with and without tax variables—are presented
with the usual tradeoff between using a small sample to test a more complete model
and vice versa. For the bigger sample, in both the fixed- and random- effect specifications, corruption and GDP per capita are significant and have the expected positive sign. Openness and the income tax variable are significant for the Ordinary
Least Square, First Order Autoregressive Model, OLS[AR(1)]. The share of agriculture in GDP and the openness index are significant and have the expected sign in
the random-effects specification but not in the fixed-effects model.

The Hausman statistic and R^2 indicate that the fixed-effects model has a better
fit. Thus, fixed-effect results were used to calculate the tax effort index for the bigger sample analysis (figure 10.1). Figure 10.2 shows tax effort index for the
OLS[AR(1)] model with the two tax variables.

This analysis indicates that when high tax rates are not accounted for, Egypt's
tax revenue-to-GDP ratio is consistent with its level of institutional and economic
conditions. Egypt's statutory corporate and income tax rates, however, are higher
than those of many developing and developed countries. Therefore, when Egypt's

FIGURE 10.1 TAX EFFORT INDEX: ECONOMIC AND INSTITUTIONAL VARIABLES, SELECTED COUNTRIES

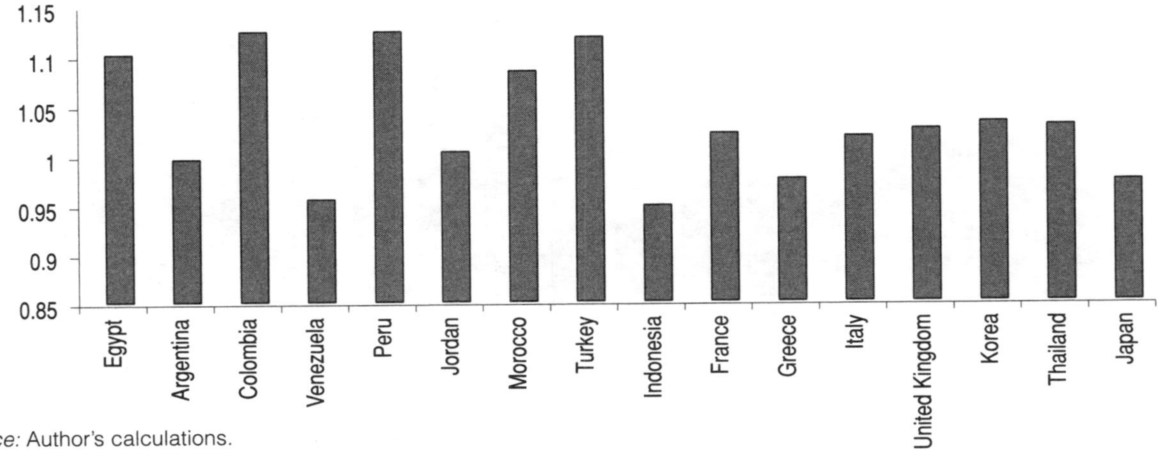

Source: Author's calculations.

FIGURE 10.2 TAX EFFORT INDEX: INCLUDING CORPORATE AND INCOME TAX, SELECTED COUNTRIES

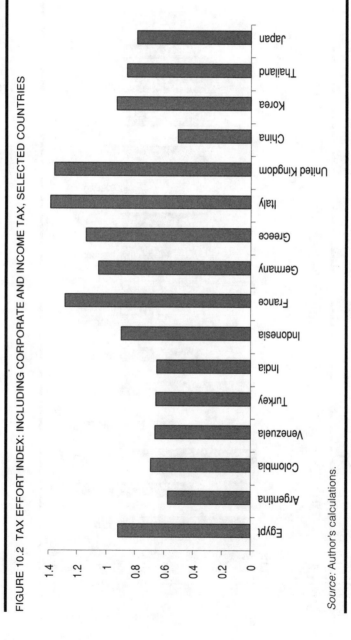

Source: Author's calculations.

166

tax rates are accounted for, the picture changes: Egypt's tax effort index in 1994 was 0.92, indicating a not-so-substantial tax evasion problem. High tax rates and tax evasion combine to produce a situation in which government tax revenue is consistent with revenue predicted—but only by maintaining high income and corporate tax rates.

Comparing Egypt with other developing countries, however, shows that its level of tax evasion, as estimated by the model, is similar to that of other developing countries such as Thailand, Korea and Indonesia, and generally lower than the level of tax evasion prevailing in Latin American countries (Egypt's tax effort index is higher).

Are Taxpayers' Transaction Costs Higher in Egypt Compared with other Countries?

While the previous section suggests that Egypt's tax administration does not adversely affect collected tax revenue, complaints from the private sector indicate that the government's methods of raising tax revenue have an adverse effect on the business environment in Egypt.[14] This paper relies on two business surveys to evaluate the private sector's transaction costs in tax administration; the first covers 154 businesses in Egypt, and the second covers 3,685 businesses in 69 countries.[15] Both surveys identify the institutions that hinder business the most. While the results do not produce a dollar value estimate or index, they help in identifying the relative rank of the tax issue (both rates and administration) as an obstacle to private business, and in clarifying how the situation in Egypt is similar to, or different from, other countries. For developing countries as a group, tax regulations and rates represent the most binding constraint to business with a severity of close to 80 percent (figure 10.3).[16] Corruption is the second greatest constraint, and in many developing countries corruption in taxation and customs represents a significant proportion of the graft perceived in the economy as a whole (figure 10.4). Surprisingly, tax regulations and rates were ranked as the primary obstacles to business activity in developed countries as well as in developing countries, but to a slightly lesser degree. Even in terms of taxpayers' evaluation of the severity of the problem, the range is small as well—with the magnitude of Egypt's problem appearing to be lower than that in developed and other developing countries (figure 10.5).

For a number of reasons, it is necessary to use caution when comparing the results of the Egyptian survey with the results of the international survey. First, in the Egyptian survey, taxpayers were not specifically asked about how they perceive tax rates as an obstacle to private sector participation. The focus was on issues that relate to the transaction between the taxpayer and the authority rather than the applicable tax rate. Second, in the Egyptian survey and the international survey, the severity of various constraints is necessarily a function of the scale of severity provided by the questionnaire. Therefore, ranking the severity of constraints from 0 to 4 in the Egyptian survey and 0 to 6 in the international survey produces degrees of severity that are not directly comparable. Finally, both sur-

FIGURE 10.3 RANKING OF CONSTRAINTS TO BUSINESS (DEVELOPING COUNTRIES)

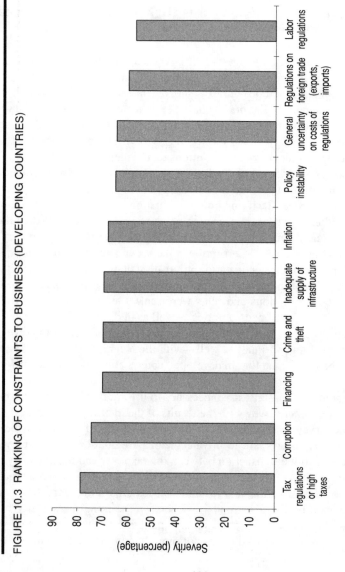

Source: Brunetti, Kinsunko, and Weder (1997).

FIGURE 10.4 RANKING OF CONSTRAINTS TO BUSINESS (DEVELOPED COUNTRIES)

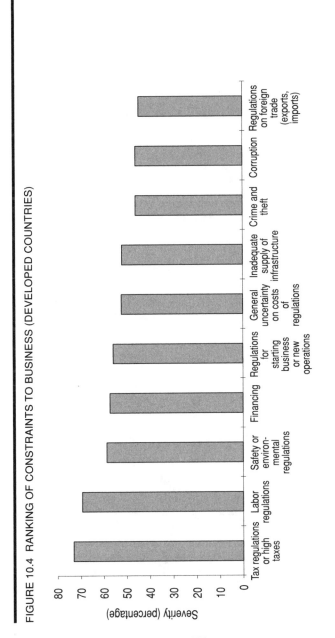

Source: Brunetti, Kinsunko, and Weder (1997).

FIGURE 10.5 RANKING OF CONSTRAINTS TO BUSINESS IN EGYPT

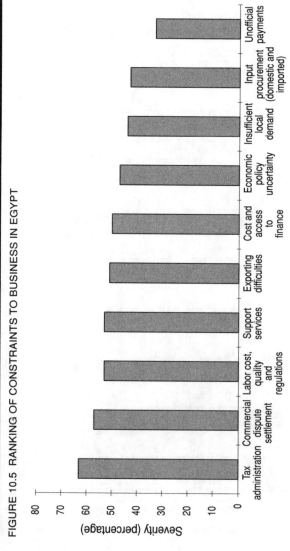

Source: Fawzy and Galal (1997).

veys are ordinal in nature. Thus, while it is adequate to rank obstacles across countries, this rank should not be taken as a proxy for comparing the magnitude of a problem across countries. Although this paper considers severity values across regions, this can be misleading. For example, a businessperson in a developed country who spends two weeks on an audit with the tax authority may perceive that cost as a severe constraint to business and would rank tax issues as severe. His or her counterpart in a developing country may not consider spending two weeks on an audit an excessive loss and thus would not rank tax regulations and rates as a severe obstacle to business.

This discussion brings us to the Egyptian survey and its treatment of various issues related to the tax authority. Two results bring the "contract," or relationship, between taxpayers and the tax authority to the forefront of the tax evasion and transaction costs debate in Egypt. When asked to rank lack of trust, arbitrary estimates and inefficiency of the dispute settlement system, respondents cited these three aspects of the tax payment and collection relationship as fairly severe obstacles to business activity in Egypt (figure 10.6). The following section analyzes the Egyptian tax payment and collection relationship's weaknesses that may be responsible for these three specific problems.

FIGURE 10.6 SURVEY RESULTS: RANKING OF TAX ADMINISTRATION CONSTRAINTS IN EGYPT

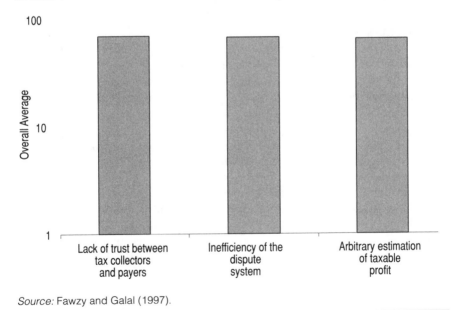

Source: Fawzy and Galal (1997).

The Main Sources of Transaction Costs in Egypt's Tax Administration

If the relationship between taxpayers and the tax authority is analyzed as a voluntary contract between two parties, it is clear that this relationship can suffer from high transaction costs because of the importance of private information, moral hazard, and adverse selection. These three problems result in higher transaction costs for both the tax authority and taxpayers. Therefore, the goal of tax administration reform must be to streamline incentives of both parties and discourage tax evasion through reducing or eliminating these weaknesses. At the same time, reform should minimize the enforcement costs for the tax authority and the voluntary compliance costs for taxpayers.

Potential Weaknesses in a Contract

This section discusses the main contractual weaknesses that can arise in any contract. Each weakness presents policymakers with a pattern of behavior that is consistent with the private interest of parties but contradicts the general efficiency of different government policies. The following section analyzes the relationship from the perspective of a potential taxpayer and provides a model that highlights possible divergences between taxpayers' incentives and the government's goal of minimizing tax evasion. It identifies the parameters that can be responsible for a taxpayer's decision not to comply with his/her tax payment obligations. The last section assesses these parameters for the Egyptian Unified Income Tax Law.

THE IMPORTANCE OF PRIVATE INFORMATION

Parties to a contract may have private information that they conceal when entering into the contract (precontractual opportunism) or they may change their position in the middle of a long-term relationship, thus holding the other party "hostage" (postcontractual opportunism). Taxpayers' private information comes from intimate knowledge of their costs, revenues, records, and so forth. The tax authority's private information comes from any discretionary power it has in interpreting and implementing various clauses of the law. The greater the discretionary power, the more room for postcontractual opportunism on the part of the tax authority. As for taxpayers, they only have the potential for precontractual opportunism (that is, taxpayers enter into that relationship with the intent to hide relevant activity and profit information). They cannot exercise postcontractual opportunism, however, because the authority's right to penalize taxpayers protects it from their opportunistic behavior. Bonuses and incentives to tax collectors are private information that influences the tax collector's behavior in maximizing the tax revenue collected. This information is not accessible to taxpayers, yet it affects tax collectors' estimates of their tax liability.

MORAL HAZARD

The problem of moral hazard arises when a change in the law or regulation causes people to change their behavior in a way that is not economically efficient or consistent with the law. The critical element in this case is that trying to verify that people actually changed their behavior is generally costly or impossible. Thus it is impossible to include penalties or other enforcement mechanisms in the new law or regulation.[17]

In the tax payment relationship, taxpayers can behave in a way that creates a moral hazard problem. When tax collectors systematically revise records upward, taxpayers come to expect this type of behavior and underreport their profits or the size of their economic activity, thus hindering the efficient collection of taxes. If tax collectors have the discretionary power to disregard taxpayers' records, some tax collectors will have a tendency to manipulate the system to extract unofficial payments. Another example of moral hazard is when taxpayers are not penalized for taking cases to trial unnecessarily. If taxpayers do not pay interest and legal expenses on contested funds, they will tend to delay cases—especially when they are using the tax dues as working capital for several years.

ADVERSE SELECTION
Adverse selection occurs when the law governing a specific economic activity discourages particular groups that would otherwise participate in that activity, while encouraging the participation of other groups who reduce the efficiency of the whole sector.[18]

Adverse selection arises in tax administration, for example, when taxpayers are discouraged from engaging in business because the law is not perceived as providing equal and transparent treatment to all taxpayers. It has been repeatedly mentioned, for example, that ambiguity in tax payment, the perception of corruption and lengthy dispute settlement discourage foreign investors from investing in Egypt. These factors also encourage small domestic investors to revert to the informal sector. Another example of adverse selection, though harder to document, is that tax collectors more prone to accepting illegal payments compete to locate themselves in industrial areas and prosperous regions that may offer more opportunities for side payments. Because of this competition, dishonest tax collectors will "crowd out" honest tax collectors in the areas where this phenomenon produces the most significant damage.

The Tax Payment Contract
Given the weaknesses of the contract discussed in the previous section, the analysis now considers how the importance of private information, moral hazard and adverse selection can influence taxpayers' incentives in their interaction with the tax authority.[19] To simplify, the discussion relies on LeBaube and Vehorn's (1992) classification of taxpayers. While the authors do not link each group of taxpayers to the contract weaknesses discussed here, the correspondence between weaknesses and each taxpayer group is apparent. According to LeBaube and Vehorn, there are four types of actual and potential taxpayers:

Group 1: Those who understand and comply willingly with the law (no contractual weakness).

Group 2: Those who want to comply but do not understand the law (private information problem).

Group 3: Those who understand the law but choose not to comply fully
(moral hazard, private information).

Group 4: Those who deliberately do not comply
(adverse selection problem).

Dividing the taxpayer population into these groups helps in devising the right
"incentive-compatible contract" for each group, thus increasing the probability of
compliance. The goal is to maximize the number of taxpayers in Group 1; discourage members in Group 1 from moving to Groups 2, 3, and 4, and encourage members of Groups 2, 3, and 4 to move to Group 1. Moving taxpayers from Group 2 to
Group 1, which entails understanding and complying with the tax laws, involves
educating taxpayers, simplifying the law and computerizing the system to reduce
the cost of compliance to taxpayers and tax collectors, thus eliminating high transaction costs in tax payment. Many countries have focused on this aspect of reforming tax administration. Table 10.5 lists countries with various types of taxpayer
information programs.

The analysis assumes, therefore, that with a simpler system and assistance from
the tax authority, transaction costs will be diminished for a subset of taxpayers by
reducing information collection costs, and that taxpayers will move from Group 2
to Group 1. The issue is more complicated for Groups 3 and 4. A taxpayer in one of
these latter groups decides whether to pay or not to pay taxes depending on the
outcome of an objective function that has the following general format:

The tax burden if the taxpayer decides to pay:

$$C^p = t * R + TC^p,$$

where C^p is the cost to the firm of paying taxes; t is the tax rate; R is the taxable
income; and TC^p is the transaction cost of filing and auditing if the taxpayer decides
to comply.

The tax burden if the taxpayer decides not to file:

$$C^e = p_d * (penalty + t * R) + TC^e,$$

where C^e is the expected cost to the taxpayer of not paying taxes (expected cost of
evasion); p_d is the probability of detection; t and R are the tax rate and taxable
income, as previously defined; and TC^e is the transaction costs of filing and auditing
in the case of detected tax evasion. In order to achieve full compliance, then, C^e
must always be larger than C^p, or:

$$p_d * (penalty + t * R) + TC^e > t * R + TC^p.$$

One way to guarantee this inequality is to have p_d equal to 1. In that case, each
taxpayer has an incentive to pay taxes for any positive penalty level as long as the
transaction costs of detected tax evasion are not less than the transaction costs of

TABLE 10.5 TAXPAYER INFORMATION PROGRAMS IN SELECTED COUNTRIES

	Argentina	Canada	Chile	Colombia	Jamaica	Mexico	Trinidad	USA
Publications								
Tax guides (instructions)	x	x	x	x	x	x	x	x
Pamphlets and bulletins	x	x		x	x	x	x	x
Technical publications		x		x	x	x	x	x
Audio cassettes for the visually impaired	x							
Newspaper supplements			x	x	x	x	x	x
Reminders in the press			x					
Media								
Radio or television commercials	x	x	x	x	x	x	x	x
Special television programs		x		x	x		x	x
Video cassettes		x				x		x
Press conferences			x			x		x
Telephone contact								
Telephone assistance	x	x	x	x	x	x	x	x
Tele-refund		x				x		x
Tele-info		x						x
Personal contacts								
Walk-in service	x	x	x	x	x	x	x	x
Correspondence								
Individually drafted letters		x	x		x		x	x
Standardized letters		x	x		x		x	x
Other programs								
Volunteers		x					x	x
High school programs	x	x	x		x	x	x	x
Rural tax scene kits		x						x
Native outreach		x						x
Training for new businesses							x	x
Seminars and conferences	x		x		x		x	

Source: LeBaube and Vehorn (1992).

paying taxes voluntarily. This policy, however, can be extremely costly to the government. In all countries, the probability of detecting tax evasion never equals 1. Therefore, a more realistic scenario must be considered in which p_d is less than 1. In this case, to guarantee that each taxpayer pays taxes, the following inequality must hold:

$$\text{penalty} > \frac{(1 - p_d) * t * R - (TC^e - TC^v)}{P_d} \; .$$

If $TC^e = TC^p$, which means that filing costs and auditing will not be higher in the case of evasion than filing costs and auditing in the case of compliance, the inequality condition reduces to:

$$penalty > -\frac{(1-p_d)}{P_d} \, t * R \qquad \text{or}$$

$$penalty > \left[\frac{1}{P_d} - 1\right] t * R.$$

The higher the tax rate (t), or the taxable income (R), the larger the penalty needed to persuade taxpayers to pay taxes, given a fixed probability of detection (p). If the penalty is not a fixed dollar value but rather a function of the tax due, the relationship becomes:

$$k(t * R) > \left[\frac{1}{P_d} - 1\right] t * R$$

where k is a constant greater than 1 that is sometimes determined on a progressive basis—that is, the larger the tax due, the larger the constant that is used to determine the penalty.

In many cases, detecting tax evasion entails a process of auditing and scrutiny that is more detailed than the original filing. In other words, detecting tax evasion involves an additional penalty that taxpayers would want to avoid. In this case, $TC^e > TC^p$ and the penalty has to satisfy the following condition:

$$penalty > \frac{(1-p_d) * t * R - (TC^e - TC^p)}{P_d}$$

While the goal of the tax authority should be to reduce transaction costs for taxpayers in both the tax compliance and tax evasion scenarios, reducing the difference between transaction costs in the two scenarios has the added benefit of reducing incentives for tax evasion. To reduce tax evasion, the following parameters are important:

- The size of the penalty, whether it is a function of the tax due or not (penalty and k), and whether there is a progressive schedule;

- The difference between transaction costs and auditing in compliance and tax evasion scenarios;

- The probability of detection and whether it increases with a history of evasion;

- The tax rate *(t)* and the comprehensiveness of the tax base *(R)*.

The following section analyzes how these parameters affect the tax payment contract in Egypt and discusses the resulting weaknesses in the relationship. The next main section, "Reducing Transaction Costs in Tax Administration," draws on other countries' experiences to provide remedies for deficiencies in the tax payment contract.

The Tax Payment Contract in Egypt

Next we look at each of the four parameters identified in the previous section and analyze how these parameters may be changed in the Egyptian case to increase the willingness of taxpayers to voluntarily pay their taxes. These parameters are 1) the size of penalty, 2) the difference between transaction costs in compliance and noncompliance, 3) the probability of detection, and 4) tax rates and tax base.

THE SIZE OF PENALTY

Two types of penalties are used to induce taxpayers to comply voluntarily—criminal and financial.[20] This section examines each of these penalties in the case of Egypt. Failure to comply with various tax obligations (such as registering, filing, keeping records, withholding) can result in a financial penalty of 10 percent of the tax due with a maximum of £E1,000. Repeated offenses within three years result in an increased penalty. Also, the law allows the tax authority to demand compensation that ranges from 25 percent to 300 percent of the amount of unpaid taxes. Failure to submit a tax return on time results in a 20 percent penalty of the tax due, which may be reduced to 10 percent if the taxpayer reconciles with the authority. From discussions with tax authority personnel, it is not clear when any of these financial penalties are actually imposed, and the information available for taxpayers about their enforcement is quite little. This clearly diminishes the effectiveness of the financial penalty as a measure to curtail tax evasion.

In the Egyptian Unified Income Tax Law 157/1981, many references to criminal penalty are vague, citing "punishment by imprisonment" as a possible penalty for failing to register with the tax authority (clause 133) or to withhold and pay third-party taxes, and submitting inaccurate records to hide taxable income.[21] These infractions are punishable by either imprisonment of up to six months or a financial penalty. The common practice in tax cases, however, is to make a distinction between tax evasion and tax fraud. The latter are cases in which the tax authority has evidence showing that the taxpayer intentionally fabricated records, failed to acknowledge a significant line of activity, or altered invoices. In these cases, the taxpayers' records for the five years prior to detection are examined. Only under those specific cases does the tax authority invoke possible criminal penalties.

The experiences of other countries suggest that high criminal penalties tend not to be used frequently, especially when it is widely believed that evasion is prevalent, whether that is actually the case or not. Therefore, countries tend to use other means to censure evasion, including financial penalties, before they turn to increasing criminal penalties. In Egypt, there has been a trend recently towards financial penalties rather than criminal penalties in tax evasion cases. Confusion about which penalties apply in which cases and doubts about enforcement increase transaction costs for taxpayers that are willing to comply. Combined with uncertainty about the tax collectors' role in determining the penalty, the present system increases transaction costs for both taxpayers and the tax authority simultaneously.

THE DIFFERENCE BETWEEN TRANSACTION COSTS IN COMPLIANCE AND NONCOMPLIANCE

Figure 10.7 is a flowchart that shows the steps for paying income tax and how these differ if the taxpayer decides to file a tax return, file on time and according to required specifications, or not file at all. The first junction (node 1.1) at which the taxpayer's decision may result in moral hazard is if the taxpayer decides to spend time and effort preparing a tax return while there is a high probability that the tax authority will reject it (node 2) as an underestimation of the taxable income. Comprehensive auditing and minimal penalties combined with a high probability that the return is rejected, create a situation in which the taxpayer can "delegate" the job of completing a tax return to tax collectors. This is a burden on the tax authority that compromises its other tax administration functions.

At node 2.2, if the taxpayer decides to file an incomplete return, which is not a fraudulent return, any arbitrariness in the tax authority's revision takes the dispute to an appeals committee. If, on the other hand, the return is considered fraudulent, the taxpayer is subject to fines or a prison sentence (node 2.3), which is usually suspended. If the tax authority does not settle the nonfraudulent record (node 3.1), the next step is to go to court. Arbitrariness in the tax collection process brings a taxpayer closer to a payoff if he or she decides not to file (node 1.2) and if he or she goes to court (node 4). There is room for the taxpayer and the tax collector to manipulate this system. At node 3, neither the tax authority nor the taxpayer have an incentive not to go to court given the advantageous delays in deciding tax cases.

THE PROBABILITY OF DETECTION

In a comprehensive audit system, each taxpayer's records are audited. Assuming the tax authority has unlimited resources, the government wastes a lot of resources making sure that each taxpayer pays accurately and promptly. Governments, however, never have unlimited resources to spend on tax collection and the budget for tax collection can be either used to perform quick and rough audits for all taxpayers or to target a sample of taxpayers through selective but detailed audits. In selective audit programs, the sample can be random, so each taxpayer has an equal probability of being audited. Or audited taxpayers can be selected according to some formula or selection criterion not known to taxpayers. In both of these approaches, tax collectors do not resort to arbitrary estimates. Taxpayers realize that if they get audited they will be subject to extensive examination, and therefore they will be meticulous in filing their records. The tax payment relationship will be characterized by fewer disputes without necessarily increasing its tax collection budget. Thus,

FIGURE 10.7 TAX PAYMENT CYCLE

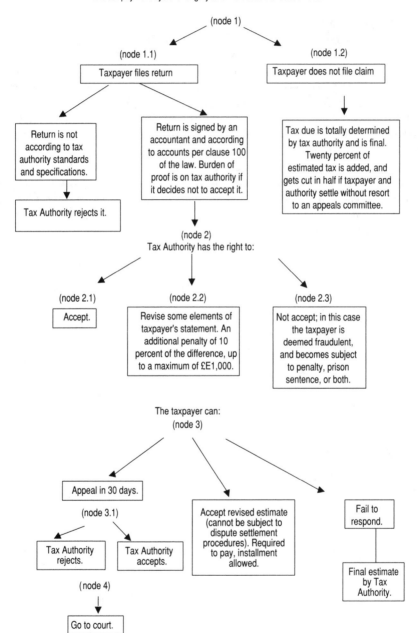

The tax payment cycle is lengthy and increases transaction costs

Source: Law 157/1981 modified by 187/1993.

increasing the "true" probability of detection reduces transaction costs for the tax authority without necessarily increasing them for taxpayers—a net welfare improvement in the system.

TAX RATES AND TAX BASE

When comparing Egypt's statutory corporate and income rates to countries in Latin America, the Middle East and North Africa, and Southeast Asia, Egypt's corporate rate is higher than most countries (table 10.6). Except for India and other Middle Eastern countries, the norm appears to be 30 percent, and many countries have even lower tax rates. In addition to a high corporate tax rate, individual income taxes, which are usually progressive for different income brackets, can represent a significant burden on the self-employed if the highest tax rate applies at a low threshold. Taking the ratio of the threshold to which the highest marginal tax rate on individual income applies relative to GDP per capita, this reveals that Middle Eastern countries in general have higher ratios than the Latin American group (with the exception of Chile) and ASEAN member countries. For Egypt, the income level at which the highest rate applies is only 4.61 times GDP per capita. That ratio is as high as one hundred times GDP per capita in some countries. Only Egypt and Morocco have a combination of high personal tax rates, a low threshold and a high corporate tax rate. Chile's individual income is heavily taxed, but its corporate rate is the second lowest rate after Iran.

TABLE 10.6 INDIVIDUAL AND CORPORATE TAX RATE

Country	Highest marginal tax rate Individual Rate (percentage) 1996	On income exceeding (US$), 1996 (a)	US$ GDP per capita 1995 (b)	Ratio (a):(b)	Highest marginal tax rate Corporate Rate (percentage) 1996
Latin America					
Brazil	20	n.a.	4,601.01		25
Argentina	30	120,060	8,054.93	14.90	30
Colombia	35	48,360	2,303.68	21.00	35
Uruguay	0	n.a.	5,594.67		30
Chile	45	6,523	4,739.37	1.38	15
Ecuador	25	64,519	1,565.36	41.23	25
El Salvador	30	22,857	1,656.67	13.80	25
Nicaragua	30	25,310	419.38	60.40	30
Paraguay	0	n.a.	1,859.63		30
Venezuela	34	n.a.	2,718.80		34
Peru	30	54,495	2,501.66	21.79	30
Middle East and North Africa					
Egypt	48[a]	4,705	1,020.97	4.61	40
Bahrain	n.a.	n.a.	n.a.		n.a.
Iran	54	17,3851	1,566.20	111.00	10

Country	Highest marginal tax rate Individual		US$ GDP per capita 1995 (b)	Ratio (a):(b)	Highest marginal tax rate Corporate Rate (percentage) 1996
	Rate (percentage) 1996	On income exceeding (US$), 1996 (a)			
Israel	50	57,256	1,5674.19	3.65	36
Jordan	n.a.	n.a.	599.34		n.a.
Kuwait	0	n.a.	1,404.20		55
Lebanon	n.a.	n.a.	n.a.		n.a.
Morocco	44	6,697	1,195.92	5.60	35
Oman	0	n.a.	5,385.90		50
Syria	n.a.	n.a.	n.a.		n.a.
Tunisia	n.a.	n.a.	2,262.99		n.a.
Turkey	55	24,7895	2,141.40	115.78	25
United Arab Emirates	n.a.	n.a.	n.a.		n.a.
Yemen	n.a.	n.a.	n.a.		n.a.
ASEAN Countries					
India	40	3,824	362.63	10.56	40
Indonesia	30	22,727	1,038.36	21.89	30
Malaysia	30	58,594	3,674.64	15.95	30
Singapore	30	273,841	28,463.48	9.62	27
Sri Lanka	35	2,101	703.80	2.99	35
Industrialized European Countries					
Austria	50	63,091	22,102.3	2.85	34
Belgium	55	76,011	20,856.8	3.64	39
Denmark	65	n.a.	30,100.6		38
Finland	39	61.140	22,269.1	2.75	28
France	n.a.	n.a.	23,758.8		33
Germany	53	77,506	20,699.3	3.74	30
Greece	45	62,474	5,426.4	11.51	40
Ireland	48	14,246	5,937.4	2.40	40
Italy	51	184,078	19,134.0	9.62	37
Netherlands	60	53,468	22,879.7	2.34	37
Romania	60	6,875	37.9	181.40	38
Sweden	30	28,024	21634.9	1.30	28
United Kingdom	40	39,844	6348.4	6.28	33
Pacific Countries					
Japan	50	300,782	38458.7	7.82	38
Australia	47	38,841	32348.9	1.20	36
New Zealand	33	19,837	36329.8	0.55	33
Papua New Guinea	35	16,969	1076.0	15.77	25

n.a. = Not available.
a. Reduced to 40 percent as of January 1998.
Source: World Bank (1997) (Tax Rate); *IFS* (May 1997) (GDP per Capita);
World Economic Forum (1996, 1997).

Reducing Transaction Costs in Tax Administration

Manipulating Parameters in the Egyptian Tax Contract

The first parameter that works against prompt compliance with the Egyptian tax system is the difference between transaction costs in evasion and transaction costs in compliance (TC^e-TC^v). The analysis in the previous sections suggests that dealing with the tax administration does not reward taxpayers, in terms of low transaction costs, who comply. While the tax reform system must focus on reducing transaction costs in both evasion and compliance scenarios to minimize delays in collecting tax revenue and implementing penalties, focusing on reducing transaction costs in compliance has the added benefit of reducing tax evasion incentives.

To encourage voluntary compliance through the probability of detection, and at the same time free resources for extensive audits, a tax system can concentrate on tax returns for the current year and block previous years from review. If any significant violation is detected, then the preceding periods not barred by a statute of limitations could be investigated. This system works better with incentives for future compliance as opposed to periodic tax amnesties that reward tax evaders and reduce the cost of tax evasion. Similar systems have been implemented in Argentina, Chile, and Mexico and have been found to produce reasonable results (Silvani 1992). Because of the large number of cases in Egypt that need to be audited, there is little expectation that audits will be thorough or complete. Even though the probability of an audit is officially equal to one, the probability of a thorough audit is significantly less than one.

The system can also manipulate tax rates and base to reduce tax evasion. A high rate (t), combined with limited personal exemptions (producing a large R), such as £E3,000 per year for a married person with children, £E2,500 for a married person with no children, and £E2,000 for a single person, creates a greater incentive for tax evasion. While reducing the tax rate may increase compliance, this policy may not be feasible now because it would reduce government revenues. Reducing the tax rate can be postponed until other policies are implemented addressing the probability of detection, enforcement of penalties, and reduction of transaction costs. An approach taken by many countries is to focus on the inequality for larger taxpayers (large R), by increasing the probability of detection for large taxpayers, extensive audits and so forth. This policy is discussed in detail later.

Rely on Third Parties

Many countries rely on a third party for specific aspects of tax administration. There are two theories behind including third parties in the process of tax payment. The first is to provide checks and balances on taxpayers and reduce the information disadvantage that the tax authority has in estimating each taxpayer's true profits. The system of additions and deductions in Egypt is an example of this. Law 77/1969 first introduced the system of additions and discounts requiring government agencies and public sector entities to deduct 10–15 percent of any payment to noncommercial professionals. The funds are submitted to the tax authority toward payment of the professional's tax liability. Law 157/1981 and later Law 187/1993 generalized these requirements to include joint venture companies, trade associations, hospitals, educational institutions, and a host of other establishments. Furthermore, these entities are required to add to the price of any good or service a similar percentage that is delivered to the tax authority on a regular basis.

The benefit of this system is that it gives the tax authority an estimate of taxpayers' activity. The tax authority is guaranteed at least the percentage withheld by the third party required to perform the collection job. This system has numerous administrative problems, which have been discussed extensively in the Egyptian press recently, including the burden on firms, especially small and medium-size firms; loopholes manipulated by third parties to avoid prompt payment; and the inability of the government to collect tax funds withheld by investment companies during their tax-exempt status. These, however, are not the focus of this discussion.

It is important instead to consider how the system of additions and deductions interacts with the contractual setting that underlies the whole relationship between taxpayers and the tax administration. If the government provides the right incentives for taxpayers to file taxes and minimizes the probability of evasion, then the system of addition and deductions becomes redundant. If, however, the government does not succeed in addressing voluntary compliance, then the usefulness of the system of additions and deductions continues to be limited. Revenue from additions and deductions accounted for 7.5 percent of total tax revenue during 1994–95 (*Al-Ahram* 1998). Any system of selective audits and self-assessment will compound the probability of tax evasion on the part of third parties. Thus, the government, again, will face an incentive problem with third parties as well as with the taxpayers.

Extensive reliance on the discretion of tax collectors can be viewed as a kind of reliance on third parties. This system, however, uses the bureaucracy to implement government policies. Principal–agent problems, lack of incentives, contradictory or unclear objectives, and room for rent-seeking are some of the usual problems encountered with this arrangement. To evaluate what kind of remuneration package can eliminate these problems in the bureaucracy, Van Rijckeghem and Weder (1997) estimate that eradicating corruption in the civil service by improving pay to public servants could require increasing the wages compared to manufacturing wages by three to seven times. The results of this report are generally weak, but they indicate how expensive raising tax collectors' wages is as a means to overcome tax evasion. Delegating assessment to taxpayers rather than collectors can be equally effective with a system that "recruits" taxpayers in addition to paid collectors. Relying on tax collectors adds one more link, thus shifting accountability further up the chain (see also Chand and Moene 1997).

The government can also rely on third parties that have a comparative advantage in specific tax administration jobs. Many Latin American countries leave printing forms, collecting payments and processing data to private sector banks or corporations. Colombia, for example, hires a private company to print and distribute tax forms through the mail. Private banks and other financial institutions are increasingly authorized to receive documents, process payments and assist the public during tax payment time. Banks also are authorized to receive tax payments, especially from large taxpayers. Payment for these services is usually in fees, but banks are sometimes allowed to use tax funds interest-free for a few months.

The question is: Can the government rely on incentives to tax accountants rather than taxpayers to get accurate profit or income records? The Mexican system utilizes this principle. This system of Expert Certification allows the taxpayer to utilize a public accountant. The tax authority considers the accountant's signature a "guarantee" on the accuracy of the return; any mistakes are the sole responsibility of the accountant. That system is voluntary, so a taxpayer chooses whether or not to rely on the accountant's services. Also, if the taxpayer decides to hire a public accountant, he or she has the freedom to choose the one that can guarantee confidentiality (Acuna 1992, p. 388).

From the experiences of other countries, it appears that the theory behind relying on a third party is relevant: if the reason is to utilize the comparative advantages of private parties, such as banks and accountants, the results are positive. If, however, the objective is to provide checks and balances, the intended results are rarely achieved unless combined with huge spending on other measures. Implementing other measures simultaneously, however, makes it difficult to evaluate the effectiveness of relying on third parties as providers of these checks and balances.

Distinguishing between Small and Large Taxpayers in the Probability of Auditing

In many countries, the tax authority has two different departments or programs to handle small and large taxpayers. Large taxpayers generally face a more extensive tax audit, a higher probability of being audited, or both in a selective audit system (table 10.7). Within that system, and over time, emphasis can be extended from the large taxpayers to small taxpayers. Publicizing this policy, however, can defeat the purpose of reducing tax evasion. While it guarantees compliance among larger taxpayers, it can cost the government extensive losses in terms of smaller taxpayers who reevaluate the probability of detection.

Other measures that distinguish between small and large taxpayers, exempt taxpayers under a specific income threshold from registration or filing. This policy reduces the tax administration authorities' paperwork, but makes detection of evaders moving in and out of that exempted level difficult. Requiring registration and filing, whether income is taxable or not, reduces the incentive to evade taxation in a specific year. The taxpayer knows that evading taxes in a specific year does not mean the tax authority does not have any record for tracing his or her activity.

Computerization, National Registration, and Tax Identification Numbers

Almost all countries embarking on tax reform introduce some measure to improve the technological capabilities of their tax collection agencies. Depending on the severity of the problem, the solution differs from one country to the other. Spain's tax reform in 1983 focused on computerization exclusively. Bolivia's tax revenue-to-GDP ratio was 1 percent before its reform program in 1985. That problem required drastic measures including hiring international consultants and establishing

TABLE 10.7 COUNTRIES WITH SPECIAL SYSTEMS TO MONITOR LARGE TAXPAYERS

Country	Collection procedures	Auditing procedures
Argentina	Yes	Yes
Australia	No	Yes
Austria	No	Yes
Belgium	No	Yes
Benin	Yes	Yes
Bolivia	Yes	Yes
Brazil	No	Yes
Burkina Faso	Yes	Yes
Canada	No	Yes
Colombia	Yes	Yes
Côte d'Ivoire	Yes	Yes
El Salvador	Yes	Yes
France	No	Yes
Mali	Yes	Yes
Mauritania	Yes	Yes
Nicaragua	Yes	Yes
Niger	Yes	Yes
Paraguay	Yes	Yes
Peru	Yes	Yes
Senegal	Yes	Yes
Spain	No	Yes
Sri Lanka	Yes	Yes
Togo	Yes	Yes
United Kingdom	Yes	Yes
United States	No	Yes
Uruguay	Yes	No

Source: Tanzi and Pellechio (1995).

FIGURE 10.8 REVENUE EFFECT OF TAX REFORM PROGRAMS IN SELECTED
COUNTRIES

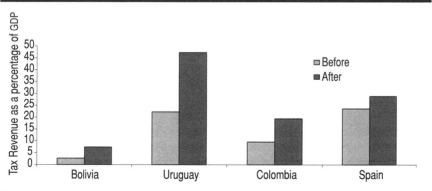

Source: IMF (1997a) (tax revenue); IMF (1997b) (GDP).

a Tax Collection Under Secretariat and the General Bureau of Internal Revenue. Uruguay implemented a more gradual approach to tax reform with a system that raised collected revenue from 11 percent of GDP in 1984 to 13 percent in 1990. Almost all countries introduced a variation of these elements, such as tax identification numbers, required registration, supplying tax returns through magnetic media for large taxpayers, and so forth. Figure 10.8 presents the revenue effect of tax reforms on selected countries.

Conclusion

This paper investigates two issues that dominate the debate on tax administration in Egypt: tax evasion and taxpayers' high transaction costs in tax administration. Empirical analysis evaluating Egypt's tax revenue relative to GDP in a cross-country analysis shows that tax evasion in Egypt is consistent, to a great extent, with its economic and institutional conditions. Adjusting for Egypt's high tax rates, the analysis indicates that tax evasion exists, though it is still not high in comparison to other countries. This combination of tax evasion and high tax rates highlights the importance of addressing tax evasion before any attempt is made to reduce corporate or income tax rates to maintain or increase tax revenue.

An evaluation of the level of transaction costs involved in tax administration, based on business sector surveys in both Egypt and 69 other countries, shows that tax issues are perceived as major obstacles to business both in developed and developing countries. The survey of Egypt shows that specific obstacles to business relate to the tax authorities' discretion and arbitrariness.

The literature on contracts and transaction costs provides tools to evaluate the tax system and incentives for both taxpayers and the tax authority. The analysis identifies contractual weaknesses that increase tax evasion and transaction costs for both taxpayers and the tax authority. Any effective attempt to reform tax administration in Egypt must address these weaknesses with an emphasis on developing a system that ensures that incentives to participants reinforce the system's efficiency instead of focusing on measures to "police" the parties involved.

Notes

1.   There are third parties that are involved in that transaction. For instance, public and private entities required to implement the system of additions and deductions bear the cost of keeping records and withholding and submitting these funds. This paper does not examine these issues, in part, because the system of additions and deductions itself is under reconsideration.

2.   An earlier version of this paper was presented at the Mediterranean Development Forum (MDF) 1998 in Marrakech. The author is grateful to Ahmed Galal and Samiha Fawzy for their comments on earlier drafts of the paper that significantly improved this version. She would also like to express her appreciation to those who participated in the "Role of the

State" Conference, which was held in Beirut in February 1998, and the MDF Cairo meeting, which was held in June 1998, for their useful comments and suggestions. The author would also like to thank Marwa Kassem for diligent research assistance.

3.   See for example, Klein, Crawford, and Alchian (1978); Klein (1988); Masten (1984); Williamson (1976); Monteverde and Teece (1982); Klein and Leffler (1981); Leffler and Rucker (1991).

4.   Based on the estimated cost of underreporting taxable income only.

5.   Documented unpaid taxes as of June 1996.

6.   Applying a 42 percent income tax rate to an estimated £E190 billion informal economy.

7.   Other estimates of tax evasion in Egypt rely on the number of tax evasion cases detected. In 1995, these were 967 cases worth £E7.2 billion (*Al-Ahrar* 1996).

8.   See also Tait, Alan A., and Barry J. Eichengreen (1978) and Tanzi, Vito (1968).

9.   A variable that captures variations in marginal effective tax rates could be more useful than statutory rates because it takes into consideration all the relevant tax holidays, exemptions, and so forth.

10.   This argument ignores possible Laffer Curve effects in which the tax rate elasticity of tax revenue may be greater than 1, thus resulting in higher tax rates and reducing total tax revenue. Accounting for that possibility in the context of a cross-country analysis is difficult.

11.   The original sample used to estimate the effect of economic variables consists of 388 observations from 70 countries. Results of this analysis are available upon request.

12.   For a presentation of the fixed- and random-effects estimation model, see Greene (1990).

13.   The way the corruption index is defined, with higher values corresponding to low corruption, translates into the expected positive relationship: the higher the index value, the higher the tax revenue-to-GDP ratio.

14.   Quantitative analysis of these two areas, especially in a cross-country context, can be extremely difficult if not impossible because it is largely subjective.

15.   For details about methodology, coverage and other results, see Fawzy and Galal (1997) and Brunetti, Kinsunko, and Weder (1997).

16.   The survey questionnaire combines tax rates and tax regulations as a single constraint. Therefore, concentrating on transaction costs separately is not possible.

17.   The classic example of moral hazard is a government requiring car owners to buy car insurance. Once a car owner buys coverage, and the more comprehensive the coverage is, the more likely it is that he or she will drive recklessly knowing that any damages to the car will be fully or partially paid by the insurance company.

18.   A classic example of adverse selection comes from the used-car market. Because it is hard to determine the quality of a used car, a buyer will only be willing to pay for the "expected" quality of the car. Even if the car appears to be in good shape, the buyer will discount the quality by the possibility that there is an undetectable problem in the car. This creates a situation in which only owners of low-quality cars will be willing to utilize that market, and owners of high-quality cars will be less willing to rely on that market to sell their cars.

19.   This paper focuses on the contract between the tax authority and taxpayers. Other contracts that affect the efficiency of tax payment and collection are the relationships between the authority and tax collectors, the taxpayer and accountants, the tax authority and other government bodies, and the tax authority and the judiciary. These contracts are discussed here only to the extent that they directly affect the contract between the tax authority and taxpayers. A more thorough analysis of these other contracts is beyond the scope of this paper.

20.   In the Egyptian Unified Income Tax Law 157/1981, financial penalties come under Chapter 10 (Penalties), and various penalties in the course of regular tax payment procedures come under Chapter 6 (General Rules) and Chapter 7 (Appeals). The discussion of the appeals mechanism is vague in the law, and many of the actual procedures are governed by internal rules established by the tax authority and not generally known to the taxpayer.

21.   Those include mainly salary witholdings and funds withheld under the additions and deductions system.

References

Abdel-Rahman, A.M. 1998. "Egypt's General Sales Tax: Recent Developments and Reforms Ahead." Working Paper No. 22. Egyptian Center for Economic Studies, Cairo. March.

Acuna, L. F. Ramirez. 1992. "Privatization of Tax Administration." In Richard M. Bird and Milka Casanegra DeJantscher, eds., *Improving Tax Administration in Developing Countries*. Washington, D.C.: International Monetary Fund.

Al-Ahram (Cairo). 1998. January 24.

Al Ahram Al Iktisadi (Cairo). 1997. May 26.

Al Ahrar (Cairo). 1996. Cairo. January 1.

Brunetti, Aymo, Gregory Kinsunko, and Beatrice Weder. 1997. "Institutional Obstacles to Doing Business: Region-by-Region. Results from a Worldwide Survey of the Private Sector." Policy Research Working Paper No. 1759. World Bank, Washington, D.C., April.

Coase, Ronald H. 1960. "The Problem of Social Cost." *Journal of Law and Economics* 3(October): 1–44.

———1984. "The New Institutional Economics." *Journal of Institutional and Theoretical Economics* 140(March): 229–31.

———1992. "The Institutional Structure of Production." *American Economic Review* (September): 713–19.

Chand, Sheetal K., and Karl O. Moene. 1997. "Fiscal Affairs Corruption." IMF WP/97/100. International Monetary Fund, Washington, D.C.

Chelliah, Raja J. 1971. "Trends in Taxation in Developing Countries." *Staff Papers* 18: 254–331. International Monetary Fund, Washington, D.C.

Fawzy, Samiha, and Ahmed Galal. 1997. *Firms' Competitiveness and the National Diamond*, ECES, Cairo.

Greene, William H. 1990. *Econometric Analysis*. New York: Macmillan.

IMF (International Monetary Fund). 1997. *Government Finance Statistics Yearbook*. Washington, D.C.: International Monetary Fund.

———. 1997. *International Financial Statistics Yearbook*. Washington, D.C.: International Monetary Fund.

Klein, Benjamin. 1988. "Vertical Integration as Organizational Ownership: The Fisher Body General Motors Relationship Revisited." *Journal of Law, Economics, and Organization* 4(1): 199–213. In Oliver E. Williamson and Scott E. Masten, eds., *Transaction Cost Economics*. Aldershot, England: Edward Elgar Publishing, Ltd.

Klein, Benjamin, and Keith B. Leffler. 1981. "The Role of Market Forces in Assuring Contractual Performance." *Journal of Political Economy* 89(4): 615–41.

Klein, Benjamin, Robert G. Crawford, and Armen A. Alchian. 1978. "Vertical Integration, Appropriable Rents, and the Competitive Contracting Process." *Journal of Law and Economics* 21(2): 233–36.

LeBaube, Robert A., and Charles L. Vehorn. 1992. "Assisting Taxpayers in Meeting Their Obligations under the Law." In Richard M. Bird and Milka Casanegra DeJantscher, eds., *Improving Tax Administration in Developing Countries*. Washington, D.C.: International Monetary Fund.

Leffler, Keith B., and Randal R. Rucker. 1991. "Transaction Costs and the Efficient Organization of Production: A Study of Timber-Harvesting Contracts." *Journal of Political Economy* 99(5): 1060–87, In Oliver E. Williamson and Scott E. Masten, eds., *Transaction Cost Economics (Volume 2)*. Aldershot, England: Edward Elgar Publishing, Ltd.

Leuthold, Jane H. 1991. "Tax Shares in Developing Countries: A Panel Study." *Journal of Development Economics* 35: 173–85.

Masten, Scott E. 1984. "The Organization of Production: Evidence from the Aerospace Industry." *Journal of Law and Economics* 27(2): 403–17. In Oliver E. Williamson and Scott E. Masten, eds., *Transaction Cost Economics*. Aldershot, England: Edward Elgar Publishing, Ltd.

Milgrom, Paul, and John Roberts. 1992. *Economics, Organization and Management*. New Jersey: Prentice Hall.

Monteverde, Kirk, and David J. Teece. 1982. "Supplier Switching Costs and Vertical Integration in the Automobile Industry." *Bell Journal of Economics* 13(1): 206–13. In Oliver E. Williamson and Scott E. Masten, eds., *Transaction Cost Economics*. Aldershot, England: Edward Elgar Publishing, Ltd..

Political Risk Services. 1995. *International Country Risk Guide*. Syracuse, NY: Political Risk Services.

Silvani, Carlos A. 1992. "Improving Tax Compliance." In Richard M. Bird and Milka Casanegra DeJantscher, eds., *Improving Tax Administration in Developing Countries*. Washington, D.C.: International Monetary Fund.

Silvani, Carlos, and Katherine Baer. 1997. "Designing a Tax Administration Reform Strategy: Experiences and Guidelines." IMF WP/97/30. International Monetary Fund, Washington, D.C.

Stotsky, Janet G., and Asegedech Woldemariam. 1997. "Tax Effort in Sub-Saharan Africa." IMF WP/97/107. International Monetary Fund, Washington, D.C.

Tait, Alan A., and Barry J. Eichengreen. 1979. "Two Alternative Approaches to the International Comparison of Taxation." IMF Departmental Memorandum 78/73. International Monetary Fund, Washington, D.C.

Tanzi, Vito. 1968. "Comparing International Tax 'Burdens': A Suggested Method." *The Journal of Political Economy* 76(5): 1978–84.

Tanzi, Vito, and Anthony Pellechio. 1995. "The Reform of Tax Administration." IMF WP/95/22. International Monetary Fund, Washington, D.C.

Van Rijckeghem, Caroline, and Beatrice Weder. 1997. "Corruption and the Rate of Temptation: Do Low Wages in the Civil Service Cause Corruption?"IMF WP/97/73. International Monetary Fund, Washington, D.C.

Williamson, Oliver. 1976. "Franchise Bidding for Natural Monopolies—In General and with Respect to CATV." *Bell Journal of Economics* 7(1): 73–104. In Oliver E. Williamson and Scott E. Masten, eds., *Transaction Cost Economics (Volume 2)*. Aldershot, England: Edward Elgar Publishing, Ltd.

World Bank. 1992–97. *World Development Report.* Oxford University Press.

———. 1997. *World Development Indicators.* Washington, D.C.: World Bank.

World Economic Forum. 1996 and 1997. *Global Competitiveness Report.* Geneva: World Economic Forum.

CHAPTER 11

International Institutions and Efficiency in Public Procurement

Bernard Hoekman

All over the world government agencies procure goods and services in order to provide public goods and services—education, defense, utilities, infrastructure, public health, and so forth. The associated public procurement markets often represent a significant share of GDP. Many governments concerned with maximizing the use of scarce financial resources have developed procedures and mechanisms to ensure that public entities procure goods and services at least cost and in a fair and transparent manner. The importance given by some countries to efficiency in public purchasing is extremely high: South Africa for example included a section on procurement principles in its 1994 Constitution, requiring that procurement be undertaken on the basis of a fair, public and competitive process by independent, and impartial tender boards (Transparency International 1997).

A common element of many procurement systems is to mimic the working of the market by requiring that public entities seek competitive bids from potential suppliers of goods and services. Over time, an increasing number of governments have also pursued more far-reaching efforts to directly subject production units to competitive forces through privatizing state-owned enterprises, encouraging entry into sectors traditionally reserved for public entities (for example, utilities), and contracting out activities to the private sector. In a survey of the empirical literature on the price and quality impact of competitive tendering and outsourcing, Domberger, Hall, and Lee (1995) conclude that savings on the order of 20 percent are common and that these do not come at the expense of quality.

In the late 1970s, a number of high-income countries negotiated an agreement on government procurement under the auspices of the General Agreement on Tariffs and Trade (GATT). The Government Procurement Agreement (GPA) extends the basic principles of the GATT—nondiscrimination, national treatment, and transparency—to the tendering procedures of specified government entities. The GPA has been renegotiated twice since 1979, greatly increasing its substantive coverage. Membership of the GPA is limited to Canada, the EU, Hong Kong, Israel, Japan, Korea, Norway, Singapore, Switzerland, and the United States. Although many developing-country governments have made efforts to improve the efficiency (lower the cost) of the provision of public services, they have refrained from signing the GPA. This is surprising, as the GPA appears to be a useful mechanism for ensuring that procurement regimes maximize value for money. Associated benefits are likely to include not only reductions in average procurement costs, but what is perhaps more important, positive spillover effects attributable to increased transparency and accountability of the public sector.

The objective of this paper is to assess existing multilateral rules on government procurement from a developing-country perspective.[1] It assumes that governments are interested in achieving and maintaining an efficient, transparent, and accountable procurement regime, and asks what could explain the hesitance of developing countries to join the GPA. This is an important topic because multilateral rules of the game must be consistent with "best practices." If there are good reasons to question the economics of the GPA's rules from a development and growth perspective, efforts are required to revise the rules. If not, the issue becomes one of political economy. Efforts must then be directed at identifying and overcoming the resistance to membership by groups in society that benefit from the status quo at the expense of society as a whole.

Procurement is a topic in which developing countries can expect to be confronted with increasing pressure in their bilateral trade relations with industrialized nations. The United States has played a lead role in this regard, making public procurement practices a priority trade policy issue and linking this to the broader issue of combating corruption. In April 1996, largely at the initiative of the United States, OECD members agreed not to allow firms to write off bribes against tax obligations; in May 1997 this was followed by an OECD recommendation to make bribery of foreign officials a criminal offense under national legislation (World Bank 1997). At the December 1996 Ministerial meeting of the World Trade Organization (WTO) in Singapore a Working Group was created with the mandate to conduct a study on transparency in government procurement practices. This is to take into account national policies and develop "elements for inclusion in an appropriate agreement" (WTO 1996, p. 7). While the GPA is not mentioned, the most straightforward way for developing countries to deal with procurement-related concerns is to join the GPA. As far as the United States is concerned, this is clearly the ultimate objective. U.S. businesses regard an "interim" agreement on transparency, openness and due process in procurement as "an important step towards a more comprehensive multilateral agreement in the WTO" (USTR 1997, p. 4).

The paper starts with a brief description of the key elements of the GPA. As one explanation that is sometimes offered for the limited developing-country interest in the GPA is a desire to maintain preference policies favoring domestic firms, this is followed by a review of the salient economic literature exploring the possible rationales for discrimination. Attention then turns to an investigation of what available data suggest concerning the operation of the GPA. Finally, a number of negotiating and political economy issues that have a bearing on increasing incentives for developing countries to accede to the GPA are evaluated.

The WTO Agreement on Government Procurement

The GPA applies to laws, regulations, procedures, and practices pertaining to any procurement by entities.[2] This includes purchase, leasing, and rental, with or without the option to buy. The Agreement applies *only* to entities that are listed in annexes for each of the signatories. There are three such "entity" annexes: one for central government entities; one listing subcentral government entities; and one for all other entities that governments decide to schedule (mostly utilities). Entities that are listed in the third annex may be partially or totally privately owned. Listed entities are subject to the rules and disciplines of the GPA with respect to their procurement of goods and services *if* (a) the value of the procurement exceeds certain specified thresholds; *and* (b) the goods or services to be procured have not been exempted from the coverage of the Agreement by a signatory. The value threshold for procurement of goods and services by central governments is generally SDR 130,000; that for subcentral bodies such as local governments is SDR 200,000; and that for other entities such as utilities is usually SDR 400,000. For most members construction contracts are only covered if they exceed SDR 5 million.

As far as *goods* are concerned a so-called negative list approach is used to determine what is covered: in principle *all* procurement is covered, unless specified otherwise in an annex. In most instances such exceptions concern military procurement. In the case of services a so-called positive list is used: only those products that are explicitly listed in each member's schedule of commitments are subject to the GPA's rules. In practice, service commitments closely parallel those made by WTO members under the General Agreement on Trade in Services (GATS) to liberalize access to service markets more generally.[3]

The Main GPA Disciplines
The primary obligations imposed by the GPA on covered entities are nondiscrimination and transparency. This extends not only to imports but also to subsidiaries of locally established foreign firms. Price-preference policies, offsets, and similar policies that discriminate in favor of domestic (national) firms are therefore, in principle, prohibited. Entities are encouraged to use competitive tendering procedures. This may comprise open tendering (any supplier may respond to a published call for tenders), or selective tendering (bids are restricted to prequalified suppliers who have demonstrated that they meet technical competence norms). So-called limited tendering, under which potential suppliers are directly solicited to bid by the pro-

curing entity, may only be used in situations in which no responses are received to an open or selective call for tenders, in cases of urgency, and for additional deliveries by an original supplier.

Procuring entities must publish calls for tender in all cases of intended procurement (unless limited tendering is used). This must state the mode of procurement, its nature and quantity, dates of delivery, economic and technical requirements, amounts and terms of payment, and so on. Individual suppliers may not be given information that could have the effect of precluding competition. Entities are obliged to award contracts to the tenderer that "has been determined to be fully capable of undertaking the contract" *and* that is (a) either the lowest tender; or (b) one that in terms of the specific evaluation criteria set forth in the notices or tender documentation is determined to be the most advantageous. As an evaluation of which tender comes closest to satisfying the criteria is open to a considerable degree of discretion, much depends on how the specific evaluation criteria set forth in the notices or tender documentation are worded. It would be a violation of the Agreement were an entity to consider a tender as the most advantageous on the basis of evaluation criteria that were not specified in the notices or tender documentation.

The nature of procurement is such that unless rapid remedial action can be taken to intervene in the procurement process, firms are unlikely to contest perceived violations of the rules. A unique feature of the GPA is that it requires members to establish bid-protest or "challenge" procedures. These consist of a mechanism under which measures can be imposed to correct breaches of the agreement and to preserve commercial opportunities. Such measures may involve suspension of the procurement process, reopening of the tender procedure, or the award of compensation for the loss or damages suffered. This is a key dimension of the GPA, as it gives firms an incentive to defend their interests. The domestic challenge mechanism is complemented by the WTO's multilateral dispute settlement process. To ensure transparency and facilitate application of the WTO dispute settlement procedures, procuring entities are required to provide pertinent information concerning the reasons why a supplier's application to qualify was rejected; why an existing qualification was terminated; why a tender was not selected; the identity of the winning bidder; as well as the characteristics and relative advantages of the tender selected.

Developing-Country Provisions

Although, in principle, entities covered by the GPA (those listed in the various annexes) may not discriminate in favor of domestic firms, developing countries may negotiate mutually acceptable exclusions from the rules on national treatment with respect to certain entities, products, or services that are included in their lists of entities (Article V, GPA). Such negotiations may also be initiated *ex post*, after signing the agreement. Some scope therefore exists for discriminating in favor of domestic firms. However, the option is limited to *certain* entities, products or services, and the scope of the pursuit such policies is therefore inherently limited by the relative negotiating power of the country seeking to apply them. Developing countries may also, at the time of accession, negotiate conditions for the use of offsets (for example, domestic content requirements). While this explicitly allows for *de facto* discrimination against foreign suppliers, offset requirements may only be used for qualification to participate in the procurement process and not as criteria for awarding contracts. Thus, if a firm offers local content that greatly exceeds the minimum requirements, this may not be a factor in awarding a contract.

Economic Issues

The major substantive disciplines imposed by the GPA are its nondiscrimination, competitive tendering and transparency provisions, complemented by the domestic and multilateral enforcement mechanisms. What is the economic rationale for these rules? Are there reasons to conclude that they may not be in the interest of developing countries? There are two potential sources of concern. First, there may be a need for discrimination in order to ensure least-cost procurement. Second, the net economic payoffs associated with the rules may be too small.

Is Nondiscrimination Always Optimal?

Intuitively the nondiscrimination rule appears to be unambiguously beneficial as it should lead to a maximization of competition, thereby minimizing procurement costs. As is often the case in economics, this is not necessarily true. Discrimination may be necessary to minimize average procurement costs. Discriminating against foreign bidders may be welfare-improving *if* domestic firms are at a competitive disadvantage in producing the products to be procured (that is, if they are higher-cost producers) *and* only a limited number of firms (foreign and domestic) bid for a contract. In such situations foreign firms may exploit their cost advantage by bidding just below what they expect domestic firms to bid (McAffee and McMillan 1989). Although the foreign firm will be the lowest bidder, the bid may be substantially above the firm's actual cost. A policy that gives preferences to domestic firms may then induce foreign firms to lower their bids by the extent of the preference margin. If so, procurement favoritism increases national welfare. Even if the cost structure of domestic and foreign firms are identical and the social cost of distortionary taxation is taken into account, discrimination may be rational simply because foreign profits do not enter into domestic welfare (Branco 1994). Thus, in principle procurement favoritism can be used as a rational profit-shifting strategy whenever there is imperfect competition (so that prices exceed marginal costs). Shifting demand to domestic firms may also reduce price-cost margins as domestic output expands (Chen 1995).

Even if there are many potential suppliers for a contract, so that competition should compress price-cost margins, discrimination may be beneficial to the procuring entity. If the products that are procured are intangible or if there are problems in enforcing contract compliance, procuring entities may increase the likelihood of performance if they restrict competition. This allows them to grant to contractors the excess profits that are necessary to get them to deliver (Laffont and Tirole 1991; Rothenberg 1993). Moreover, if there is an incentive to pay a premium over the suppliers' cost to ensure contract performance, the required premium may increase as the number of potential bidders rises (because each supplier will take into account the higher probability of not getting repeat business) (Breton and Salmon 1995). Minimizing expected costs of procurement in such settings may require limiting the number of potential suppliers. If so, governments can be expected to favor domestic over foreign suppliers. Expected sourcing costs will not be affected, while political benefits may arise because domestic firms are part of their constituencies. Such situations are more likely to arise if services are an important dimension of what is being procured, because of their intangible nature. Services are often the largest category of purchases by governments—increasingly so in countries that have been pursuing outsourcing and contracting strategies. In the United States, for example, most federal non-defense procurement comprises services (Francois, Nelson, and Palmeter 1997).

Problems of asymmetric information may also induce entities to choose suppliers that are located within their jurisdictions, as this can reduce monitoring costs. Such proximity incentives will make it more difficult for foreign firms to bid successfully, even in the absence of formal discrimination. They increase the incentives for foreign firms to contest procurement markets through foreign direct investment (FDI). This incentive is of course not procurement-specific but will apply in all instances in which buyers of goods or services prefer to deal with "local" suppliers. The policy issues that then arise are how entities decide whether suppliers are local "enough," and what, if any, the barriers against establishment (direct investment) by foreign suppliers are.

While there are a number of situations in which discriminatory procurement may lower procurement costs, simulation studies suggest that the net welfare benefits are likely to be modest at best. Procurement favoritism will generate greater profits for domestic firms, but any cost savings for public entities will tend to be offset by increased prices (Deltas and Evenett 1997). The net welfare impact depends on the government's objective function, in particular the relative weight put on domestic industry profits as opposed to expected procurement costs. (The latter will generally be a multiple of the former.) In most instances the optimal preference policy will be difficult to determine and generally will vary depending on the specifics of the situation; in practice, favoritism can be expected to be more costly than a policy of nondiscrimination. In many situations the information required to judge whether diverging from nondiscrimination is beneficial will not be available. Even if it is, generally worded regulations calling for discrimination—for example, a universal price preference of 15 percent—are too rigid. In many cases markets will be competitive and products relatively homogenous, so that the considerations discussed above do not arise.

Nonetheless, in principle there is a potential tradeoff or tension between the GPA's nondiscrimination rules and economic efficiency. One way to address this would be to give entities the discretion to apply a "rule of reason" and require them to justify their decisions. A serious drawback to this approach is that it ntroduces the potential for arbitrary decisions and will make it more difficult, if not impossible, to apply to the GPA's enforcement and dispute settlement provisions.

The experience obtained with competitive procurement regimes indicates that in most situations competition is the best rule of thumb. The available evidence suggests competitive and transparent procurement regimes allow substantial cost savings to be realized. For example, Transparency International (1997) has concluded that procurement costs may increase as much as 30 percent if noncompetitive procedures are applied. Estimates of the cost savings associated with international competitive bidding that have been done for World Bank loans are in the same range. In the case of a recent balance of payments loan to the Russian Federation, a comparison of average procurement costs of identical items in previous years with those incurred following competitive bidding suggested that cost savings were 30–40 percent on average and rose to 75 percent for certain pharmaceutical products (World Bank 1994).

In practice, discrimination may be motivated not by cost minimization or contract compliance considerations, but by a desire to promote the development of domestic industry. In this case, procurement favoritism is an "infant industry" policy. Much has been written on the pros and cons of infant industry protection. The conventional wisdom is that targeted intervention by governments to support specific industries has a high probability of failure—the infants frequently never grow up and become a vested interest that lobbies for indefinite support. What matters in the current context is not whether there are rationales for intervention on infant industry grounds, but that procurement favoritism is unlikely to be the optimal policy to use in pursuit of this objective. In effect, the discrimination in favor of domestic firms is equivalent to a subsidy that is financed by a tax on domestic taxpayers, as government purchasing costs increase and these must be financed. But preferences are less transparent than a direct subsidy from the budget, and as a result provide greater potential for rent-seeking and corruption. Debroy and Pursell (1997) provide an interesting review of the experience of India, which has sought to use procurement regimes to support infant industry policies. The government recently decided to reduce significantly the extent to which domestic firms are favored in procurement on efficiency and cost grounds.

Benefits and Costs

Even if it is accepted that nondiscrimination is the best rule of thumb, and that significant cost savings can be realized, it may be that net benefits are minor. Costs that are incurred in the pursuit of nondiscrimination must be taken into account. These costs can be substantial, as entities must satisfy many procedural requirements to ensure due process and transparency. While these procedures are undoubtedly burdensome, they have advantages as well. An important potential benefit arising from nondiscrimination, transparency, and accountability provisions is that these principles may constrain rent-seeking activities. Allowing procuring entities to discriminate may facilitate bribery of procurement officials. Although the issue of corruption extends beyond procurement, rent-seeking in the public purchasing context is particularly prominent because the amounts involved are often significant and foreign interests are frequently directly affected. Case studies have demonstrated the cost of corruption to be high, leading to excess costs per project in the 25–50 percent range (Wade 1982; Rose-Ackerman 1995a). The result of corruption and rent-seeking is a reduction in the economy's growth performance as the most efficient suppliers are not allocated contracts, resource allocation is distorted, and governments impose excess tax burdens—or more commonly, pursue deficit or monetary financing (Mauro 1995; Murphy, Schleifer, and Vishny 1993; Schleifer and Vishny 1993; Bardhan 1997).

Regardless of variation in cultural norms across countries, effective anti-corruption strategies must reduce the magnitude of the benefits that can be granted by officials, increase the costs of bribery for the private sector, and limit the market power of officials (Rose-Ackerman 1995a, 1995b; Bardhan 1997). Of the various strategies and suggestions made in the literature, the following are particularly relevant for procurement: effective deterrents through *ex post* punishments that exceed the gains realized (including banning firms caught in attempts to engage in bribery from bidding for contracts for a number of years); the creation of external monitoring devices and institutions (including encouragement and protection of "whistle blowers"); public transparency-enhancing mechanisms (published audits by independent auditors; a free press); privatization and hard budget constraints; requirements to use standardized products or goods that have well-established market positions; use of general retail or wholesale market prices for goods similar to those to be procured as comparators; and creation of incentives for losers of corruption to complain.

Although the GPA lacks an explicit corruption standard or norm, it is consistent with—or embodies many of—these principles. Of particular importance are the challenge procedures that are required by the GPA. This provides firms with an opportunity to protest before the procurement decision process is completed, as well as thereafter. Multilateral monitoring and the threat of initiation of WTO dispute settlement procedures will also help to ensure that entities abide by the GPA's substantive and procedural disciplines. As argued by Alam (1995), the opportunities for losers to take countervailing actions can be a key factor constraining rent-seeking activities. In the procurement context, the set of losers is usually small. In discretionary, nontransparent procurement systems, losing firms have little incentive to protest against irregularities because of the power of procuring entities to blacklist them. The GPA's rules and procedures aim to maximize the incentives to obtain and use information concerning possible violations. However, as discussed further below, given the sunk costs of participation in the bidding process there is only an incentive to protest if expected returns outweigh expected costs of protesting. Ensuring that this is the case may be difficult.

Operation of the GPA

The GPA requires signatories to report annual statistics on procurement by covered entities to the WTO Committee on Government Procurement, which oversees the operation of the GPA. This Committee comprises representatives from all member countries, and meets periodically in Geneva. Regular data reporting was intended to help parties determine how the Agreement was functioning, by providing comparable cross-country information on sourcing practices. Signatories began reporting statistics for the year 1983. Because the latest year available for some countries is

1992, the analysis that follows is restricted to the 1983–92 period. During this period the GPA applied only to the procurement of goods by central government entities. As a result, most procurement activities by the public sector broadly defined were excluded. In the case of the United States, for example, Francois, Nelson, and Palmeter (1997) note that in 1993 goods accounted for less than five percent of total federal non-defense-related purchases.

Coverage

Total procurement of goods by entities covered by the GPA in 1992 was some US$62 billion. The largest procurement market, by a substantial margin, opened up under the GPA is that of the United States. Average annual purchases by covered U.S. entities reported to the GATT was some US$29 billion in 1992 (table 11.1). This compares to the procurement of $16 billion by EU-12 entities, $9.2 billion by Japan, and $1.6 billion by Canada. In order to allow cross-country comparisons, it is helpful to relate these numbers to total non-defense-related central government expenditures on goods and services and capital expenditures by the central government. Relative to total central government expenditures on goods and services—which includes items such as wages—large countries such as France, Germany, Italy, Japan, and the United Kingdom tend to have below-average coverage; the United States and the Nordic countries above-average. On both measures, Germany and Italy have the lowest ratios, suggesting that they may have sought to limit the coverage of their GPA obligations. Israel and Singapore have scheduled substantially less than OECD countries.

It is extremely difficult to estimate how much additional procurement was brought under the GPA's umbrella in 1996, when it was extended to cover services and subcentral government. It is not always clear whether specific services are covered, or whether the nondiscrimination rule applies fully for all services (many countries made commitments conditional upon reciprocity). Information on average contract sizes across entities and types of goods and services purchased is also not available. An attempt can nonetheless be made at guesstimating the potential size of aggregate procurement markets of GPA members. Total central government non-defense expenditures on goods and services of GPA signatories is about US$2.1 trillion (table 11.1). Available data (IMF 1996) suggest that total expenditures on goods and services by subcentral government bodies adds at least another $1 trillion. Not all of this is available for international competition. In particular, the average size of noncentral government contracts may be lower than those of central government entities. If it is assumed that one-third of total outlays could be subjected to GPA rules, the total potential market is therefore some $1 trillion per year. Applying the historical GPA rate for the share of procurement of goods that falls below the threshold value (about 50 percent—see table 11.2), some $500 billion could be open to international competitive bidding. This is likely to be an overestimate, however, as threshold values for noncentral government entities and services are significantly higher than those that apply to central government entities. Thresholds for construction contracts are at least SDR 5 million, and are SDR 15 million in the cases of Korea and Japan. A more realistic figure is therefore US$300 billion.

TABLE 11.1 GDP AND CENTRAL GOVERNMENT EXPENDITURE IN 1992
US$ million and percentage

	Gross domestic product	Total government expenditure (A)	Total non-defense goods and services by central government (B)	Capital expenditure by central government (C)	Value of total contracts under GPA[a]	Value of total contracts relative to:		
						(A)	(B)	(C)
Austria	185,235	40,282	29,842	4,750	433	1.08	1.45	9.12
Belgium[b]	218,836	64,197	44,540	4,973	407	0.63	0.91	8.19
Canada	493,602	128,155	96,959	1,965	2,399	1.87	2.47	122.12
Denmark	123,546	47,219	35,782	1,539	1,646	3.49	4.60	106.92
Finland	93,869	30,020	23,045	1,912	834	2.78	3.62	43.58
France[b]	1,319,883	256,711	178,104	19,273	3,279	1.28	1.84	17.02
Germany[b]	1,789,261	215,669	149,629	35,832	2,055	0.95	1.37	5.74
Ireland	43,294	16,986	13,236	1,269	208	1.23	1.58	16.43
Israel	69,762	25,270	13,001	3,500	68	0.27	0.53	1.95
Italy[b]	1,222,962	335,439	232,725	17,983	1,994	0.59	0.86	11.09
Japan[b]	3,670,979	479,158	332,436	58,360	9,507	1.98	2.86	16.29
Luxembourg	12,638	2,394	1,784	364	34	1.43	1.92	9.44
Netherlands	320,290	92,698	75,644	6,505	1,281	1.38	1.69	19.70
Norway	112,906	25,399	19,276	1,255	775	3.05	4.02	61.76
Singapore	46,025	8,889	3,424	2,272	30	0.34	0.89	1.34
Sweden	220,834	75,172	61,158	3,386	1,162	1.55	1.90	34.31
Switzerland	90,649	8,973	5,784	1,096	252	2.81	4.36	22.99
United Kingdom	903,126	338,259	211,108	33,755	5,740	1.70	2.72	17.00
United States	5,920,199	1,037,354	631,924	56,354	29,120	2.81	4.61	51.67
Total	n.a.	3,228,246	2,159,399	256,343	61,227	n.a.	n.a.	n.a.
Unweighted average	n.a.	n.a.	n.a.	n.a.	n.a.	1.64	2.60	30.35

n.a. not applicable.

a. Average of the sum of 1991 and 1992 total contracts

b. Estimates; Switzerland, 1984; Hong Kong has been excluded because of data inconsistencies.

Sources: WTO Secretariat, Annual reports to the Government Procurement Committee, 1984–94; IMF (1996).

TABLE 11.2 INDICATORS OF GPA PERFORMANCE, 1983–92
US$ million and percentage

	Value of covered procurement		Share of limited tendering		Share of procurement covered domestically		Share of procurement that falls above SDR threshold	
	1983–85	1990–92	1983–85	1990–92	1983–85	1990–92	1983–85	1990–92
Austria	179.4	403.9	43.2	43.2	51.3	1.5	46.9	43.5
Belgium[a]	129.9	407.2	10.3	8.6	100.0	100.0	40.0	57.5
Canada	968.5	2,163.9	9.7	7.4	92.3	77.4	42.9	46.0
Denmark[a]	447.9	1,651.7	4.0	1.4	95.6	79.8	5.8	12.6
Finland	256.3	800.8	0.3	0.1	95.7	69.1	39.4	18.1
France[a]	937.9	3,089.5	33.3	29.6	97.6	97.2	35.1	85.5
Germany[a]	845.6	2,029.3	13.3	24.0	97.2	99.1	24.9	61.7
Hong Kong	154.5	348.6	22.1	28.2	5.8	3.2	67.7	71.2
Ireland[a]	47.8	185.8	1.8	5.6	100.0	84.8	20.6	29.1
Israel	30.1	67.9	5.0	3.3	13.7	25.6	84.0	91.1
Italy[a]	382.4	1,937.5	1.0	5.9	99.2	97.8	5.0	60.5
Japan	3,379.4	9,274.1	12.3	21.0	86.1	85.5	37.4	43.7
Luxembourg[a]	14.9	35.8	39.8	23.9	100.0	97.8	30.9	28.4
Netherlands[a]	547.1	1,407.7	16.8	13.5	98.7	86.4	12.1	37.7
Norway	384.7	721.4	7.1	8.3	48.6	40.4	44.5	58.9
Singapore	48.5	31.0	0.0	0.0	45.1	67.3	57.9	51.1
Sweden	624.4	1,200.5	4.0	4.8	43.7	43.6	27.9	36.9
Switzerland	265.0	806.2	25.1	27.7	35.7	38.3	43.8	39.8
United Kingdom.[a]	1,329.7	5,375.0	13.7	6.6	99.4	98.2	29.3	49.0
United States	24,080.8	28,891.2	11.5	9.6	86.3	90.4	80.1	66.8
Memo: EU countries	7,967.2	16,119.4	19.0	15.0	98.3	94.9	21.2	54.1
Average (unweighted)	n.a.	n.a.	13.1	13.0	74.6	71.2	38.8	49.5
Average (weighted)	n.a.	n.a.	13.3	14.1	86.1	87.3	59.7	57.4

n.a. not applicable.
a. Average of 1984–85.
Source: WTO Secretariat, Annual reports to the Government Procurement Committee, 1984–94.

Foreign Sourcing

Smaller countries, on average, procure much more on international markets than do large countries. If Canada, the EU, Japan, and the United States are excluded, about 60 percent of purchases by covered entities exceeding the GPA thresholds were allocated to national suppliers. This compares to more than 90 percent for the large players. Unfortunately, EU statistics define "domestic" as intra-EU sourcing. It is not surprising, therefore, that reported self-sufficiency ratios for the EU-12 are above 98 percent on average during 1983–92. Three of the smaller EU countries source disproportionately from non-EU sources: Denmark, Ireland, and the Netherlands (table 11.2), but the extent of non-EU sourcing remains limited, averaging around 16 percent. In interpreting these statistics it should be noted that no distinction is made between domestic firms "proper" and foreign firms that have established a local presence. As long as large countries do not differ from smaller ones in the share of FDI in total investment this should not affect the cross-country comparisons.

In the EU, Japan, and the United States, the share of domestic firms in total procurement by covered entities remained virtually unchanged during 1983–92. The average weighted share across all GPA members is relatively constant; the unweighted average falling by three percentage points, from 74.6 percent to 71.2 percent (table 11.2). For the smaller countries, however, with the exception of Singapore and Switzerland, the share of procurement from national sources has declined over time. For some countries the decline is quite significant, for example, Norway, Finland, Canada, Austria, Sweden, and Hong Kong. Although it is impossible to attribute such changes in sourcing patterns to the GPA—regional developments also played a role; for example, the NAFTA in North America, efforts to liberalize EU procurement markets, and unilateral deregulation and privatization policies—the finding that smaller GPA members became less "nationalistic" in their purchasing decisions appears to be robust. But for most of the large players there has been no change.

This conclusion is supported by the few empirical studies analyzing the quantity impact of government procurement practices in OECD countries. These use a methodology suggested by Baldwin (1970) and Baldwin and Richardson (1972), the basis of which is to suppose that in the absence of discriminatory policy, government entities would behave the same way as private firms. Thus, under total nondiscrimination the government's demand for imports of a good as a share of its total consumption would equal that of the private sector as a whole. The difference between this hypothetical public sector import propensity and the actual import share of total government consumption can be used to construct a preference margin. Baldwin (1970) estimated that the preference margin in the United States was some 20 percent in 1958. After adjusting for the fact that certain large import items such as oil were not subject to discriminatory policies, the margin for the residual set of covered goods increased to some 40 percent. More recent estimates of preference margins in 1992 for a number of countries using the Baldwin-Richardson method give an estimated preference margin for U.S. purchases of 16.3 percent (Francois, Nelson, and Palmeter 1997). This suggests that there has been a small decline in preference margins. If preference margin calculations are done on a sectoral level, positive margins in OECD countries may be as high as 50 percent, but in many cases they are negative (table 11.3). Margins are invariably the highest for procurement of services.

Estimates of preference margins using the Baldwin-Richardson methodology are obviously sensitive to the assumption that, other things being equal, the government would import the same share of a good as the private sector, and that all differences can be attributed to formal or informal preference policies. One source of bias that arises is that private sector imports may be distorted because of tariffs and other trade policies. Alternatively, private sector demand for certain products may be very low or even zero because government is the dominant supplier of output that embodies particular products (defense, utilities, certain types of transport services, and so on.).

Limited Tendering
Under the GPA, open competitive tendering procedures are in principle to be used for all contracts that exceed the threshold value. Limited tendering procedures (which involve an entity contacting and negotiating with potential suppliers individually) is only allowed under certain conditions. The use of limited tendering varies across signatories, from a reported low of zero (Singapore) to a high of over 30 percent on average for France, Italy, Switzerland, and Hong Kong (table 11.2). Across all signatories the weighted and unweighted average share of limited tendering was about 13 percent. The share of limited tendering has been falling over time for the EU-12 (decreasing some 7 percent per year on average during 1983–92), but rising for the United States. By 1992, the EU and the U.S. use of limited tendering stood at 10 percent, largely as the result of a significant decline in the use of this method by France and Germany during the 1980s. Japan's use of limited tendering rose from around 12 percent during 1983–85 to 21 percent during 1990–92. Hong Kong and Switzerland make even more intensive use of such procurement mechanisms.

TABLE 11.3 ESTIMATED PREFERENCE MARGINS FOR CORE GOVERNMENT PURCHASING, 1992
Baldwin-Richardson approach

Country	Machinery	Other goods	Trade, transport, communication	Utilities	Other services
Canada	..	..	..	..	39.6
United States	18.4	17.9	..	18.8	42.6
Western Europe	..	9.2	13.7	14.9	48.3
Japan	..	32.0	26.2	34.0	46.6
Australia	49.8	49.7	..	..	41.5
New Zealand	13.9	19.7	49.8	..	50.0
Korea	30.6	20.8	..	..	48.2

Note: .. denotes a preference margin that is less than or equal to zero.
Source: Francois, Nelson, and Palmeter (1997).

Data of the type reported to the GPA Committee is not available for developing countries. Indeed, little is known about the product composition of procurement across countries, average contract size, or the "import propensity" of government entities. One benefit of membership of the GPA would be that data on procurement flows will have to be collected and reported to the WTO. This would be a valuable source of information not just for researchers, but more important, for the governments concerned. While somewhat burdensome, the regular reporting requirements imply that mechanisms must be put in place to track procurement and thus monitor the behavior of public entities.

Transparency, Disputes, and the Challenge Mechanism

A fundamental requirement for procurement procedures to achieve efficiency is that potential suppliers are aware of demand and have sufficient time to respond to calls for tenders. The GPA requires that such calls be published and that potential foreign suppliers be given enough time to respond. It does not monitor compliance with these requirements; that is left to the private sector. As a result, many violations may not be remarked on. Even in the EU, where procurement opportunities must be published in the Official Journal and can be obtained through electronic networks (by accessing a database called "Tenders Electronic Daily"), a recent study found that procuring entities often did not publish or if they did, they provided insufficient time for responses. Moreover, many potential suppliers did not monitor the Official Journal and were thus unaware of the potential market (Gordon, Rimmer, and Arrowsmith 1997). In part, these problems were attributable to ambiguities in the wording of the rules regarding the coverage of the EU procurement regulations.

No experience has been obtained with the GPA's challenge mechanism, as this only entered into force in 1996. The key requirement for these procedures to be an effective deterrent for procuring entities is that a participant in a procurement process can either obtain rapid intervention by a judicial or administrative body or has the opportunity to obtain significant financial compensation after the fact for violations of procurement disciplines. Once a tender has been closed and a contract awarded it may be difficult to reopen the proceedings. In such cases, significant financial compensation must be available for enterprises to have an incentive to complain about violations of the rules. A problem with this is that it may give rise to problems of moral hazard and excessive litigation. Ensuring that firms have access to an effective and speedy mechanism through which they can challenge a procurement process or award is therefore very important. A recent evaluation of EU procedures and disciplines—which were an important model for much of the GPA—suggests that the challenge mechanism has not been used to great effect by EU suppliers because it is perceived as being too slow (Gordon, Rimmer, and Arrowsmith 1997).

Negotiating Accession: Issues and Political Economy Considerations

The available data suggest that large countries did not experience changes in sourcing patterns following membership in the GPA. Small countries are more open to foreign suppliers, and appear to have become more so over time. These findings are consistent with what economic theory would predict. The larger are countries, the greater the number of potential domestic suppliers and the higher the probability that domestic firms attain minimum efficient scale. Thus, large countries can be expected to continue to source predominantly from national suppliers even if they abide fully with the GPA. Small countries, in contrast, will generally have fewer national firms that can provide the goods needed by the government at least cost—particularly in cases involving specialized, capital-intensive items, for which scale economies are important (for example, telecommunications, transport, or power generating equipment).

The discussion in the section on WTO agreement on government procurement led to the conclusion that economic rationales for not joining the GPA are weak and that hesitancy may in large part be driven by political economy factors. The issue then is to seek to offset the opposition of groups that have an interest in maintaining the status quo. The political economy problem that arises is similar to liberalizing trade: losers from the status quo (taxpayers, consumers) will have less of an individual incentive to push for reform than incumbent industries and procurement officials have to oppose it. In the trade liberalization context, the problem arising from the asymmetric distribution of costs and benefits can be addressed by providing those who gain from reform a greater incentive to engage in the political process in pursuit of their interests. One way to mobilize support in favor of liberalization is to promise exporters better access to foreign markets, something that the government can demand as a quid pro quo from trading partners for liberalizing the domestic market. The data suggest that accession will not have much of an impact in terms of increasing developing countries' share of OECD procurement markets. Thus, mobilization of domestic industries that have an interest in exports to foreign procurement markets is not relevant.[4] However, there is no formal constraint on demanding concessions in other areas as part of the accession negotiation. Efforts could be made to seek improvements in access to export markets that are of interest to developing countries. Although barriers to trade imposed by industrialized countries are relatively low on average, a significant amount of tariff escalation remains. Tariffs and other trade barriers tend to be substantially higher for labor-intensive products such as footwear or clothing than for other types of manufactures. Achieving reductions in these barriers is difficult. Linking accession to the GPA to reductions in trade barriers by OECD countries may help to mobilize support in export sectors for domestic liberalization of procurement markets.

Another way to attenuate opposition is to seek to change the rules of the game in a manner that allows some of the concerns associated with implementation of the GPA to be met. One option that has been suggested in the literature is to allow developing countries to apply price preferences that favor procurement from national suppliers. Although a strong presumption exists that the GPA's nondiscrimination, transparency, and enforcement provisions will be beneficial for developing countries, many nations have procurement regimes that provide preferences for domestic firms. Such provisions may be motivated by infant industry arguments; they may reflect an attempt to offset higher input costs for domestic bidders that are attributable to other policies (for example, high import tariffs); or they may be motivated by imperfect competition or asymmetric information considerations discussed earlier. As mentioned earlier, imperfect competition and infant industry arguments are not compelling in practice, given recognition of the drawbacks of discretion and discrimination. In principle the optimal policy to deal with policy-induced distortions such as tariffs is to eliminate or significantly reduce them, thereby allowing the elimination of the domestic preferences as well. Some countries have embarked on a such a process—for example—India, but local content requirements and price preferences continue to prevail in many jurisdictions.

Attempts could be made to amend the GPA to allow developing countries to apply price preferences as long as these are applied in a transparent and accountable fashion. It was argued earlier that the case for policies that discriminate in favor of domestic suppliers is not compelling. However, there may be value in permitting the time-bound transitional use of price preferences as a facilitating device to encourage membership. It can be noted that such preferences are allowed subject to certain conditions and limits by multilateral financial institutions such as the World Bank. The World Bank permits a maximum price preference of 15 percent for procurement of goods, and 7.5 percent for works. Provisions for the use of price preferences are also included in the United Nations Committee on International Trade Law (UNCITRAL) Model Law on Procurement (Beveglia-Zampetti 1997). An advantage of price preferences over other policies to favor domestic procurement is that they allow the price mechanism to continue to work. As such they are superior to local content and offset requirements or policies that the GPA currently allows developing countries to apply. One option that might be considered would be to seek agreement to convert offset and similar policies into price preferences. This would be akin to the "tariffication" of quotas and related measures that occurred in the Uruguay Round for agriculture (see Hoekman and Kostecki 1995). Even if price preferences in some countries turned out to be relatively high after the "tariffication" process, they would become the focal point for future multilateral negotiations to reduce discrimination. Of course, the use of such preferences should be optional and not be used to create a preference margin that exceeds that currently implied by existing policies in a nation; and tariffication should not be sought in instances in which preference policies do not already exist.

Potential Negotiating Leverage

What negotiating leverage might developing countries have to pursue better access to foreign markets or temporary exceptions to GPA disciplines? Given the mercantilist nature of bargaining in the WTO context, the size of nonmember (developing-country) procurement markets is perhaps the best indicator of developing-country leverage. Unfortunately, data on the size of procurement markets are scarce. Total central government expenditures on goods and services by non-OECD countries in the early 1990s was some US$300 billion (table 11.4). This includes conservative estimates for a number of large countries that do not report data—for example, India, Indonesia, Pakistan, and South Africa.[5] Data on expenditures by subcentral government entities in developing countries are even patchier. If it is assumed that purchases by such entities equal central government expenditures, the total will be

TABLE 11.4 GOVERNMENT FINANCE AND OFFICIAL DEVELOPMENT
ASSISTANCE
US$ million and percentage

	GDP 1992 (A)	Total non-defense expenditure on goods and services (B)	Capital expenditure	Multilateral development bank loans 1992	Development assistance committee loans 1992	Ratio multilateral development bank loans/ Total non-defense expenditure (B)
Average of low-income countries (N=46)	23,704	2,053	1,637	n.a.	n.a.	n.a.
Total low-income countries	1,090,384	94,447	75,296	17,076	32,931	18.1
Average of lower-middle-income Countries (N=42)	31,151	2,237	921	n.a.	n.a.	n.a.
Total lower-middle-income countries	1,308,362	93,960	38,682	13,972	15,337	14.9
Average of upper-middle-income countries (N=16)	80,384	6,602	1,496	n.a.	n.a.	n.a.
Total of upper-middle-income countries	1,286,158	105,631	23,943	6,135	1,239	5.8

n.a. = Not available.
Note: Multilateral Development Bank loans refer to loan approvals; Development Assistance Committee data pertains to net disbursements and includes bilateral assistance.
Source: World Bank, Asian Development Bank, Inter-American Development Bank, African Development Bank and OECD Development Assistance Committee, Annual Reports; IMF Government Finance Yearbook (1996).

at least $600 billion. How much of this will be available to foreign suppliers depends on the share of contracts that exceed the GPA's threshold values. These are likely to have a greater effect in developing countries, since the average size of each contract can be expected to be less than in a high-income country. It is also important to recognize that many expenditures by developing-country governments are financed through official development assistance funds, both bilateral and multilateral. Official bilateral development aid is often tied to the sourcing of goods and services from the donor country; the recipient government cannot subject purchases using such finance to international competition. Absent agreement from donors to eliminate tying of aid, such projects will be exempt from GPA rules. Conversely, procurement financed through multilateral development assistance usually already will be subject to international competitive bidding.

Available data on the relative importance of aid flows as a share of government expenditure suggest that aid finances a significant share of total purchases of goods and services by developing-country governments. The ratio of official aid flows (bilateral and multilateral) to total expenditure is equivalent to 35 percent of total expenditures on goods and services for low-income countries (table 11.4). For lower-middle-income nations, total aid accounts for 16 percent of expenditures; for upper-middle-income economies the figure drops to 6 percent. This suggests that for poor countries in particular, much procurement either cannot be subjected to the GPA or is already subject to international competitive bidding. However, GPA accession negotiations can be expected to focus mostly on the higher-income developing countries in which aid plays only a minor role. It can also be noted that what matters in the WTO context is not so much the actual policy stance of a government, but the extent to which countries bind (lock in) their policies. Even if countries are already relatively open, this does not mean they have nothing to offer in the WTO negotiating context. Negotiating leverage for developing countries is therefore substantial.

Concluding Remarks

Government procurement is a key interface between the public and private sectors. Not only is efficiency in public purchasing of fundamental importance in ensuring that the best value for money is obtained by public entities, but procurement practices will also figure prominently in the way potential investors and civil society at large view a country. Many developing countries have adopted procurement legislation and regulations that aim to ensure that public entities source goods and services through an open and competitive process. To what extent actual practice is consistent with the formal rules and principles is often difficult to determine, in part because the incentives to contest violations of the formal rules of the game are often small. The GPA provides a unique international mechanism through which governments can credibly commit themselves to a transparent and competitive procurement regime and provide participants with more effective enforcement mechanisms than may be available under the status quo. Enforcement is a necessary condition for any set of rules to be effective. This applies as much to industrialized as to developing countries.[6]

Governments desiring to minimize procurement costs have options that go beyond the adoption of efficient purchasing practices and related procurement regimes. These include privatization and allowing entry into markets serviced by public entities, in cases in which such entry is feasible. The potential benefits of such initiatives are increasingly recognized. Procurement disciplines may be second-best (if not redundant) if market forces can be applied to the activities of public entities. The greater the extent to which public entities operate in a competitive environment and are subject to hard budget constraints (that is, they do not obtain direct or indirect financing from the government), the smaller the likelihood of inefficient purchasing decisions will be. However, in cases in which entities have a dominant position, competition laws and policies are required to ensure that they do not abuse their market power. The same is true in terms of dealing with problems of collusion and restrictive business practices more generally—maters on which the GPA has nothing to say (see Wood 1997). This does not imply that procurement regimes will become irrelevant—quite to the contrary. Governments (both central and local) will remain important purchasers of goods and services. Indeed, the more activities are contracted out by government agencies, the greater the need for transparent and efficient procedures to allocate contracts.

More research is required to determine the extent to which current procurement regimes in developing countries are compatible with the GPA. Surprisingly little is known about actual practices and their economic impact. Accession would imply collection of data of the type required by the GPA Committee on Procurement and would be a valuable improvement in the knowledge base. It could also help provide a framework to collect additional information that is not required by the GPA but which would be useful to governments in analyzing and monitoring the operation of the procurement regime. Examples include data on the composition of procurement; the import propensity of government entities at various levels as compared to the private sector; the extent to which procurement costs diverge from market price–based comparisons; differences in procurement efficiency across similar entities and contracts as a function of ownership and market structure; and the incidence of reopening of negotiations *after* contracts have been awarded.[7]

It is unclear why developing countries have been hesitant to join the GPA. Potentially the GPA could be of great value in increasing the transparency and efficiency of the procurement process. Although there are valid theoretical justifications for being able to discriminate in the procurement context, any associated economic benefits are likely to be small in practice, especially if one considers the potential for inappropriate discrimination, rent-seeking, and corruption. Nonparticipation in the GPA is probably best explained by a combination of rent-seeking, second-best considerations, infant industry objectives, and mercantilism. Given the trend towards liberalization of trade and greater reliance on market forces, second-best and infant industry rationales for procurement favoritism have become less relevant. This suggests that the main problem may be that the accession process does not generate enough benefits for governments to allow them to overcome the opposition of those groups in society that benefit from nontransparent or discretionary procurement regimes. After all, the main quid pro quo of accession in mercantilist terms is that it provides reciprocal access to the procurement markets of existing GPA members. This is not very useful to developing countries. Seeking better access to export markets more generally appears to be the best approach, complemented by efforts to seek transitional periods in which to phase in those aspects of the GPA that requires institutional strengthening. Insofar as governments currently allow for price preferences in favor of domestic firms to offset the effect of high import tariffs, they should consider making the elimination of such preferences conditional upon more general liberalization of the trade regime.

Notes

1.   This paper draws heavily on Hoekman (1998). Thanks are due to Marie-Helene Le Manchec and Faten Hatab for excellent research assistance; Annet Blank and Dick Westin for their help in obtaining data; and members of the World Bank Research Observer Editorial Board, Simon Evenett, Petros C. Mavroidis, Garry Pursell, Stephen Johnston, and Alan Winters for helpful comments on an earlier draft. The views expressed are personal and should not be attributed to the World Bank.

2.   This section draws on a more detailed discussion of the GPA's disciplines in a number of the contributions to Hoekman and Mavroidis (1997).

3.   See Hoekman and Kostecki (1995) for an introduction to the GATS and references to the literature.

4.   Some countries may have a comparative advantage in providing certain services. The problem that arises is not so much existing procurement regulations in high-income countries as the need to first achieve liberalization of market access to the services markets concerned. Service industries remain much more subject to restrictive regulations than goods markets.

5.   Data reported in the IMF (1996) on the average ratio of expenditure on goods and services to total central government expenditures of all the developing countries reporting both variables was used to estimate data for missing countries.

6.   In the EU, for example, many members states have been slow to implement EC Directives relating to procurement, and the directives are often violated. In 1994 the Commission of the European Communities initiated some 250 legal actions against member states or entities for inconsistency with procurement rules (Hoekman 1998).

7.   This is potentially a significant loophole in any procurement regime as it may reflect or induce corruption and collusion between the entity and a favored supplier, who will bid low to win the tender in the knowledge that the contract will be renegotiated ex post.

References

The word *processed* describes informally reproduced works that may not be commonly available through libraries.

Alam, M.S. 1995. "A Theory of Limits on Corruption and Some Applications." *Kyklos*, 48: 419–35.

Baldwin, Robert. 1970. *Nontariff Distortions of International Trade*. Washington, D.C.: Brookings Institution.

Baldwin, Robert, and J. David Richardson. 1972. "Government Purchasing Policies, other NTBs, and the International Monetary Crisis." In H. Edward English
and K. Hay, eds., *Obstacles to Trade in the Pacific Area*. Ottawa: Carleton School
of International Affairs.

Bardhan, Pranab. 1997. "Corruption and Development: A Review of Issues." *Journal of Economic Literature* 35: 1320–46.

Beveglia-Zampetti, Americo. 1997. "The UNCITRAL Model Law on Procurement
of Goods, Construction and Services." In Bernard Hoekman and P. Mavroidis,
eds., *Law and Policy in Public Purchasing: The WTO Agreement on Government
Procurement*. Ann Arbor: University of Michigan Press.

Branco, Fernando. 1994. "Favoring Domestic Firms in Procurement Contracts."
Journal of International Economics 37: 65–80.

Breton, Albert, and Pierre Salmon. 1995. "Are Discriminatory Procurement Policies Motivated By Protectionism?" *Kyklos* 49: 47–68.

Chen, Xiangqun. 1995. "Directing Government Procurement as an Incentive of Production." *Journal of Economic Integration* 10: 130–40.

Debroy, Bibek, and Garry Pursell. 1997. "Government Procurement Policies in India." In Bernard Hoekman and P. Mavroidis, eds., *Law and Policy in Public Purchasing: The WTO Agreement on Government Procurement*. Ann Arbor:
University of Michigan Press.

Deltas, George and Simon Evenett. 1997. "Quantitative Estimates of the Effects of
Preference Policies." In Bernard Hoekman and P. Mavroidis, eds., *Law and Policy
in Public Purchasing: The WTO Agreement on Government Procurement*. Ann
Arbor: University of Michigan Press.

Domberger, Simon, Christine Hall, and Eric Ah Lik Lee. 1995. "The Determinants
of Price and Quality in Competitively Tendered Contracts." *Economic Journal*
105:1454–70.

Francois, Joe, Douglas Nelson, and David Palmeter. 1997. "Government Procure-
ment in the U.S.: A Post-Uruguay Round Analysis." In Bernard Hoekman and P.
Mavroidis, eds., *Law and Policy in Public Purchasing: The WTO Agreement on
Government Procurement*. Ann Arbor: University of Michigan Press.

Gordon, Harvey, Shane Rimmer, and Sue Arrowsmith. 1997. "The Economic Impact of the EU Regime on Public Procurement: Lessons for the WTO." Processed.

Hoekman, Bernard. 1998. "Using International Institutions to Improve Public Procurement." *World Bank Research Observer* 13: 249–69. World Bank, Washington, D.C.

Hoekman, Bernard, and Michel Kostecki. 1995. *The Political Economy of the World Trading System.* Oxford: Oxford University Press.

Hoekman, Bernard, and Petros C. Mavroidis, eds. 1997. *Law and Policy in Public Purchasing: The WTO Agreement on Government Procurement.* Ann Arbor: University of Michigan Press.

IMF (International Monetary Fund). 1996. *Government Finance Statistics Yearbook.* International Monetary Fund, Washington, D.C.

Laffont, J.J., and Jean Tirole. 1991. "Auction Design and Favoritism." *International Journal of Industrial Organization* 9: 9–42.

Mauro, Paolo. 1995. "Corruption and Growth." *Quarterly Journal of Economics* 109: 681–712.

McAfee, R. Preston and John McMillan. 1989. "Government Procurement and International Trade." *Journal of International Economics* 26: 291–308.

Murphy, Kevin, Andrei Schleifer, and Robert Vishny. 1993. "Why Is Rent-Seeking So Costly to Growth?" *American Economic Review* 83: 409–14.

Rose-Ackerman, Susan. 1995a. "The Political Economy of Corruption." *Viewpoint* No. 74 (April). World Bank, Washington D.C.

Rose-Ackerman, Susan. 1995b. "Redesigning the State to Fight Corruption." *Viewpoint* No. 75 (April). World Bank, Washington D.C.

Rothenberg, Julio. 1993. "Comment." In Jim Leitzel and Jean Tirole, eds., *Incentives in Procurement Contracting.* Boulder: Westview Press.

Schleifer, Andrei, and R. Vishny. 1993. "Corruption." *Quarterly Journal of Economics* 107: 599–617.

Transparency International. 1997. *The TI Source Book: Applying the Framework.* Internet address: www.transparency.de.

USTR (United States Trade Representative). 1997. "Annual Report on Discrimination in Foreign Government Procurement." April 30. Internet address: www.ustr.gov/reports/special/title7.html.

Wade, Robert. 1982. "The System of Administrative and Political Corruption: Canal Irrigation in South India." *Journal of Development Studies* 18: 287–327.

Wood, Diane. 1997. "The WTO Agreement on Government Procurement: An Antitrust Perspective." In Bernard Hoekman and P. Mavroidis, eds., *Law and Policy in Public Purchasing: The WTO Agreement on Government Procurement*. Ann Arbor: University of Michigan Press.

World Bank. 1994. "Rehabilitation Loan: Pre-Identified Import Component Distribution Monitoring Report." December 9. Processed.

World Bank. 1997. *Helping Countries Combat Corruption: The Role of the World Bank*. Washington D.C.: World Bank.

WTO (World Trade Organization). 1996. "Singapore Ministerial Declaration." WT/MIN(96)/DEC. World Trade Organization, Geneva.

Index